THE HILLTO
a Victorian Colony am

ALLEN Charles Grant Blairfindie
ALLINGHAM William
BARING-GOULD Rev Sabine
BEVERIDGE Annette Susannah
  (née AKROYD)
BLOUNT Godfrey & Ethel (née HINE)
BROWN George Douglas
BUCKTON George Bowdler FRS
BURROUGHS John
CARRINGTON Richard Christopher FRS
COSTELLOE Benjamin Francis Conn
DAKYNS Henry Graham
DOYLE Sir Arthur Conan
ELIOT George (Marian EVANS)
  later Mrs Cross
GALTON Sir Francis FRS
GARNETT Lucy Mary Jane
GILCHRIST Anne (née BURROWS)
HAMILTON Bernard
HARRISON Frederic
HOLL Henry
HOPKINS Manley
HUNTER Sir Robert
HUTCHINSON Sir Jonathan
KER David
KING Joseph MP
KING Maude Egerton (née HINE)
LE GALLIENNE Richard
LEWIS George Henry
MANGLES James Henry
METHUEN Sir Algernon Methuen
  Marshall, Bt (né STEDMAN)
MURRAY George Gilbert
NETTLESHIP Edward FRS
NEVILL Lady Dorothy (née WALPOLE)
OLIPHANT Mrs Margaret (née WILSON)
PINERO Sir Arthur Wing
POLLOCK Sir Frederick, 3rd Bt

PONSONBY Arthur Augustus William
  Harry, 1st Baron Ponsonby of Shulbrede
ROGERSON Mrs Christina ('Chrissie')
  Adelaide Ethel Athanasia
  (née STEWART) later STEEVENS
ROSSETTI Christina
RUSSELL Lady Mary Agatha
RUSSELL Bertrand Arthur William,
  3rd Earl Russell
RUSSELL Hon Francis Albert Rollo
SALVIN Osbert FRS
SHAW George Bernard
SILLICK William Austen
SMITH Hannah (née WHITALL)
SMITH Lloyd Logan Pearsall
STORR Rayner
STRACHEY Rachel Conn ('Ray')
  (née COSTELLOE)
SWANTON Ernest William
TENNYSON Alfred, 1st Baron Tennyson
TENNYSON Lady Emily
  (née SELLWOOD)
TENNYSON Hallam, 2nd Baron Tennyson
THOMPSON Flora Jane (née TIMMS)
TYNDALL John FRS
WALES Hubert (William PIGGOTT)
WARD Mrs Mary Augusta (née ARNOLD)
  [known as 'Mrs Humphry Ward']
WEBB Sidney James, 1st Baron Passfield
WEBB Martha Beatrice (née POTTER)
WELLS Herbert George
WESTON Dame Agnes Elizabeth
WHITE Montagu
WHITEWAY Richard Stephen JP
WHYMPER Edward
WOLSELEY Garnet Joseph,
  1st Viscount Wolseley
WRIGHT Thomas

The Hilltop Writers

a Victorian Colony among the Surrey Hills

W. R. Trotter

The Hilltop Writers

First published 1996 by The Book Guild Ltd

This illustrated edition published 2003,
with extra material supplied by Haslemere Museum

Typeset and published by John Owen Smith
19 Kay Crescent, Headley Down, Hampshire GU35 8AH

Tel: 01428 712892
wordsmith@johnowensmith.co.uk
www.johnowensmith.co.uk

ISBN 978-1-873855-31-7

Printed by CreateSpace

Publisher's Note

In producing this new edition of *The Hilltop Writers* we have taken the opportunity to add illustrations of many of the authors and their houses, and maps to show where they lived.

We have also added a section on William Austen Sillick, the journalist on whose work much of this book is based, and a preface introducing the reader to Bob Trotter whose book this is.

Other than that, the text has remained unchanged except for a few minor corrections of fact which have been made here and there.

As well as echoing Bob's own acknowledgements which are listed later, we would like to add our own thanks to the staff and volunteers of Haslemere Museum who have helped with the gathering of additional information and illustrations needed to prepare for this volume.

About the Author

Wilfred Robert (Bob) Trotter was born into a medical family in London in 1911. His father, Wilfred Batten Lewis Trotter, a distinguished surgeon, physiologist and philosopher was appointed as honorary surgeon to King George V in 1928. Another of Mr Trotter's relatives, Ernest Jones, wrote a biography of Sigmund Freud.

Bob followed his father's footsteps by qualifying in medicine at Oxford and University College Hospital in 1935. During the Second World War he served as a major in the Royal Army Medical Corps, and researched the treatment of malaria.

After the war he became a consultant physician at University College Hospital, London, where he specialised in thyroid cases. He was also a senior lecturer at London University. He wrote widely on medical matters and retired to Haslemere in 1973.

With his wife, Enid, he shared an interest in archaeology and when a local archaeology group was started at Haslemere Museum they both joined up. Together they took part in field walking, surveying and occasionally making small excavations.

By the 1980s the archaeology group had broadened its scope to include local history and worked on a number of projects. During this time Bob also wrote articles on a variety of subjects including literature, local history, gardens and archaeology.

One project that he particularly enjoyed researching was the diary of James Simmons, master paper maker at Sickle Mill. This is one of the few first hand accounts of life in Victorian Haslemere and is therefore of intense interest to local historians. Working with a small team of fellow enthusiasts a full transcript of the Simmons diary was produced in 1990.

It was during his research work in the archives of Haslemere Museum that Bob came across the 'literary scrapbook' of William Austen Sillick which, as he explains in his Acknowledgements, formed the inspiration for this book. It took him some years of further research to complete the work, which was then 'launched' publicly at Haslemere Museum in August 1996.

Bob kept active by helping to sort and catalogue manuscripts and other archive material at the museum, right up until the week before he died, in November 1998.

Cross and view from Gibbet Hill, Hindhead

Contents

᧧᧧᧧

Publisher's Note..5
About the Author 7
List of Illustrations 10
Acknowledgements...17
Introduction...19
Section One: Chronology..29
    Beginnings...29
    Growth...33
    Climax 35
    Decline...38
Section Two: The Hilltop Community.................................43
    The Writers and their Houses 43
    Their Politics...44
    Social Issues 47
        'Degeneracy' 47
        The 'Woman Question' 50
    Religion 62
Section Three: Biographical Notes 81
Bibliography..235
Index 241

Illustrations

∾ ∾ ∾

Cross and view from Gibbet Hill, Hindhead........................8 and Front Cover
Map of the Hilltop Writers area 12
Map of Haslemere, circa 1867 15
View of the Devil's Punch Bowl in the early 1900s...................................20
'The Huts' at Hindhead, circa 1890 24
Haslemere High Street, looking north in 1887...29
Aldworth, the Tennysons' house on Blackdown 31
Inval, the Hutchinsons' home at Haslemere 33
Tyndall's hut at Hindhead in the 1880s 34
Pitfold House, the Beveridges' house on Woolmer Hill where George
       Bernard Shaw spent his honeymoon 36
The 'Fox & Pelican' in Grayshott, soon after its opening in 1899 38
The Croft, the house of Grant Allen at Hindhead 42
Tyndall's 'Hind Head House' 44
Crossways Road in Grayshott, circa 1900: Flora Thompson worked here...46
Undershaw at Hindhead, built by Arthur Conan Doyle 48
Haslemere High Street, looking south, circa 1894....................................51
Waggoners Wells near Grayshott – Richard Le Gallienne lived close by at
       Kingswood Chase...54
View from Blackdown, near to Fernhurst...56
Shulbrede Priory, home of Arthur Ponsonby...58
Barford, the home of Gilbert Murray 60
Brookbank, where George Eliot and GH Lewes stayed in 1871 63
Rayner Storr, photographed by George Bernard Shaw...............................67
Highcombe Edge, home of Rayner Storr at Hindhead................................69
George Herbert Aitken, Rector of Haslemere...71
Hill Farm, Camelsdale, home of Joseph and Maude King in the 1920s.......73
Haslemere Town Hall, when used as a 'lock-up' 76
Grant Allen...81
William Allingham 89
Godfrey Blount 93
George Bowdler Buckton...95
Jumps House and Carrington's observatory in 1871 99
Sir Arthur Conan Doyle..107
Beacon Hotel, where Doyle held his Christmas party in 1898 109
Walt Whitman, to whom Anne Gilchrist was attracted 120

Bernard Hamilton...122
Frederic Harrison 125
Sir Robert Hunter...131
Sir Jonathan Hutchinson 133
Joseph King..138
Richard Le Gallienne 139
Henry Mangles...145
Gilbert Murray 148
Edward Nettleship..150
The Georgian Hotel, Haslemere High Street 152
Sir Frederick Pollock 159
Arthur Ponsonby 161
Rollo Russell..173
George Bernard Shaw 177
William Austen Sillick..179
Rayner Storr...187
Ernest William Swanton 191
Alfred Tennyson, with his whistle 194
The Tennysons with sons Lionel and Hallam, circa 1862 199
Flora Jane Thompson – from the bust erected in Liphook.....................202
John Tyndall FRS..205
One of Tyndall's screens, viewed from Hindhead Road 207
Sidney and Beatrice Webb..213
Garnet Joseph Wolseley...222

Sources:

All illustrations are from the archives of Haslemere Museum, except—
Barford (p.60) – Olivia Cotton
Jumps House (p.99) – Melene Barnes
Shulbrede Priory (p.58) and Arthur Ponsonby (p.161) – the Ponsonby family
Waggoners Wells (p.54), Flora Thompson (p.202), View from Blackdown
(back cover) – John Owen Smith

Map of the Hilltop Writers area (pp.12/13) – drawn by Greta Turner

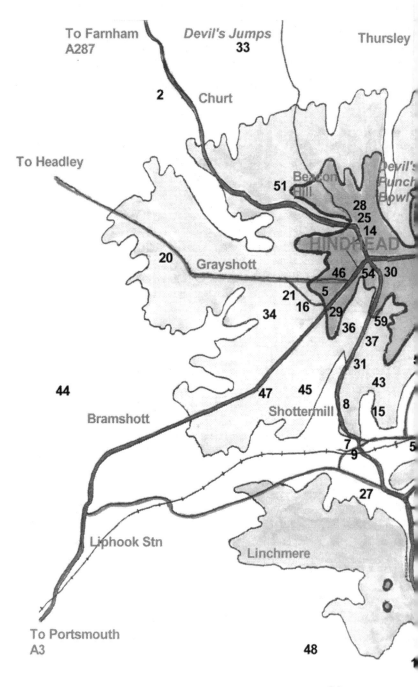

To Farnham
A287

Devil's Jumps
33

Thursley

2

Churt

To Headley

51 Beacon
Hill

*Devil's
Punch
Bowl*

28
25
14

HINDHEAD

20

Grayshott

46 **54** **30**

21
16

5

34

29

59

36

37

31

43

44

47

45

Shottermill

8

15

Bramshott

7
9

5

27

Liphook Stn

Linchmere

To Portsmouth
A3

48

24
To Midhurst
A286

12

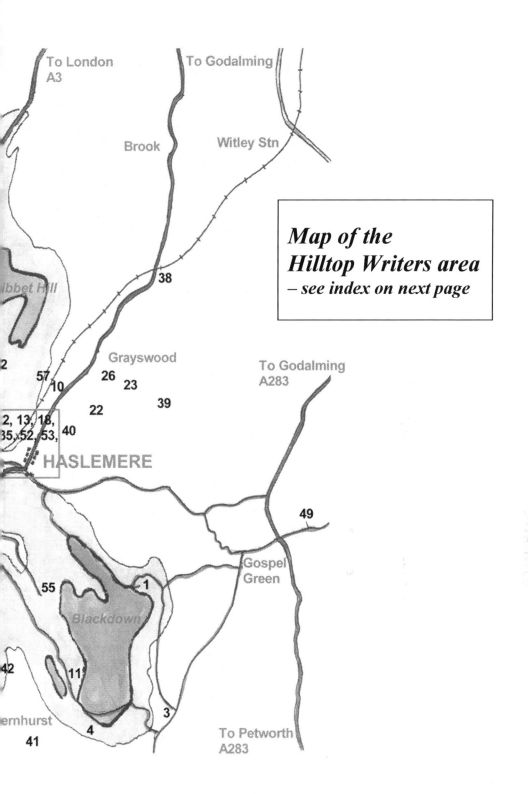

To London
A3

To Godalming

Brook

Witley Stn

*Map of the
Hilltop Writers area
– see index on next page*

ibbet Hill

38

Grayswood

To Godalming
A283

2

57
10

26
23

39

22

2, 13, 18,
35, 52, 53,
40

HASLEMERE

49

Gospel
Green

55

1

Blackdown

42

11

3

ernhurst

4

To Petworth
A283

41

13

Locations of Writers

1   Aldworth, Blackdown – The Tennysons
2   Barford Court, Churt – George Gilbert Murray
3   Blackdown Cottage – Frederic Harrison; Henry Holl; George Bernard Shaw
4   Blackdown House – Henry Holl
5   Blen-Cathra, Hindhead (now St Edmund's School) – George Bernard Shaw
6   3 Bridge Road, Haslemere – William Austen Sillick
7   Brookbank, Shottermill – George Eliot; Anne Gilchrist; George Lewes; Christina Rossetti
8   Brownscombe, Hindhead Rd – Richard Whiteway
9   Cherrimans, Shottermill – George Eliot; George Lewes; Christina Rossetti
10   Chesham Cottage, Grayswood Road – David Ker
11   Cochet Farm, Blackdown – H G Wells
12   Brockton, College Hill (now not known) – E W Swanton
13   under Courts Hill, Haslemere – William Allingham
14   The Croft, Hindhead (now Forest House) – Grant Allen
15   Dunrozel, Farnham Lane – Rollo Russell
16   Ensleigh, Crossways Rd, Grayshott – Dame Agnes Weston
17   Friday's Hill House, Fernhurst (not the present house) – Frank Costelloe; Hannah Smith
18   The Garth, High Lane, Haslemere – Gerald Manley Hopkins
19   Goodwyns, corner of Well Lane/High Street, Haslemere – Montagu White
20   Grayshott Farm (now Grayshott Hall) – The Tennysons
21   Grayshott Post Office (not the present building) – Flora Thompson
22   Grayswood Beeches – Mrs Humphrey Ward
23   Grayswood Place – Mrs Humphrey Ward
24   Hawksfold, Vann Rd, Fernhurst – Osbert Salvin
25   Highcombe Edge, Tilford Road, Hindhead – Rayner Storr
26   Highercombe, Grayswood – Henry Daykins; Sir Arthur Wing Pinero
27   Hill Farm, Camelsdale Road – Joseph & Maude King
28   Hindhead Brae, Hindhead (next to Highcombe Edge) – Bernard Hamilton
29   Hindhead Copse (now part of The Royal School) – Sir Frederick Pollock
30   Hindhead House – John Tyndall
31   Honey Hanger, Hindhead Road – Sir Algernon Methuen
32   Inval, Bunch Lane, Haslemere – Sir Jonathan Hutchinson
33   Jumps House, Devils Jumps, Churt – Richard Carrington
34   Kingswood Lane, Grayshott – Richard Le Gallienne
35   The Lodge (now Haslemere Museum), High Street – Montagu White
36   Log (or Long) House, Hazel Grove, Hindhead – Margaret Oliphant; Christine Rogerson; Hubert Wales
37   Longdown Hollow, Hindhead – Edward Nettleship
38   Lower Birtley, Grayswood – Joseph King
39   Manor House, Three Gates Lane, Haslemere – Garnet Wolseley
40   Meadfields, Three Gates Lane, Haslemere – Sir Robert Hunter
41   Millhanger, Lickfold Road, Fernhurst – Bertrand Russell
42   The Mud House, Friday's Hill, Fernhurst – Logan & Mary Pearsall Smith

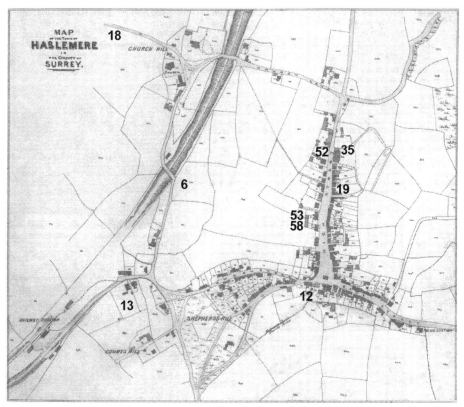

Map of Haslemere, circa 1867
— *showing approximate locations of Hilltop Writers' houses* —

43   New Place, Farnham Lane, Haslemere – Sir Algernon Methuen
44   Passfield Corner, Bramshott – Beatrice & Sidney Webb
45   Pitfold House, Woolmer Hill – Annette & William Beveridge; G B Shaw
46   Rozeldene, Hindhead – Lady Agatha Russell
47   Seven Thorns Inn (now derelict), Bramshott Chase – Richard Le Gallienne;
      Margaret Oliphant
48   Shulbrede Priory, Linchmere – Arthur Ponsonby
49   Stillands Farm, Gospel Green – Sir Arthur Wing Pinero
50   Stoatley Farm (or Great Stoatley, now gone) – Sir Jonathan Hutchinson;
      The Tennysons
51   Tilden Cottage, Grove Road, Beacon Hill – David Ker
52   The Town House, High Street – Edward Whymper
53   Tudor Cottage (now part of Georgian Hotel), High St – Lady Dorothy Nevill
54   Undershaw (now a hotel), Hindhead – Sir Arthur Conan Doyle
55   Valewood House, Fernden Lane, Blackdown – James Mangles
56   The Weaving House, King's Road, Haslemere – Godfrey & Ethel Blount
57   Weycombe House (now gone), near Puckshot Farm – George Buckton
58   The White House (now Georgian Hotel), High Street – Rayner Storr
59   Yaffles (now Anthony Place), Polecat Hill, Hindhead – Sir Francis Galton

57	Weycombe House (now gone), near Puckshot Farm – George Buckton
58	The White House (now Georgian Hotel), High Street – Rayner Storr
59	Yaffles (now Anthony Place), Polecat Hill, Hindhead – Sir Francis Galton

Unknown locations:—
Briar Cottage, Hindhead – George Douglas Brown
Homeward Heath, Hindhead – Hubert Wales
Sandy Croft, Haslemere – Lucy Garnett

Acknowledgements

This book was conceived among the archives of Haslemere Education Museum. It was there that I discovered the literary remains of William Austen Sillick (c.1877–1955), a remarkable local journalist who served on the staff of the Haslemere Herald for more than fifty years. Sillick took a great interest in the history of the locality, but particularly in the many literary figures who had resided in the neighbourhood. Following his death, Sillick's widow donated his many papers and notebooks to the museum; among these was his literary scrapbook which covered a period of about a hundred years and which contained notes and newspaper cuttings on 148 local writers.

This scrapbook alerted me to the fact that there had been a great deal of literary activity in the neighbourhood of Haslemere, but from his notes it became apparent that Sillick's main interest had been in the Victorian authors. True, there were no really outstanding names among the more recent writers mentioned – similar lists might have been compiled in comparable towns throughout southern England – but what did stand out as being unusual was the tight cluster of Victorian authors who had arrived during the last few decades of the nineteenth century. As well as the number of eminent figures in this small group, other distinctive features were the timing of their arrival soon after the railway came to Haslemere, and their predilection for the wild and uninhabited uplands. It was not difficult to infer from this that most of them had settled in this particular area for the same, or at least similar, reasons. Although Sillick himself does not explicitly recognise their existence as a special group, the length of his entries on the Victorian writers (particularly Tennyson) compared with his much briefer notes on their successors, is an implicit acknowledgement of special status. So, I have much to thank William Sillick for, and regret that I am unable to do so in person.

My gratitude to Sillick is coupled with recognition of the debt I owe to the institution which houses his literary remains. I gladly acknowledge the Curator of Haslemere Educational Museum, Diana Hawkes, not only for permitting me to spend many hours rummaging in the Museum's copious archives and well-stocked library, but also for encouraging me to persevere in the writing of this book. I am also grateful to my fellow voluntary workers in the Museum, John and Greta Turner and Cyril and Vi Queen, who freely shared their comprehensive knowledge of local history and local personalities. In particular, Greta Turner has been invaluable in helping to identify the houses inhabited by various writers.

Another valuable source of information has been the Local Studies Library at Guildford, where John Janaway and his staff have given every possible assistance.

Personal contacts have also been useful. I would particularly like to thank Mrs Melene Barnes for sharing her great knowledge of the Carrington tragedy with me; and Anna Powell and David Unwin for letting me see letters, diaries and photographs relating to their grandfather, Rayner Storr.

Local sources have therefore been invaluable in determining where and when the Hilltop Writers came to live in the district, how they spent their time, and what they wrote while they were here. But the Hilltop Writers were not just local heroes: they were part of the great Victorian literary culture, and had to be seen also in a wider context. The extensive research which this entailed was carried out at the London Library and the British Library, and I am grateful for help from the staff of both these institutions. I wish to thank the Manuscript Division of the British Library, and the Trustees of the National Library of Scotland for permitting me to use material in their possession to assist in dating Margaret Oliphant's visits to Hindhead. I am particularly indebted to Mr J.F. Russell, of the National Library of Scotland, for scanning Oliphant's numerous letters in order to identify those bearing a Hindhead dateline. I am grateful to Rosemary Ashton, biographer of G.H. Lewes, for permitting me to see a photocopy of part of Lewes' diary, in order to describe his and George Eliot's activities during a typical week while they were living at Shottermill. The diary is in the possession of the Beinecke Rare Book and Manuscript Library, Yale University, and I am grateful for permission to make use of extracts from it. I also wish to acknowledge my gratitude to Cambridge University Press for permission to quote from *My Apprenticeship* by Beatrice Webb, 1979; to Victor Gollancz for permission to quote from *Remarkable Relations* by Barbara Strachey, 1980; to the London School of Economics and Political Science for permission to quote from *The Diaries of Beatrice Webb*, 1982; to Oxford University Press for permission to quote from *The Letters of Alfred Lord Tennyson*, 1990, *The Autobiography of Margaret Oliphant*, 1990 and *Gilbert Murray OM 1866-1957* by Duncan Wilson, 1987; and to A.P. Watt Ltd, Literary Executors of the Estate of H.G. Wells for permission to quote from *Experiment in Autobiography* by H.G. Wells, 1996.

I am especially grateful to Maxine Merrington and Liz Ball for compiling the index.

W.R. Trotter, 1996

Introduction

During the last decades of the nineteenth century, writers working in London were presented with an enticing possibility. The new railway line to Portsmouth, opened in 1859, had carved its way through the as-yet unsullied highlands of south-west Surrey. The station at Haslemere, which could be reached after a journey of no more than an hour and a half from London, gave access to these heights, and a means of escape from the murk and stench of the capital, without loss of its facilities. The heather-covered hilltops, with their wide views and wholesome air, held out the promise of a writers' paradise.

Many writers, from Virgil and Horace to Wordsworth and Thoreau, have felt the appeal of the wilderness. Few have been in a position to respond to it; wildernesses tend to be a long way from cities, with their libraries and publishers, and the company of like-minded folk. But the new railway line offered Londoners a unique opportunity to escape to a real wilderness. The gateway to the promised land was Haslemere, then no more than a small village perched on a ridge marking the watershed between the headwaters of the rivers Wey and Arun. The ridge is not much more than four hundred feet above sea-level; a trivial height, yet, with a light dusting of snow, Haslemere can even now give a passable imitation of an Alpine village. To the east, the Wealden plain stretches across Sussex to Kent; to the west, a semicircle of sandstone hills rises to 895 feet at Hindhead, and 918 feet at Blackdown. E.C. Matthews described the geology and landscape of this tract of rugged hill country as it appeared in Edwardian times: 'in their great elevation, their abruptness of form, and the deep ravines which furrow their sides, these Southern Highlands more nearly resemble true mountainous country than anything else in this part of England. They stand, an isolated tableland, with a steep escarpment both to north and south, rising into wild hills and high, treeless, heather-clad commons.'[1]

The prospect of being able to live in such wild country, yet remain within easy reach of the metropolis, appealed to writers of all descriptions, and in the late-nineteenth century many of them came to make a permanent home, rent lodgings or stay with friends, while writing their books. They were a fairly representative cross-section of the late-Victorian literary and intellectual community. There were some distinguished names among them: poets, such as Alfred Tennyson, Christina Rossetti and William Allingham; the novelists George Eliot, Conan Doyle, Grant Allen, Richard Le Gallienne, Margaret Oliphant, Mrs Humphry Ward and H.G. Wells; playwrights Bernard Shaw and Arthur Pinero; the essayist, Logan Pearsall Smith; and Flora Thompson, re-creator of the rural past. There were also a number of people who were not primarily writers, but who were distinguished in other walks of life, and came to the hill country to set down their accumulated expertise in published works: scientists like John Tyndall and Francis Galton; social reformers like the Webbs and Arthur Ponsonby; the historian Frederic Harrison; Gilbert Murray, the classical scholar; the lawyer, Frederick Pollock; Bertrand Russell, the philosopher and mathematician; medical men like Jonathan Hutchinson and Edward Nettleship; the mountaineer, Edward Whymper; and – defying classification, but of great intellectual stature – George Henry Lewes.

View of the Devil's Punch Bowl in the early 1900s

There were many others too, writers who may not have produced great literature, but who in the range of their expertise, and the deep seriousness with which they went about their business, were as truly representative of the late-Victorian intellectual community as those who are better known. And what they perhaps lacked in literary finesse they often made up for by the interest of their personalities, or of their life-histories. There was, for instance, Manley Hopkins (father of Gerard, the poet), an average adjuster by profession, who wrote a history of the Kingdom of Hawaii, as well as a book of arithmetical conundrums, and a lot of bad poetry; Rayner Storr, the Positivist whose Concordance to *De Imitatione Christi* was praised by the Pope;

James Henry Mangles, the railway director who hybridised Himalayan rhododendrons, and walked with Tennyson on Blackdown, and recorded their conversation. Then there was Anne Gilchrist, the respectable middle-aged widow who, as well as completing her late husband's *Life of William Blake* and introducing Tennyson, George Eliot and Christina Rossetti to the hilltop country, still found time for a passionate transatlantic affair with Walt Whitman; Richard Carrington, the eccentric astronomer who made tunnels in The Devil's Jumps, with disastrous consequences for himself and his wife; and Hannah Pearsall Smith, connoisseur of bizarre religious sects, and scourge of the male sex.

One of the most notable – though now largely forgotten – of the Victorian writers who settled on the Surrey hills was Grant Allen, novelist and science writer. He decided to call his two best-known books Hilltop Novels, and it is from him that I have borrowed the term for the title of the present work. In the Introduction to one of these, *The British Barbarians*, Allen explained what the hills meant to him:

> I am writing in my study on a heather-clad hilltop. When I raise my eye from my sheet of foolscap, it falls upon miles and miles of broad open moorland. My window looks out upon unsullied nature. Everything around is fresh and clean and wholesome. Through the open casement, the scent of the pines blows in with the breeze from the neighbouring firwood. Keen airs sigh through the pine-needles. Grasshoppers chirp from deep tangles of bracken. The song of a skylark drops from the sky like soft rain in summer; in the evening, a nightjar croons to us his monotonously passionate love-wail from his perch on the gnarled boughs of the wind-swept larch that crowns the upland. But away below in the valley, as night draws on, a lurid glare reddens the north-eastern horizon. It marks the spot where the great wen of London heaves and festers. Up here on the free hills, the sharp air blows in upon us, limpid and clear from a thousand leagues of open ocean; down there in the crowded town, it stagnates and ferments, polluted with the diseases and vices of centuries.2

His fervent delight in distancing himself from the grime of London suggests something more than merely physical relief. In effect, Allen and the other 'hilltop writers' were expressing their distaste for the overcrowded cities and ruined countryside brought about by the Industrial Revolution, as well as their joy in the purity and freedom of an as-yet unspoiled land. Yet it was the great surge in middle-class wealth, together with advances in paper-making and printing, that had given authors the means to make their escape from the consequences of that revolution. They were indeed a fortunate generation; but in return for the good fortune which permitted them to build their sturdy houses in a desirable wilderness, they left as their legacy some outstanding works of literature, together with a deep sense of the enduring virtue of an all-embracing culture.

The delight of the Hilltop Writers in the pure air and wide views of their wilderness seems oddly at variance with earlier accounts of the same area. When J.M.W. Turner passed this way in November 1807, his sketch (later engraved) *Hind Head Hill* reveals a gloomy, uninviting landscape of bare and barren hills.[3] And a few years later, William Cobbett denounced Hindhead as 'certainly the most villainous spot that God ever made'.[4] That was in 1822; like Turner, he was there in November, it was raining heavily, and the guide had annoyed him by bringing him over Hindhead, which he wanted at all costs to avoid. But he was also displeased by the infertility and uselessness of the wide expanse of heathland. It was in fact used only as common land for the grazing of a few sheep and cattle, owned by farmers living in the valleys below; this was enough to restrain the growth of Scots pines, and so preserve the heather cover. Apart from marauding bands of robbers, the only human inhabitants of these upland heaths were the so-called 'broom squires', who made besoms from birch twigs and heather. They lived in primitive huts, where they plied their trade for markets in London and Portsmouth. But by the middle of the century they were gradually becoming extinct, owing to competition from factory-made brooms. By the 1870s and 1880s, when the coaching trade had also vanished – and with it, many of the robbers who preyed upon it – the Hindhead plateau and the surrounding hills were more empty than they had been in the past, or would be in the future. Louis Jennings, who walked that way in 1878, testified to the beauty and the loneliness of these remote hilltops:

> At every step some new beauty bursts upon you. There is not a human being near – but one house, a solitary farm faraway on the ridge of Hindhead, is to be seen ... It is with surprise that in this lonely waste one sees, between the Devil's Punch Bowl and the top of the hill, a fine, broad and well-kept road, nor is that surprise diminished when you come upon it, and find that it is as hard and smooth as any road in a private park can possibly be. There are very few marks of wheels to be found upon it, but abundant traces of sheep ... I declare that I stood looking at that road in amazement for pretty nearly a quarter of an hour, and I am inclined to think that if I had stayed there till now I should not have seen anybody or anything coming along it in either direction.[5]

The contrast between Cobbett's displeasure and the ecstasies of later writers was in large part due to the change in taste which came about during the course of the nineteenth century, as the increasing squalor of the enlarging cities encouraged appreciation of the beauties of the untouched countryside. So once writers had discovered this empty land, they began to realise that it was ideally suited to their needs. There was peace and quiet in abundance, and a sense of freedom. Furthermore, the surrounding heaths invited a stroll in the intervals of composition. The wide views from the hilltops seemed to induce a sense of philosophic detachment, while the air was invigorating and, it was widely believed very good for the health. Hallam Tennyson relates that the 'fine air' of Blackdown cured his father of the troublesome attacks of hay-fever.[6] Many other writers testified to the remarkable properties of the air of the hilltops, and are quoted in the Biographical Notes (Section Three). None was more eloquent than the novelist Helen Mathers, who frequently came to Hindhead to recover from the stresses of London. She wrote in *TPs Weekly* for 1903: 'in its thin pure buoyant air you feel splendidly well, and cannot tire yourself however far you walk or cycle, while your slumbers are those of the blest'. Yet a short ride in a pony-trap would bring you to the station, where the train would whisk you up to London to study in a library, or haggle with a publisher over terms for your forthcoming book.

Some of the early literary settlers bought or rented existing houses in the valleys, contenting themselves with arduous walks on the heathery uplands. But to get full value from the wilderness, one had, like Grant Allen, to live in the midst of it, which meant building a new house on a most inaccessible site. This required a technical infrastructure which was only just becoming available. Tennyson's Aldworth, built 800 feet up on Blackdown in 1868–69, was a pioneering effort, only possible for a relatively wealthy person. But it showed what could be done, for despite the remote situation, it was equipped with all the conveniences then required by the increasingly sophisticated middle class (it even had a bath, something that Tennyson's other house, Farringford, lacked).[7] This demonstration that it was possible to site a comfortable house on these wild hilltops must have done much to make the area known in literary circles. Others soon followed the example, and ventured on to Hindhead, the other main eminence in the locality. Concomitantly, an infrastructure grew up: a brick-making industry started up in the valley at Hammer, and steam lorries carried its products up on to the heights. At the foot of the valleys settlements grew up to house the workers who serviced the developments on the uplands. Coal was needed in large quantities to make the winters endurable; and for writers an adequate postal service was a necessity. Many of the houses springing up on Hindhead were serviced from the nearby village of Grayshott, and – as Flora Thompson, who worked in the post office there, vividly described – the literati came there to send their telegrams.

For a time, writers almost had their wilderness to themselves, but it was not long before their example was followed by business people, and hotel and lodging-house keepers. Hindhead, in particular, became recognised as a health resort. True commuters – now the dominant element – only appeared after 1900, when the motor-car eased the journey from the railway station to the hilltops. A pony-trap, while adequate for writers, who only needed to make occasional forays to London, would not have suited businessmen returning from a hard day's work in the City. Large-scale building on Hindhead started in the early 1900s, and very soon converted much of the wilderness into the suburb that it is today. Alarm at the threat of development eventually protected some of the remaining hilltops. Most of the heathlands salvaged from the speculative builders gradually came under the care of the National Trust. The consequence was that all of the original wilderness was either suburbanised, or else packaged in enclaves rigorously protected from ambitious builders.

'The Huts' at Hindhead, circa 1890

The Hilltop Writers, and the commuters who followed them, not only transformed the physical countryside; they also changed the social climate. For they were alien, middle-class invaders of a land of small farmers, agricultural labourers, broom-makers and petty shopkeepers, and had little real contact with the indigenous inhabitants, other than as servants and builders of their homes. Ironically, of all the Hilltop Writers, the one who seems to have had the closest contact with the natives was an American, John Burroughs. The original colony of Victorian writers dispersed early in the new century, but they had launched a middle-class invasion, the effect of which was to turn Hindhead into a prosperous if unattractive suburb, while Blackdown, jealously guarded by the National Trust, remained inviolate.

The migration of writers to the hills of south-west Surrey was noted by several contemporaries. Thomas Wright (see Biographical Notes), living at

Olney in Buckinghamshire, knew of Hindhead's reputation as a centre of intellectual activity well before his visit there in 1897. It was, he believed, 'the loftiest settlement in the British Isles', and he had heard of the 'picturesque race of aborigines who get their living ... by working the landscape into brooms'. Above all, he knew of the place as 'the literary Olympus, the abode of so many cultured notables that some wag felicitously suggested that the name should be altered to Mind Head'. When he actually got there in 1897, he was quite carried away by the unspoilt beauty of the scenery: 'never have I witnessed scenery one half so lovely or a tithe so striking as that of the blowing woodlands and ample commons of aëry, amethystine, and oderiferous Hind Head'.[8]

Shortly afterwards, F.W. Bockett, cycling through the Surrey lanes in search of the homes of his literary heroes, came to Haslemere, in the south-west corner of the county, in the summer of 1900.[9] 'The neighbourhood of Haslemere,' he wrote, 'has, during the past ten or twelve years, become quite a famous haunt of literary men. Not only have they congregated in the village, but they have climbed to the topmost heights of Hindhead ...' But, he added, these same heights were 'now being overrun not only by people who are merely rich, but also by lodging-house keepers and hotel proprietors'. He feared that the next step would be the construction of 'a cable tram from the village to the head, or perchance an American-made electric lift'.[10]

As Bockett noted, by 1900 the literary migration to the hills of south-west Surrey was coming to an end. Many of the early settlers were departing; among them was Rayner Storr, who left Hindhead for Hampstead in 1908. From there he wrote to journalist and Haslemere historian W.A. Sillick on 11th November 1913: 'I am quite bewildered at the disappearance of so many of my old and useful friends at Hindhead and Haslemere. Is that privileged district to come down from its proud pre-eminence as the chosen home of public-spirited and enlightened men?'[11] Shortly afterwards, the same theme was expressed more dramatically by a character in Shaw's *Misalliance*: 'The writing is on the wall! Rome fell! Babylon fell! Hindhead's turn will come!'

For a time, as the nineteenth century approached its end, it looked as if the writers who had come individually to the Surrey hilltops might, with all their common interests, come together to form a close-knit community with definable characteristics, like the Bloomsbury Group. The *New Age* had indeed forecast that 'Hindhead may become in time the nineteenth-century representative of the Mermaid Tavern and Will's coffee-house.'[12] But before anything like this could happen, their paradise disappeared under bricks and mortar. They had shown the rest of the world that it was possible to live in a wilderness, and yet retain close contact with civilisation; and now the rest of the world wanted to join in on the act. And so, as the entrepreneurs, contractors, businessmen and hotel-keepers moved in, the writers deserted their by-now suburbanised hilltops.

So the colonisation of the Surrey hilltops was no more than a brief episode. Yet it deserves a niche in literary history because it brought together, in one relatively circumscribed area, a representative collection of writers at a crucial turning-point in intellectual development. Before 1900, it was possible for an intelligent person, with the necessary application, to grasp the whole sweep of human knowledge; and a number of the Hilltop Writers did just that. But after 1900 came Planck's quantum theory, Einstein's relativity, Freud's psycho-analysis, Joyce's *Ulysses*, abstract painting, atonal music; and, inevitably, specialisation. The Hilltop Writers belonged to the last generation of 'complete men', in the tradition of the Renaissance; and as they left their hilltops, that tradition also faded. It was an inevitable development, but it seems fitting to recall, not without a tinge of regret, the breadth and diversity of their knowledge, and the impressive seriousness with which they studied the arts and sciences. Late-Victorian *gravitas* may today seem unduly ponderous, even at times pompous, but it testifies to a common purpose to push the human intellect to its limits.

The plan of this book is first, to introduce the writers chronologically, as they settled in among the hills; next, to look briefly at their collective attitudes to the main issues of the day; and finally, to treat each of them severally in a short biographical sketch, with the emphasis on their activities whilst they were living – and writing – on the Surrey uplands.

Footnotes to Introduction

[1] Matthews, E.C., *The Highlands of South-West Surrey*, pp. 2–3.

[2] Allen, Grant, *The British Barbarians: A Hilltop Novel*, p. xvii.

[3] Herrman, Luke, *Turner's Prints: The Engraved Works of J.M.W. Turner*.

[4] Cobbett, William, *Rural Rides*, p. 118.

[5] Jennings, Louis J., *Field Paths and Green Lanes*, pp. 132–33.

[6] Tennyson, Hallam, *Memoir*, vol. 2, p. 209.

[7] Tennyson, Charles, *Aldworth: Summer Home of Alfred Lord Tennyson*, p.8.

[8] Wright, Thomas, *Hindhead, or the English Switzerland, and its Literary and Historical Associations*.

[9] Frederick William Bockett (1858–1913) became successively a printer, journalist, sub-editor and finally printing clerk to the London County Council 1889–1912. In 1897 he moved from London to Woking. Eight of his cycling forays are described in his book, the seventh being to Haslemere. The book is dedicated 'To you pilgrims who have discarded staff and sandals for the more comfortable and expeditious rubber-tyred wheels'. Bockett had an extensive knowledge of literary people and their homes. He got to know Frederic Harrison early in the 1880s and joined the Positivist Society – in which Harrison was the leading figure – in 1883. In 1886 he delivered an address to a meeting at Newton Hall on 'The Workman's Life'. The address was subsequently published as a booklet, price tuppence. In it he contended that 'Positivism was a religion for the common people, as well as for the rich and clever.'
See Newman, Robert, *Positivist Review*, vol. 21, 1913, pp. 91–93, 'In Memoriam Frederick William Bockett'.

[10] Bockett, *Some Literary Landmarks for Pilgrims on Wheels*, pp.218–19.

[11] Quoted from an autographed letter in the Sillick Collection, Haslemere Museum.

[12] Whittington-Egan, Richard and Smerdon, Geoffrey, *The Quest of the Golden Boy: The Life and Letters of Richard Le Gallienne*, p.290.

Section One: Chronology

Beginnings

When the railway came in 1859, Haslemere was a quiet little market town or village of barely 952 inhabitants. The houses huddled together on a narrow ridge separating the catchment areas of the rivers Wey and Arun. The ridge was about 400 feet above sea-level, but the surrounding Greensand hills rose to about twice that. Not surprisingly, the first literary migrants settled either in Haslemere itself or in the neighbouring valleys, since to have built a house to middle-class expectations on the desolate hills around the town would have meant a major and expensive undertaking.

Haslemere High Street, looking north in 1887

Among the first arrivals was the Whymper family, who came to Town House in the High Street, in early 1859 (James Simmons, the Shottermill diarist, noted that Josiah Wood Whymper, head of the family, spoke at a Bible meeting in Haslemere in April of that year.)[1] Josiah Wood Whymper was a well-known wood-engraver; his second son, Edward, was also an engraver, but became better known as a mountaineer, and as the author of graphic accounts of his experiences. The youngest daughter, Annette, born in Haslemere soon after the family arrived, wrote some religious stories. Edward was a friend of John Tyndall, the scientist and fellow mountaineer, who came to live at Hindhead in 1883; they had known each other well before this, and were rivals in attempts to climb the Matterhorn. This seems to have been Edward's only contact with other Haslemere authors. Many other members of the Whymper family became prominent citizens of Haslemere, though their talents lay more in art than literature.

James Henry Mangles, the second of our authors to settle in the Haslemere area, would not ordinarily be thought of as a literary figure. He is, however, known to garden historians as an early hybridist of the newly introduced Himalayan rhododendrons, and his collection of this genus was much admired by contemporaries. He had settled at Valewood House, in a valley beneath Blackdown, in September 1859; it was in order to grow rhododendrons that he had come to the area, as conditions there were particularly favourable for this purpose. However, Mangles is also known to Tennyson scholars in a quite different context. Soon after the poet was installed at Aldworth, on the opposite side of Blackdown, Mangles struck up an acquaintance with him, and had many conversations during the period 1870–72, the gist of which he recorded in his diary. This diary was only published long after Mangles's death, and does much to reveal the human side of the Laureate.[2] After completion of his diary, Mangles's interests seem to have been confined to his rhododendrons, and to the London & South-Western Railway, of which he was a director.

Neither the Whympers nor Mangles played much part in the general development of the future literary community. But the next to arrive, Anne Gilchrist, proved to be a key figure in its early evolution. Even before she settled at Brookbank, in the outlying hamlet of Shottermill in early 1862, she was already integrated into London literary society, having lived next door to, and on the friendliest of terms with, Thomas and Jane Carlyle. Very soon after settling in at Brookbank she was engaged in completing her late husband's *Life of William Blake* (1863), in which task she was assisted by Dante Gabriel and William Rossetti. This, in turn, initiated her friendship with Christina Rossetti, who stayed and wrote at Brookbank. So right from the start of her occupancy, her little cottage was a centre of literary activity.

A few years later, Anne Gilchrist was also largely responsible for securing Alfred Tennyson as a resident of the Surrey hills. Walter White, assistant secretary of the Royal Society and writer of travel books, was an old friend of Anne's. He was also on friendly terms with Tennyson. When the two met in November 1864, the poet was complaining about the encroachment of buildings round his house at Farringford in the Isle of Wight. This led White to suggest that he might be interested in an estate at Churt.[3] White put the Tennysons in touch with Anne Gilchrist, and they duly turned up at Brookbank in August 1866. For the next two years, Anne, with the assistance of her neighbour, James Simmons, was active in helping them to find a site for their new house. Without her help and local knowledge, it is very likely that the Tennysons would not have succeeded in building Aldworth at Blackdown.

The Tennysons moved into the house in the summer of 1869. Two years later, G.H. Lewes and Marian Evans (George Eliot) rented Brookbank from Anne for the summer months. The arrival of such literary giants as Tennyson and Eliot made the name of Haslemere familiar in intellectual circles, and instilled the idea that this could be a point of entry to wild and attractive hilltop country, where authors might settle and write their books, without losing touch with the capital. All this flowed from Anne Gilchrist's move to the little cottage at Shottermill in 1862. This, more than any other, was the seminal event that initiated the literary migration to the hills round about Haslemere.[4]

Aldworth, the Tennysons' house on Blackdown

Tennyson's decision to build on a windswept ledge, high up on Blackdown, was an audacious one. It demonstrated, first, that it was possible to construct a house with the amenities which the middle-classes were beginning to see as essential, on such an out-of-the-way spot; and secondly, that an author could now live in comfort in an attractive wilderness, and yet remain in touch with the literary life of the capital. No-one followed him on to the heights of Blackdown, but his example suggested that other similar hills – notably Hindhead – might suit the needs of other writers. In view of his immense reputation, Tennyson's example was undoubtedly important in starting the move of literary people to the Surrey hills; but once settled there,

31

he did not encourage further local contacts, other than with his old friend William Allingham, who settled in Haslemere for some months in 1880, James Henry Mangles, Frederic Harrison and with the Leweses during their brief stay at Shottermill.

Brookbank played an important role for the second time in 1871. George Eliot and G.H. Lewes rented it from Mrs Gilchrist for the summer months, and a large section of *Middlemarch* was written there. Both of the Leweses were absorbed in their writing, and had little time for social life. Their only literary contact while they were there was with the Tennysons. Eliot's reputation was already high, and rose higher still after the publication of *Middlemarch*, so she must also have done much to make the name of Haslemere well known in literary circles.

Meanwhile, the district's charms had been discovered quite independently by Jonathan Hutchinson, an enterprising and successful London surgeon, in 1863. He began a series of summer visits to Haslemere, staying in rented lodgings, until 1872, when he built Inval as a family home. It was a less audacious venture than Tennyson's, being situated on a lower eminence, and nearer the town centre; but the idea behind it was the same – to build a comfortable home in a wild area of country, with ready access to London.[5]

In the course of time, Hutchinson became a dominant figure in the cultural life of Haslemere, mainly through the museum which he founded, and the immensely popular lectures he gave there. He started the museum in 1888, and in 1891 it became linked with the independently founded Haslemere Microscope and Natural History Society. The connection persisted, and as in the course of time many of the authors who came to the area joined the Society, they necessarily came in contact with Hutchinson. In contrast to many of the other Hilltop Writers, Hutchinson stayed on at his Haslemere home until his death in 1913. He, and his museum, provided the continuity which kept alive the literary and cultural tradition into the early years of the twentieth century.

In 1865, George Buckton, astronomer and entomologist, and his daughter Alys, known later as a poet and playwright, settled at Weycombe House. Both played a part in the cultural life of Haslemere, and both Buckton and his daughter visited Tennyson at Aldworth.

Four years later, the strange and isolated figure of another astronomer appeared among the three small conical hills, north of Hindhead, known as The Devil's Jumps. Richard Carrington, an astronomer of some distinction and author of many publications on the subject, built his highly original observatory on the middle of the three hills, and lived a secluded life with his young and lovely bride, until overtaken by the mysterious and tragic sequence of events related in Biographical Notes.

The next to arrive, Rayner Storr, became an important figure in the affairs of the Haslemere Microscope and Natural History Society, as well as presiding over the Grayshott and District Refreshment Association's attempt to civilise the English pub, and taking a practical interest in the state of the local drains. He was also a keen student of medieval literature, an admirer of Dante, and the compiler of a Concordance to *De Imitatione Christi*. Storr came in 1875, and lived in a house in the centre of Haslemere until 189. He then felt the call of the wild hill-tops, and moved to a new house overlooking the Punch Bowl at Hindhead.

Inval, the Hutchinsons' home at Haslemere

The arrival of Robert Hunter, co-founder of the National Trust, in 1881 was immensely important for the amenities of the area, since he, more than anyone, saved Blackdown from the fate of Hindhead. However, although he wrote some influential works, he made no particular impact on the literary community. The same is true of the biologist Osbert Salvin, who settled at Fernhurst in 1882; and of John Burroughs, who came fleetingly to Shotter-mill in the same year from across the Atlantic, in the hope of hearing the nightingale. He, too, it seems likely, came as a result of his friendship with Anne Gilchrist.

Growth

Apart from Tennyson on his Blackdown eyrie, the literary settlers had so far shunned the higher uplands. But in 1883, perhaps responding to Tennyson's initiative, John Tyndall, the eminent scientist, and his wife camped in a primitive hut which they had put up in the grounds of their future home near the summit of Hindhead. In the same year, Rollo Russell settled on the lower slopes. They were both writers as well as scientists, and they foresaw the future of Hindhead for people of their sort, and invested in some of the waste there. This was the start of the major inflow of literary settlers.

33

Tyndall's example made a particular impact. Well known as a mountaineer, he had a house in the Swiss Alps, and had come to Hindhead as a more convenient location at which to enjoy the benefits of the mountain air. Whether or not he invented the actual phrase, it was as a direct result of his influence that Hindhead became known as 'the English Switzerland'. The news gradually spread that the Hindhead air was especially beneficial – an important factor in attracting future migrants. The first to come was Frederick Pollock, who settled in Hazel Grove, just below the Hindhead plateau, in 1884. By profession a lawyer, he too was a mountaineer, and had come to Hindhead as the nearest handy substitute for the Alps. Thus Tyndall, Russell and Pollock together demonstrated that it was possible to live in comfort on these wild uplands.

Tyndall's hut at Hindhead in the 1880s

Frederic Harrison, the historian and Positivist, struck out on his own when he took Blackdown Cottage in 1886, on a ten-year lease. Situated a little below the summit, on the south-east corner of Blackdown, this was perhaps the most remote location of all. But it did allow him to walk over to Aldworth to visit Tennyson, with whom he had a slightly edgy friendship. Despite the remoteness, he seems to have been able to travel to London quite frequently, for during part of his time at Blackdown he was serving as Professor of Jurisprudence to the Council of Legal Education.

Some of the new arrivals in the 1880s still preferred relatively lower locations. Manley Hopkins, who settled with his family in Haslemere in 1887, and Lord Wolseley, who spent the summer of that year there, both settled in the village. But a number of authors compromised, choosing sites on some of the lower hills nearer to the centre. The minor eminence of Grayswood was particularly popular: Arthur Pinero and Mrs Humphry Ward were both there in 1890; Henry Dakyns in 1892; Joseph and Maude King in 1894. But when Margaret Oliphant came for the first of her four visits in 1888, she was a guest of her friend, Mrs Rogerson, on the heights of Hindhead, very near the house of Frederick Pollock.

A new and important colony was established on one of these lesser heights when the Pearsall Smith family from Philadelphia, which included the matriarchal Hannah Smith, her son Logan and two daughters, acquired Friday's Hill House, overlooking Fernhurst, in 1889. Sidney Webb stayed with them in 1890, while Beatrice lodged with the Frederic Harrisons at Blackdown Cottage; and they were both at Friday's Hill in 1901. Soon after the Pearsall Smiths had moved in, Rollo Russell walked over from his house in Farnham Lane with his young nephew, Bertrand Russell, who happened to be staying with him. Bertie fell in love with the Pearsall Smiths' younger daughter Alys, who became the first of his four wives. The young couple later occupied a cottage in Fernhurst village, where Bertie wrote the first of his many books. So Friday's Hill became another centre of literary activity: Logan Pearsall Smith started his writing career there; the Webbs stayed there while engaged on one of their books; and Hannah's granddaughter Ray Strachey – who would later edit Hannah's remarkable account of bizarre religious sects – also wrote her first novel there.

Climax

The literary influx reached its peak in the 1890s at Hindhead. Margaret Oliphant stayed there on four occasions between 1888 and 1895, writing her novel *The Cuckoo in the Nest*, with a local setting. In 1893, Grant Allen came to Hindhead for the sake of his health, and to write his Hilltop Novels, in his house overlooking the Devil's Punch Bowl. In 1894, the Beveridges, with their son William, settled at Pitfold House, on Woolmer Hill, a little below the summit of Hindhead. In 1895, Richard Le Gallienne came seeking consolation from Grant Allen after the death of his first wife. He stayed to build his own house further along the Portsmouth Road in Kingswood Lane and wrote *The Quest of the Golden Girl*. It was probably also in 1895 that Revd S. Baring-Gould came to stay with his friend the vicar of Thursley, and was encouraged to write his novel *The Broom Squire*, which also had a local setting. In 1896, Arthur Conan Doyle built Undershaw at Hindhead crossroads, and there wrote his historical novels and some of the Sherlock Holmes stories. In 1897, Algernon Methuen, better known as a publisher though also a writer on his own account, acquired Honeyhanger, a short way down the hill from Tyndall's Hindhead House. This phase of the development of the literary community is fully documented by Thomas Wright (see entry in Biographical Notes), when he came to the nearby village of Grayshott, to write his account of the hilltop community, *Hindhead, or the English Switzerland* (1898).

Unnoticed by Wright, and unknown to any of the literary community, the young Flora Thompson came to nearby Grayshott in 1898, not to write, but to take up the humble post of assistant to the local postmaster. There she quietly absorbed the beauty of the surrounding heathlands and noted the quirks of the local inhabitants, much later writing about both in the posthumously published *Heatherley*.

Pitfold House, the Beveridges' house on Woolmer Hill
where George Bernard Shaw spent his honeymoon

1898 was memorable for the arrival of George Bernard Shaw, at first at the Beveridges' house on Woolmer Hill, and then at Blen-Cathra, at the junction of Hindhead and Grayshott. As might be expected, he added considerably to the already active intellectual life of the area, expressing his vigorous opinions in a public address on 'Why I Am a Socialist', and causing dismay to the local schoolteacher by advising children to disobey their elders. Next year a friend of Shaw's, the Greek scholar Gilbert Murray, came to Barford near Churt, and engaged in some lively correspondence with him.

A notable focus for the intellectual life of Haslemere at this time was provided by the Haslemere Microscope and Natural History Society. The Society had its origin in a class started in 1888 by a Colonel William H. Mason, to enable working men to study nature with the help of a microscope. The Colonel left Haslemere in the following year, but the Society flourished.

The secretary for the first year was Charles Pannell jun., a local shoemaker from an old Haslemere family, who also wrote books: *A Short account of the Land and Freshwater Molluscs of Haslemere* (1903) and *120 Years of Non-conformity in Haslemere* (1908)). In 1891, Rayner Storr was appointed Honorary Secretary, and the Society metamorphosed from a means of instruction for working men into a forum for middle-class intellectuals to exchange information and ideas.[6]

At about the same time, Jonathan Hutchinson started his museum, with which the Society became closely associated. Many of the authors mentioned in this book – Tennyson is a notable exception – belonged to the Society, and took part in its debates. A large contingent came regularly to the meetings from Hindhead, where a partly separate group had formed round John Tyndall, Rollo Russell, Grant Allen, Conan Doyle, Frederick Pollock and later Rayner Storr, Bernard Shaw and Gilbert Murray. The Society did much to create a sense of community among a set of individualists. Its title was not an accurate description of its activities in its early days, for, like Hutchinson's lectures at the museum, they covered virtually all aspects of human endeavour, including the arts as well as all branches of science. Only after the break-up of the literary community did it devote itself wholly to natural history.

Another communal project, the Grayshott and District Refreshment House Association, was supported by Frederick Pollock, Rayner Storr, Edward Nettleship and George Bernard Shaw. It was formed in 1898 when a local brewer threatened to install a conventional public house at Grayshott, on the same high ground as Hindhead, but just across the Hampshire border. At that time there was a good deal of alarm at the spread of drunkenness among the working class, and temperance societies were active. The Association sought to steer a path between excessive drinking and total abstinence. They managed to pre-empt the brewer's action by building The Fox and Pelican, a refreshment house which was to be run on' a modification of the Gothenburg system', i.e. it was intended to be a non-profit-making place of refreshment and entertainment for families, in which the consumption of alcoholic drinks was permitted, but not encouraged.[7] To that end, the only source of alcohol provided was 'a little three-handled beer engine, hidden modestly away behind a curtain'. All the same, this was much more often in use than 'the prominently displayed stores of minerals, or the barrel of draught ginger beer'. In addition to the bar, there was also a large coffee room, with a small library – the books were donated by Shaw and included works by Tolstoy, Milton, Wordsworth, Pope and Herbert Spencer – and there were facilities for holding meetings and concerts, and for playing dominoes. The name was chosen by Pollock because of his association with Corpus Christi College, Oxford, which had been founded by Bishop Fox of Winchester, whose device was the pelican. The inn-sign was painted by Walter Crane – a Socialist friend of Shaw's and a distinguished artist, much involved in the Arts and Crafts movement – and blessed by Bishop Stubbs of Oxford.

It was an auspicious start, and the high-minded enterprise, launched by such distinguished names, seems on the whole to have been successful, even though an unfortunate incident occurred only two months after the launch. The *Surrey Advertiser* for 7th October 1899 reported that a stonemason from Shottermill, who had spent the whole day on the premises, became so drunk that he had to be taken home in a wheelbarrow. He was fined five shillings, while the Committee of Management, represented by Rayner Storr, was prosecuted at the same time and fined ten shillings.

The 'Fox & Pelican' in Grayshott, soon after its opening in 1899

F.W. Bockett, on his cycling tour of Surrey in 1900, stopped off at The Fox and Pelican, and was very favourably impressed. 'Here,' he wrote, 'in a clean and cheerful wainscoted room, you can lunch like a king for less than two shillings, with a huge glass tankard of good ale thrown in. And bookshelves too!'[8] Flora Thompson, when living at Grayshott between 1898 and 1901, was evidently referring to the same meals – but without the tankard of ale – when she wrote of 'the ninepenny dinners which were a feature of the new model inn'. These she had sent over to her when she was unable to leave her duties at the telegraph office. They consisted of 'a thick cut off the joint, two or more vegetables, and a wedge of fruit tart or a round roly-poly, sufficient for three dinners for one with her appetite'.[9]

Decline

Although there were so many fresh arrivals among the Surrey hills in the 1880s and 1890s, the community was at the same time diminished by a number of deaths of distinguished authors who had come there earlier: G.H.

Lewes died in 1878, his partner George Eliot in 1880, Anne Gilchrist in 1885, Alfred Tennyson in 1892, John Tyndall in 1893, Christina Rossetti in 1894, Margaret Oliphant in 1897, Grant Allen in 1899.

Thus by the turn of the century the literary community had already lost most of its greatest names. Two lesser novelists came to the area: David Ker in 1899, and George Douglas Brown in 1900. But Brown, a young Scottish writer of considerable promise, spent only a year at Hindhead before dying of consumption. An even later arrival, Francis Galton, died four years after his arrival in 1907 (included here, despite the late arrival, because he was so preeminently a Victorian).

At the same time, some of the older inhabitants were leaving, while the new recruits tended to stay only briefly. Richard Le Gallienne had left Kingswood Chase in 1899 for nearby Chiddingfold, but he only remained there until 1901. Flora Thompson left Grayshott in 1901, only returning to the district much later to assist her husband in the post office at nearby Liphook. In an address in 1901, Frederick Pollock had deplored the fact that the rapid increase in houses on Hindhead had resulted in much loss of wild-life; and in 1904 he decided that the time had come for him to depart. As noted in the Introduction, F.W. Bockett had commented on the overrunning of Hindhead 'by people who are merely rich', when he visited the area in 1900.

Netta Syrett, the novelist, often stayed with her uncle, Grant Allen, between 1893 and 1899, when Hindhead was 'still unspoilt by buildings, and very beautiful' – the implication being that after those dates it had lost its charm.[10] The changes which took place at the turn of the century must have been at least partly responsible for the departure of Conan Doyle for Crow-borough in 1907, and of Rayner Storr for Hampstead in 1908. Although there was far less new building in the Fernhurst area, Hannah and Logan Pearsall Smith left Friday's Hill for Oxford in 1906.

It was during this period of decline that H.G. Wells, who had twice before visited Hindhead, stayed in 1911 at remote Cochet Farm, on the western flank of Blackdown, which had escaped the suburbanisation that had over-taken other parts of the uplands. Wells's stated purpose was to complete some work; but he was also aware that recently widowed Elizabeth von Arnim, to whom he had become attracted, would be staying at the same time in Fernhurst, just over the hill from Cochet.

By 1914, little literature of any distinction was being written in Haslemere or on the surrounding hills. Arthur Pinero was still turning out plays, but he was past his best, and his reputation was beginning to decline. Hubert Wales was still writing his novels, usually about the adventures of young men with older women. David Ker, who came in 1899, and Bernard Hamilton, who came in 1900, continued to churn out undistinguished novels. Maud Diver arrived in Farnham Lane in 1910 to write stories and semi-fiction about the Raj. The last authors to come to the area before the Great War were Agnes and Egerton Castle, joint authors of a series of historical romances, and also of four whimsical accounts of life in their Italianate villa at Hindhead.

It would, nevertheless, be quite wrong to give the impression that all literary activity in the Haslemere area ceased after 1914. Arrivals after that date included several well-known novelists: A.S.M. Hutchinson, author of *If Winter Comes*; Alastair Maclean, of *The Guns of Navarone*; Oliver Onions and his wife Berta Ruck, both of them authors of best-sellers. Then there were a number of writers distinguished in other fields: Sir Arthur Bowley, economic statistician; the broadcaster Richard Dimbleby; S.F. Edge, pioneer motorist and author of the classic *My Motoring Experiences*; Sir Humphrey Rolleston, a distinguished physician, best known for his textbook on the endocrine system; Dr Marie Stopes, paleobotanist but better known for her work on birth control; Ernest Tristram, art historian, who made a comprehensive survey of all medieval wall-paintings in England; Oliver Warner, naval historian and biographer. And there were many others.

After 1918, however, the only incomer of real distinction was David Lloyd George, who came to Churt in 1922 to write his *War Memoirs* (1933–6), and *The Truth about the Peace Treaties* (1938). He also had other motives: it was a convenient place to lodge his mistress, Frances Stevenson, while his wife remained in North Wales, and it also enabled him to cultivate an advanced fruit farm. The sandy soil needed large quantities of manure, which Lloyd George obtained from the barracks at Aldershot, remarking memorably that 'it was the only use he had ever found for cavalry'.

All these, and many others, made Haslemere and its hinterland something more than just a bed-and-breakfast home for businessmen working in the City. But the authors who settled there could have done their writing equally well in many other places. After 1900, Haslemere and its hills were no longer uniquely attractive to literary people, and it could no longer muster names like Tennyson, Eliot, Shaw or Doyle.

Footnotes to Section One

[1] A transcript of Simmons's diary covering the period 1831–68 is in the Haslemere Museum.

[2] Knies, Earl A., *Tennyson at Aldworth: The Diary of James Henry Mangles*.

[3] White, Walter, *The Journals of Walter White*, p. 158.

[4] Alcaro, Marion Walker, *Walt Whitman's Mrs G.: A Biography of Anne Gilchrist*, pp. 92–115.

[5] Hutchinson, Herbert, *Jonathan Hutchinson: Life and Letters*.

[6] Swanton, Ernest William, *The Rise and Development of the Haslemere Natural History Society*.

[7] Quoted in the *Surrey Times*, 10th September 1898; see also the *Haslemere Herald*, 9th September 1949.

[8] Bockett, F.W., *Some Literary Landmarks*, p. 225.

[9] Thompson, Flora, *A Country Calendar, and other writings*, selected and edited by Margaret Lane, p. 238, and *Heatherley* (1998 publication), p. 93.

[10] Syrett, Netta, *The Sheltering Tree: An Autobiography*, p. 46.

The Croft, the house of Grant Allen at Hindhead

Section Two: The Hilltop Community

The Writers and their Houses

Sixty-three authors are described here as Hilltop Writers. I have not attempted to define this term any more closely than to say that it applies to the Victorian writers who migrated to the tract of wild hill country accessed by means of the railway from London to Haslemere. 'Victorian writers' is not a term susceptible of precise definition, since many of them did much of their writing after the death of the Queen in 1901. So there is inevitably a subjective element in the process of selection of the authors, as there is in deciding on the limits of the hilltop country.

Writers tend to be individualists, and these people certainly were; it is that that makes them so interesting. But they had one thing in common: they nearly all belonged to the middle class, the only exceptions being the three aristocratic Russells, Lady Dorothy Nevill and, at the other end of the social scale, Flora Thompson, daughter of an Oxfordshire stonemason. So this was a middle-class invasion of a countryside previously inhabited almost exclusively by small farmers, agricultural labourers, a few workers in small industries. There were no big estates, and only a sprinkling of owners of enough land to feel that they were entitled to be called gentlemen. There seems to have been very little real social contact between the invaders and the natives, the latter being regarded by the former just as providers of essential services. There are no records of actual squabbles between the two groups, probably because they were in a sense complementary: the middle-class could not run their large houses without servants; in so doing – and by employing builders and tradesmen – they brought wealth to an impoverished part of the country. It was in a way like the Norman invasion of 1066, without the violence and the language problem: the uncompromising brick mansions of the middle class rose above the picturesque but tumbledown cottages much as the Norman castles had towered over the hovels of the Saxon peasants. There are not many instances recorded of fraternisation between the two groups; one of the few we have is a pleasing glimpse of George Eliot, at the height of her fame, sitting on the grass with the wife of a local farmer, discussing the merits of different sorts of butter.[1]

The houses constructed by these authors on their hilltops were, for the most part, typical of those favoured by the middle class of the day. They were nearly all built in red brick – except for Tennyson's Aldworth, for which the local sandstone was used – and, like most late Victorian buildings, they favoured solidity rather than charm. Their main characteristic was a sort of

43

sullen robustness, as if they were aware that they were alien intruders in a countryside with older, gentler traditions, but didn't greatly care. Although they did not, like Norman castles or the grander Georgian mansions, attempt to dominate the countryside, it was clear that neither did they intend to be dominated by anyone else. And it was true enough that, in such exposed situations, solidity was a prerequisite. The fact that so many survive today is a testimony to their sturdy construction.

Tyndall's 'Hind Head House'

For the most part, the writers came of English stock, though there was a contingent of five born in Ireland: Allingham, Costelloe, Shaw, Tyndall, Wolseley – all, save Costelloe, from the Protestant Ascendancy – plus a small overseas group: Allen from Canada, Murray from Australia, White from South Africa, Burroughs and the Pearsall Smiths from the United States.

Their Politics

The Hilltop Writers tended to take a liberal view on most topics, so it is not surprising that the more politically-minded among them tended to support the Liberal Party. Three of them eventually became Liberal Members of Parliament: William Beveridge, Joseph King, Arthur Ponsonby (he and King both changed later to Labour). Aneurin Williams (1859–1924), who lived at Hindhead and wrote two political books, was also a Liberal MP, but is not included among the hilltop community, as he cannot be thought of as a Victorian. Frederic Harrison was an unsuccessful Liberal candidate in the election of 1886, and had shocked his friends by his defence of Trade Unionism, though he was opposed to the forceful tactics of the Marxists. Algernon Methuen also failed to get into Parliament as a Liberal. Gilbert Murray was offered the Liberal candidature for Leeds at the time of the Boer War, but refused.[2] H.G. Dakyns, Rollo Russell and the Rector, Revd Aitken, all attended meetings of the local branch of the Liberal Association. Bertrand Russell, Bernard Shaw and the Webbs were of course noted Socialists.

A minority of the Hilltop Writers supported the Conservatives, or their allies, the Liberal Unionists and the Tariff Reformers. Tennyson liked and admired Gladstone as a friend, but disagreed with his policies. He took no active part in politics. Conan Doyle stood twice for Parliament, both times unsuccessfully, once as a Liberal Unionist – the group which had broken with Gladstone's administration over Home Rule for Ireland – and once as a follower of Joseph Chamberlain's movement for Tariff Reform. Mrs Humphry Ward had similar affinities, actively supporting Liberal Unionists and Tariff Reformers; her son Arnold was one of the latter, and got into Parliament with much strident support from his mother.[3] Lady Dorothy Nevill was a Conservative, but had many Radical friends, including Richard Cobden. She claimed that the Primrose League originated at one of her dinner-parties, at which Lord Randolph Churchill was a prominent guest.[4] She herself gave the League only nominal support, but her daughter Meresia was an active worker for the cause. None of the Hilltop Writers became a Conservative (or allied) MP.

The main political issues of the time were Irish Home Rule and the problem presented by the two breakaway Boer republics. On both questions, the Hilltop Writers were divided according to their political affinities. So Frederic Harrison and Bernard Shaw were fervent supporters of Home Rule for Ireland, though Shaw of course had much else to say about the relationship between the English and the Irish, while Harrison was intolerant of Sinn Fein. Tennyson, on the other hand, disapproved of the 1886 Home Rule Bill so strongly that he refused at first to meet Gladstone at a dinner. Later he relented, and so persuasive was Gladstone that Tennyson admitted: 'He has quite converted me.' However, next morning he recanted, saying: 'It is all wrong, this Home Rule, and I am going to write and tell him so.'[5] Mrs Humphry Ward, who up till then had been vaguely Liberal in her politics, spent a week in Dublin in 1880 with her uncle, who was then Chief Secretary; Ireland was in turmoil, and she became convinced that what was needed was coercion, rather than Home Rule. Her opinion was further strengthened by the Phoenix Park murders and by Parnell's adultery.[6]

Those who favoured Home Rule for Ireland were for the most part also opposed to British intervention in South Africa, where the Boers were prepared to fight to keep out the foreign financiers who were infiltrating their country. Frederic Harrison, Algernon Methuen, Gilbert Murray, Bertrand Russell, Rayner Storr were all what was termed 'pro-Boer'. It is possible that Montagu White, who had represented the two Boer republics as Consul-General in London, and consequently lost his job at the outbreak of war in 1899, knew of this strong local sentiment in favour of his country's cause when he decided to retire to Haslemere. Even White's Conservative friend, Lady Dorothy Nevill, was 'not over-enthusiastic' about the war, while another friend of hers, Frederic Harrison, was vehemently opposed, writing her long and vehement letters, and threatening to leave for Ireland, after the 'material and moral ruin of his country', in consequence of its attitude to the Boers.[7] White's stay in Haslemere seems to have been untroubled, apart from a minor riot on Guy Fawkes night in 1899, when thirty or forty drunken local youths threw insults and stones at his house.[8]

Flora Thompson, who was living at nearby Grayshott during the war, and moved in lowlier circles, wrote that in contrast to the intellectuals, most of the people with whom she came in contact – namely, tradespeople and their families – supported the war, the only exception being Ernest Chapman, the local builder, but he was only mildly cold-shouldered by the other inhabitants. There do not seem to have been any instances of riots or window-smashing at Grayshott.

Crossways Road in Grayshott, circa 1900: Flora Thompson worked in Walter Chapman's shop (right); the entrance to his brother Ernest Chapman's builder's yard can be seen to the left

Three of the Hilltop Writers did come out in favour of the war: Conan Doyle, Bernard Hamilton and Mrs Humphry Ward. Doyle went out to South Africa at the first opportunity, and served in a field hospital. At the end of the war he wrote his influential pamphlet, *The War in South Africa: Its Cause and Conduct* (1902), which sold more than half a million copies and did much to influence foreign opinion in favour of the British cause. In recognition of these services, another Hindhead resident, the novelist Bernard Hamilton – author of a silly allegorical booklet, boosting Cecil Rhodes and denigrating Paul Kruger – organised a public presentation to Doyle. By the time the South African crisis was looming, Mrs Humphry Ward, who had left Haslemere by then, had become a fervent imperialist, eager to teach the Boers a lesson and show them who was running the world. 'We *are* fit to rule, and are meant to rule,' she declared. So as far as the Boers were concerned, English rule was 'the natural discipline appointed for them by Providence'.[9]

The great wave of imperialistic sentiment which swept over the country in the last decade of the nineteenth century met with a muted response from most of the Hilltop Writers. Indeed, escape from it may well have been one of the reasons leading many of them to seek asylum among the Surrey hills. Frederic Harrison was always ready to spring to the defence of any whom he thought of as underdogs – Irish, Poles, Hungarians, Arabs, Afghans, Zulus, Boers – and so was perhaps inevitably anti-imperialist. His complex reactions to home and foreign politics were summarised by his son as 'Royalist for England, Republican for France and anti-Bismarck for Europe, though pro-Mazzini, pro-Garibaldi, and pro-Boer'.[10] Bernard Hamilton was the only example of the jingoism which pervaded the country in the run-up to the Jubilee of 1897, though Conan Doyle, Mrs Ward and perhaps Tennyson could be described as imperialists of a more dignified sort. It seems rather likely that the surge of imperialist feeling, like the *fin de siècle* movement which also flourished in the capital in the 1890s, influenced many writers in deciding to leave London for the purer – metaphorical as well as literal – atmosphere of the Surrey hills. The Hilltop Writers remained attached to the solid Victorian past, and distrusted strident movements of any sort. They probably looked forward to the new century with some misgiving – and who can blame them?

Social Issues: 'Degeneracy'

Two main social issues troubled the late Victorians: the 'degenerate' state of the lower classes in the great cities, and what they called the 'woman question', now more commonly known as feminism (a term first used in 1894). The full extent of the first of these did not become apparent till after the Boer War, so it is more of an Edwardian than a Victorian problem, and only requires brief treatment in the present context.

Throughout the nineteenth century, concern had been gathering about the state of the masses cast up by the Industrial Revolution and deposited in slums in all the major cities. They included a great variety of unfortunates: 'paupers, syphilitics, epileptics, dipsomaniacs, cripples, criminals and degenerates'.[11] This state of affairs had long been deplored, and charitable organisations had done what they could to alleviate the worst of the suffering. It was seen as an unfortunate, even disgraceful, state of affairs, but not as a real threat to the future of the nation until recruitment for the Boer War in 1899–1900 revealed that between 26 and 60 per cent of volunteers had to be rejected as physically unfit.[12]

Undershaw at Hindhead, built by Arthur Conan Doyle

'Degeneracy' was in the first instance a biological concept, carried over from Darwin's theory of evolution, and developed by his disciple, the great zoologist Ray Lankester. The general idea behind it was that evolution was not a one-way street, producing ever more advanced and complex creatures; organisms could on occasion become less advanced and less complex with time, as in the case of many parasites which had necessarily evolved after their hosts.[13] So, by analogy, the people of a country like Britain, hitherto seen as continuously 'improving', could also be pictured as going into reverse. How far this degeneration was thought of in biological, rather than social terms, depended on the individual point of view: for Francis Galton it was a biological problem, for Sidney and Beatrice Webb, a social one.

Many different remedies were proposed. It so happens that most of the suggested measures had distinguished advocates among the Hilltop Writers. The most drastic proposal was that of Lord Wolseley, who recommended widespread euthanasia with chloroform for the inmates of gaols and hospitals. This, he thought, would save 'much trouble and expense'. In those pre-Holocaust times, this was not considered to be such an outrageous proposal as it seems today. Others favoured similar solutions: William Allingham remarked to Wolseley that Dr Bodichon of Algiers (husband of George

Eliot's friend Barbara Bodichon) had advocated juries of scientific men to decide which of these assorted unfortunates should be permitted to continue to live.[14]

The remedies proposed by those who favoured gentler measures were of two types, according to whether the problem was seen as primarily genetic or primarily social. Francis Galton was the leading proponent of the former, by his advocacy of eugenics. In his ideal world, only those who had been shown to be physically and mentally fit would be allowed a licence to breed. In this way he hoped to encourage 'health, energy, ability, manliness and courteous disposition'; as the degenerate city-dwellers were conspicuously lacking in these qualities, they would in course of time be automatically eliminated, without the need for the drastic measures favoured by Wolseley.[15]

Rollo Russell saw it as a social problem, and felt that what was needed was to reverse the huge influx of people from the countryside to the towns. In his book on epidemics, he wrote of the 'pestiferous dens where fever always lodges' in the towns, the results of overcrowding and foul air.[16] In 1904, influenced by the findings in the Boer War recruits, he was deeply pessimistic about the prospects for the country, and deplored the lack of 'great men', compared with Victorian times. Most great men, he believed, were brought up in the countryside. Not only were the people in the industrial towns exposed to foul air, their diet was also deplorable – too much meat – as were their habits: alcohol, tea, coffee and – interestingly – cigarettes.[17] In a later work, Russell contrasted the depopulated English countryside with that in France and Germany, inhabited by a healthy and prosperous peasantry. The reason, he thought, was the 'oligarchic despotism' prevailing in England, with the countryside divided into a small number of huge estates. He considered that the best remedy for this state of affairs would be wholesale nationalisation of land, which would encourage the re-population of the countryside with large numbers of smallholders. However, he despaired of ever getting such a measure through Parliament.[18]

None of these proposals seemed likely to have much effect on the problem. The approach of Beatrice and Sidney Webb, and their protégé William Beveridge, was a great deal more professional. They believed that no progress was possible until the facts had been thoroughly ascertained, and in a series of immense labours they investigated every aspect of an industrialised society. In the course of time, their Fabian approach paid off and, very gradually, some of their labours – and those of their disciples – led to practical steps which went some way towards alleviating the worst horrors of degeneracy.

Social Issues: The 'Woman Question'

Problems concerning the relationship between the sexes were know collectively to the Victorians and Edwardians as the 'woman question'. Perhaps surprisingly, it was only with the publication of Mary Wollstonecraft's *Vindication of the Rights of Woman* in 1792, that there had been any public recognition that women had anything in particular to complain about; and even then, feminism did not become a major issue until the 1890s. But that decade can be regarded as seminal: women had been admitted to Oxford and Cambridge, though not as full members; a few women had qualified as doctors; the question of women's suffrage had at least been discussed in Parliament; and there was a flood of feminist literature. Two inventions had widened the horizons for women's work and leisure: the typewriter and the safety bicycle. The liberating effect of the latter was celebrated in a popular ditty:

> Mother's out upon her bike enjoying of the fun,
> Sister and her Beau have gone to take a little run,
> The housemaid and the cook are both a-riding on their wheels,
> And Daddy's in the kitchen a-cooking of their meals.

Quoting this rhyme, Flora Thompson, a strong supporter of women's rights, expressed the hope that 'the knell of the selfish, much awaited-upon, old-fashioned father of the family was sounded by the bicycle bell.'[19] But even a hundred years later, Daddy still seems reluctant to spend much time a-cooking in the kitchen. Yet the 1890s saw at least the foundation laid for the more spectacular suffragist campaigns in the Edwardian era.[20] So the debate on women's rights was well under way at the time that the hilltops were being actively colonised by literary people.

Victorian women had much to put up with. With so few possible careers open to them except domestic service or factory work for the lower classes, school-teaching or governessing for the middle, many had no real alternative to marriage. Within marriage, it was the husband who made the decisions and took care of the cash. Most galling of all must have been the universal assumption of the inherent inferiority of women for any activity other than child-bearing, child-rearing and looking after the home. Only the simplest education was thought to be necessary or desirable as preparation for such humble occupations. Even someone as enlightened as Havelock Ellis, the pioneer sexologist, and a hero to many 'advanced' women, could write in 1894: 'Nature has made women more like children in order that they may better understand and care for children.'[21]

It might have been expected that the response of the intelligent and articulate women among the Hilltop Writers would have been uniformly favourable to attempts to improve the female lot. In fact, their attitudes were very varied.

George Eliot was of course well aware of the problems that beset women. She touched on them in her novels as they cropped up in the course of the narrative. In *The Mill on the Floss*, for instance, she emphasised the contrast between the treatment of Tom Tulliver, who was given a full education from which he was too dim-witted to benefit, and that of his intelligent sister Maggie, to whom it was denied. The same contempt for female intellect is apparent in their father's deliberate selection of his wife because 'she wasn't o'er cute ... for I wasn't going to be told the rights o' things by my own fire-side'.

Haslemere High Street, looking south, circa 1894

Eliot's attitude was revealed more directly in 1870, when she forwarded to Octavia Hill, the social reformer and co-founder of the National Trust, a copy of the speech by Lady Amberley on 'The Claims of Women'. This was the speech which so enraged Queen Victoria – 'Lady Amberley ought to get a good whipping' – by advocating suffrage and equal rights in education, professions, employment and wages, as well as property rights for married women. In an accompanying note, Eliot commented: 'I could find little of which I cannot say that I both agree and keenly sympathize with.'[22]

But Eliot did not feel it necessary to indulge in any public propaganda for women's rights. Even in the matter in which she probably felt most strongly – the right of women to higher education – she contented herself with a gift of £50 to the Girton College fund. The fact was that she herself, despite these handicaps and the additional stigma of her union with an adulterer, had man-aged eventually to attain a position of great eminence in intellectual society. Her *salons* at The Priory in St John's Wood attracted anyone with literary pretensions. At one dinner, Tennyson recited *Maud*; at another, the Princess Louise humbly requested to be presented to George Eliot; at yet another, the

Princess Royal and the German Crown Prince were present. Although she had been disadvantaged in her earlier career, Eliot eventually showed that even Victorian society could not prevent a really talented woman from reaching the ultimate heights.[23]

It was otherwise with Margaret Oliphant, who had to support a gaggle of children and ineffectual males by her writing, yet who because of her sex was not eligible for an editorial job, which would have brought her a regular income. She felt resentful of male writers, on the one hand, because they could secure steady jobs and at the same time escape domestic duties; and of favoured female writers, on the other, who were not expected, as she was, to be wage-earner, child-minder and housewife simultaneously. She was particularly envious of George Eliot, though she recognised the superiority of the latter's genius, and wondered if she might have done better herself 'if I had been kept, like her, in a mental greenhouse and taken care of?'[24] In her novels she does not directly complain about women's problems, but seems to be showing, through a series of resolute heroines, how they can be overcome. These strong-minded girls know what they want, and usually get it. Miss Marjoribanks, Kirsteen, Patty of the Seven Thorns, are all examples of determined young women who, by the use of female strategies, succeed in getting their way in a predominantly male world. They reflect Mrs Oliphant's own determined character, which at least kept her and her feeble relations afloat through difficult times – and even provided occasional minor triumphs, as when, in 1879, she was feted by Oxford dons.[25]

Oliphant's attitude to sex and marriage, however, was conventional, as shown by her response to the novels of Thomas Hardy and Grant Allen, which she attacked in a forthright article entitled 'The Anti-Marriage League'.[26] She was concerned that English novelists were imitating the depraved French, by treating of 'subjects hitherto considered immoral'. Love was all right as the subject of novels, but 'what is now freely discussed as the physical part of the question ... has hitherto been banished from the lips of decent people, and as much as possible from their thoughts'. Oliphant had admired Hardy's *Tess of the d'Urbervilles* as a work of art, but deplored its morals. She was even more horrified by *Jude the Obscure*: 'nothing so coarsely indecent as the whole history of Jude in his relations with his wife Arabella has ever been put in English print – that is to say, from the hands of a Master.' When – several pages later – Mrs Oliphant has finished with Hardy, she turns on Grant Allen, 'not a man of genius, but a professor of literature, whose crow upon his hill-top ... is rather an outcry to burst the bosom of the gallant bird who makes it, than to arouse the world'. She was relieved that the first of Allen's two Hilltop Novels, *The Woman Who Did*, did not, like *Jude*, treat explicitly of what she calls 'a certain act common to men and beasts', but she was shocked by its attack on the institution of marriage. The desire of the heroine, Herminia, to be liberated from the bondage of marriage was interpreted by Oliphant as a wish to be 'free to exchange her companion if she discovers another more fit to be loved. And if one, also another no doubt, and another.' (In fact Herminia remained constant to the memory of her only lover, after he died.) Allen's *The British Barbarians* was equally obnoxious, all the more so because, when the strange being from the other world persuaded the heroine, Frida, to leave her husband and come away with him, the place the couple decamped to was none other than Hindhead, 'which, for some whimsical reason best known to themselves, the Anti-Marriage Brigade have chosen for their happy hunting-ground. They all go to Hindhead, which but a little while ago was the abode of Innocence and Science.'

Mrs Oliphant seldom refers to the question of women's suffrage. However, her attitude is plainly revealed in one offhand comment in 1866, about 'Stuart Mill and his mad notion of the franchise of women'.[27] It was John Stuart Mill's book, *The Subjection of Women*, which brought the 'woman question' to a sharp focus on the single issue of whether women should be given the vote – an issue which had been exacerbated by extension of the franchise in 1867 and 1884 to include some men of the labouring class. Yet some intelligent women, like Mrs Oliphant, were apparently content to subscribe to the proposition that they were less capable of casting an informed vote than an uncouth farm labourer. Her more advanced friend, Christina Rogerson, did indeed accuse Mrs Oliphant of 'going back to the dark ages when the men were reckoned superior beings'.[28]

The response of another famous female Hilltop novelist, Mrs Humphry Ward, was equally forthright, and equally negative. Although in her younger days, when living at Oxford, she had been a founder, and the first secretary, of Somerville Hall (later College), by 1889 she had reversed her opinion of women's rights, and initiated an 'Appeal against the Extension of the Parliamentary Franchise to Women'.[29] She induced 104 other prominent women to join in this appeal, which asserted that 'the emancipating process has now reached the limits fixed by the physical constitution of women', and that women were biologically 'lacking in sound judgement'. Her reasons for mounting this campaign against the interests of her own sex are obscure. She was the principal earner of her family, and a respected and dominant figure in the literary world. Most members of her family, including her two sisters and her daughter Janet, were ardent suffragists. Her biographer, John Sutherland, has considered her motives in depth, and concluded that there were three main reasons for her strangely passionate anti-feminism. One was to help men whom she looked up to and respected, like Frederic Harrison, who had encouraged her in her appeal; another, that women, in appealing for the suffrage, made themselves ridiculous; a third, her horror of 'militancy', then associated in people's minds with Irish revolutionaries.[30]

As well as Mrs Oliphant, Mrs Ward and Mrs Frederic Harrison, other female Hilltop Writers opposed to giving women the vote were Miss Lucy Garnett and Mrs Annette Beveridge, who became secretary of the Shottermill branch of the League Against Women's Suffrage.

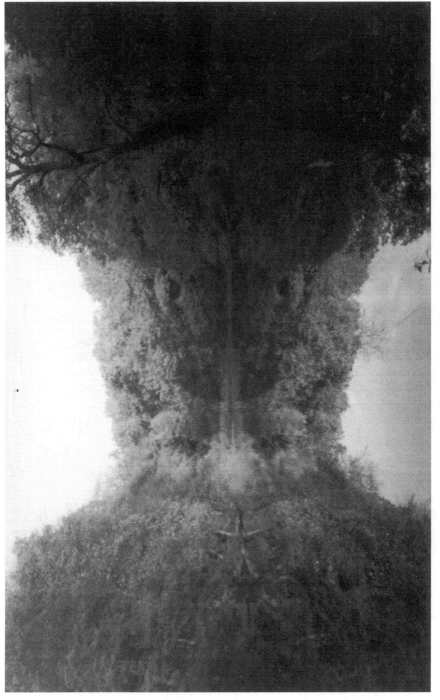

Waggoners Wells near Grayshott – Richard Le Gallienne lived close by at Kingswood Chase

One might be forgiven for suspecting an element of hypocrisy in assertions of female inferiority by someone so conspicuously successful as Mrs Humphry Ward. But there can be no reason to question the sincerity of Christina Rossetti's conviction of the inherent inferiority of women; it was in tune with the humility which was her outstanding characteristic. In her book of religious prose, *Seek and Find* (1879), she wrote: 'Woman must obey ... She by natural constitution is adapted not to assert herself, but to be subordinate ... Her office is to be man's helpmeet ... the man is the head of the woman, the woman is the glory of the man.'[31] A few years later, Christina got into an argument with another female poet, Augusta Webster, who was what was then known as a 'strong-minded woman', that is, a feminist. Christina wrote a cordial but firm letter to Mrs Webster, setting out her own position:

Does it not appear as if the Bible was based upon an understood unalterable distinction between men and women, their position, duties, privileges? Not arrogating to myself but most earnestly desiring to attain to the character of a humble orthodox Xian, so it does appear to me; not merely under the Old but also under the New Dispensation. The fact of the Priesthood being exclusively man's, leaves me in no doubt that the highest functions are not in this world open to both sexes: and if not all then a selection must be made and a line drawn somewhere ... Many who have thought more and done much more than myself share your views – and yet they are not mine. I do not think the present social movements tend on the whole to uphold Xianity, or that the influence of some of our most prominent and gifted women is exerted in that direction: and thus thinking I cannot aim at 'women's rights'.[32]

The opposition of Mrs Oliphant, Mrs Ward and Christina Rossetti to agitation in favour of women's rights, was counterbalanced by the formidable voice of Mrs Hannah Pearsall Smith. Hannah had migrated from Philadelphia to Friday's Hill at Fernhurst with her family. She had married early, and soon became disillusioned with her thriftless husband Robert, whom she described in her emphatic way as 'a bad husband and an unsatisfactory human being'. Further observation led her to conclude that other men were not much better. When her daughter Mary was contemplating her first marriage in 1886, Hannah wrote to warn her: 'What I object to is the present usual relation of the sexes in marriage, by which the man is considered, and considers himself, *master*. From this *my whole soul revolts*, and until this is righted I cannot encourage any woman to enter into this legal slavery.'[33]

Final proof of the vileness of men, and the need for strong measures to deal with them, was provided by the trial of Oscar Wilde. In a letter to the same daughter in 1895, Hannah wrote:

55

Everybody thinks that Oscar Wilde is going to get off after all! It is outrageous, for no human being doubts his guilt. I believe the judge and jury are all guilty of the same thing, and dare not convict him. We are writing our resolutions for our [British Women's Temperance Association] Annual Council, and I handed one to Lady Henry which read as follows – 'Resolved that it is the sense of this Council that all men should be castrated'. It is the only effectual remedy that I know.[34]

History does not record whether this resolution was ever debated, and, if so, what the conclusion was.

View from Blackdown, near to Fernhurst

Of Hannah's two daughters, Alys shared her mother's views, though she did not express them quite so forcefully. In 1894, Mrs Frederic Harrison, a signatory of Mrs Humphry Ward's 1889 appeal against women's suffrage, had published an article in the *Nineteenth Century* about the lack of discipline among modern daughters. Alys published 'A Reply from the Daughters' in the same journal.[35] Hannah's other daughter, Mary, seems to have had no strong feelings on the subject, though Mary's own daughter, Ray Strachey, became a leading figure in the Edwardian suffragist movement and also its first historian.

Mrs Humphry Ward's appeal also brought a swift riposte from indignant feminists, with upwards of two thousand female signatories. The names of only a quarter of these were published. They include those of Lady Dorothy Nevill and Lady Agatha Russell, both of them Hilltop Writers.[36]

Early in her adult life, Beatrice Webb (then Beatrice Potter) had been firmly opposed to the movement for women's rights. This was a reaction against the opposing views of her father, Richard Potter, who, she wrote, 'worshipped his wife, admired and loved his daughters; he was the only man I ever knew who genuinely believed that women were superior to men, and acted as if he did; the paradoxical result being that all his nine daughters started life as anti-feminists!'[37] But when, in 1883–84, she was in love with Joseph Chamberlain and contemplating marriage, Beatrice drew back in alarm at the prospect:

> If the fates should unite us (against my will) all joy and light heart-edness will go from me. I will be absorbed into the life of a man whose aims are not my aims; who will refuse me all freedom of thought in my intercourse with him; to whose career I shall have to subordinate all my life, mental and physical, without believing in the usefulness of his career, whether it be inspired by earnest con-viction or ambition … If I married him I should become a cynic as regards my own mental life.[38]

Yet in 1889, she was prepared to put her name – still Beatrice Potter – to Mrs Humphry Ward's anti-suffrage petition. Mrs Webb later analysed the reasons for her attitude at this time:

> Conservative by temperament, and anti-democratic through social environment, I had reacted against my father's overvaluation of women relatively to men; and the narrow outlook and exasperated tone of some of the pioneers of women's suffrage had intensified this reaction. I remember at a luncheon given by an American lady to American suffragists {who had not given me a cigarette to soothe my distaste for the perpetual reiteration of the rights of women) venting this irritation by declaring provocatively – 'I have never met a man, however inferior, whom I do not consider to be my superior!'

But then Frederic Harrison – like his wife, a convinced anti-suffragist – intervened with a letter to Beatrice. Mrs Ward's anti-suffrage appeal had been immediately followed by a rebuttal by Mrs Millicent Fawcett, a leading suffragist, and Harrison wanted Beatrice to counter this with a published article. His letter stung Beatrice into reconsidering her position, and she real-ised that she had made a mistake in signing the petition. She declined to accede to Harrison's request, though she 'delayed [her] public recantation for nearly twenty years'.[39]

So women were divided in their attitudes. On the whole, most of them seem to have been content to accept the *status quo*, meekly agreeing that men were inherently superior beings. However, this attitude was not necessarily quite as supine as it seems, for Victorian ladies, supreme in their drawing-rooms and their soirees, exercised a surprising amount of behind-the-scenes political influence, and must have been aware of the fact. But in the 1890s, the tide was beginning to turn, as an increasing number of women came to share the Pearsall Smiths' more overtly belligerent attitude, and were prepared to fight tooth and nail for equality with men in marriage, Parliament and university.

Shulbrede Priory, home of Arthur Ponsonby

The male Hilltop Writers were more muted; they were, after all, in possession of the field. It must have seemed to many that the best policy was to lie low and hope that it would all blow over. So it is difficult to discover just where many of these writers stood on the various issues concerning women's rights. Arthur Ponsonby was in favour of giving women the vote.[40] So, too, was George Bernard Shaw; but although he wrote much about women it is not easy to say just what he thought about other aspects of the 'woman question'.[41] Similarly, Frederic Harrison – and his wife – were against women's suffrage, but thought that women's education ought to be improved.[42]

Tennyson, on the other hand, was silent on the matter of suffrage, but revealed his thoughts about higher education for women in *The Princess*, a long narrative poem, in parts light-hearted but in others deadly serious, in which the heroine, Princess Ida, a redoubtable feminist, ultimately succumbs to the hero and accepts the traditional role of a wife.

The action centres on a remarkable all-female university established by the Princess, where the students are taught:

By violet-hooded Doctors, elegies
And quoted odes, and jewels five-words-long
That on the stretch'd forefinger of all Time
Sparkle for ever: then we dipt in all
That treats of whatsoever is, the state,
The total chronicles of man, the mind,
The morals, something of the frame, the rock
The star, the bird, the fish, the shell, the flower,
Electric, chemic laws, and all the rest,
And whatsoever can be taught and known ...

This seemingly idyllic institution is infiltrated by the Prince and two companions, disguised as women. They are discovered and expelled, and in no
time are engaged in bloody combat with an invading army. After some
typical male mayhem, the hero is wounded, and only revived by the
Princess's devoted nursing, the university having by now been converted into
a hospital. In the end, the convalescent Prince declares his love, the university
is forgotten, and the story lapses into a conventional happy ending. The
Prince tells the Princess how he sees the ideal relationship between men and
women. In his *Memoir* Hallam Tennyson assures us that this was also how
his father saw it:

> ... seeing either sex alone
> Is half itself, and in true marriage lies
> Nor equal, nor unequal: each fulfils
> Defect in each, and always thought in thought,
> Purpose in purpose, will in will, they grow,
> The single pure and perfect animal,
> The two-cell'd heart beating, with one full stroke,
> Life.[43]

The Princess agrees:

> ...A dream
> That once was mine! What woman taught you this?

The clear implication is that, so far as women are concerned, family life is
what really matters – so they can forget all this nonsense about higher
education.

Of the male Hilltop Writers, the one who was least equivocal in his
support of women's rights was Gilbert Murray, the great classical scholar. He
was a strong supporter of higher education for women, of votes for women –
though he disapproved of the more militant suffragettes – and of changing the
divorce laws. Murray was sensible of the 'unconscious oppression' of intelli-

gent wives by their husbands, which made them appear stupid: 'an anxious and incessant pressure of trivial cares and duties has left them no time to read, no energy to think or use their imagination'.[44]

Barford, the home of Gilbert Murray

The attitude of Grant Allen, on the other hand, was distinctly ambiguous. Although widely regarded, both by his contemporaries and by posterity, as an ardent feminist, his article in the *Fortnightly Review* is in fact a forthright attack on advocates of careers for women.[45] He claims to have 'the greatest sympathy with the modern woman's demand for emancipation. I am an enthusiast on the Woman Question ... I should like to see her a good deal more emancipated than she herself as yet at all desires. Only, her emancipation must not be of a sort that interferes in any way with this prime necessity.' The 'prime necessity' is, of course, the breeding of children. Sympathetic though Allen is to women's aspirations for a life of the intellect, he feels that this must not be allowed to interfere with their function as procreative machines. To maintain the existing population, Allen calculated that women should have four to six children – a not unreasonable estimate, in view of the infant mortality then prevailing. The exact figure depended on the proportion of women who became wives and mothers: the more the burden was spread, the fewer children each woman needed to produce. What worried him was that 'both in England and America, the women of the cultivated class are becoming unfit to be wives or mothers. Their sexuality (which lies at the basis of everything) is enfeebled or destroyed. In some cases they eschew marriage altogether – openly refuse or despise it, which surely shows a lamentable weakening of wholesome feminine instincts.' Allen purports to be a supporter of higher education for women, but he thinks it has taken a wrong direction. Women should, he thought, be 'educated to suckle strong

60

and intelligent children, and to order well a wholesome, beautiful, reasonable household'. It was for this reason that Herminia, heroine of Allen's novel *The Woman Who Did*, left Cambridge in disgust at the academic nature of the teaching. It is strange indeed to find this benign, learned man prepared to deny women the normal curriculum of a university, in favour of technical training in the art of rearing children. It also seems at first sight surprising that, in a period when the population was growing fast, anyone should worry about maintaining the birth-rate. But his remark above about the unfitness for child-bearing of 'the women of the cultivated class' betrays Allen's real concern that if too many girls went to university, the middle-class birth-rate would fall and be overtaken by the greater fecundity of the labouring class.

Mrs Millicent Fawcett, then emerging as one of the leaders of the women's movement, had no doubt that Allen should be ranked as an anti-feminist. In an article charged with venom she wrote: 'Mr Grant Allen has never given help by tongue or pen to any practical effort to improve the legal or social status of women. He is not a friend but an enemy.' His supposedly feminist novel, *The Woman Who Did*, was, she wrote, 'a story feeble and silly to the last degree ... it may be asked, why take any notice of it? It only seems worthwhile because its author purports to be writing in support of the enfranchisement of women ...'[46]

The issue which concerned Allen most deeply, and which earned him his reputation with the general public as a feminist, was the subjection of married women. This was the intended theme of the novel which so roused Mrs Fawcett's wrath. She of course accepted that the position of married women was a legitimate subject for feminist protest, but she was contemptuous of Allen's treatment. 'The central idea of Mr Grant Allen's book is that marriage means slavery; but he only reiterates this again and again, without attempting to prove it.' This was ungenerous. Mrs Fawcett was certainly right to brand him an anti-feminist for his coldly biological view of women as breeding machines with no need of a conventional university education, but she might have given him credit for wanting to change the conditions of marriage in women's favour. Allen thought it not surprising 'that independ-ent-minded women should hesitate to accept the terms of marriage as they now and here exist'. 'But,' he added, 'if they really have it at heart to alter those terms, to escape from slavery, to widen the basis of the contract between the sexes, to put the wife on a higher and safer footing, most sensi-ble men, I feel sure, will heartily cooperate with them.'[47] This was a senti-ment which feminists might be expected to applaud; Mrs Fawcett's bitter attack was clearly determined by the need for the suffragists to dissociate themselves from Allen's advocacy of free-love, which might otherwise have been used to smear their campaign for women's votes.

H.G. Wells was another fighter for the rights of women, who yet found much to criticise in *The Woman Who Did*. He condemned it on literary grounds, as being, in effect a homily disguised as a novel; and on feminist grounds, because if, as Allen advocated, marriage were to be abolished, it would merely leave women even more exposed to the lust of predatory males.[48]

The Woman Who Did and *The British Barbarians* were what Grant Allen called his Hilltop Novels, because they expressed sentiments about which he felt deeply, and which seemed to him to partake of the purity of the mountain air. While the former warned women against getting trapped in marriage, the latter seemed to advise them that if they should find themselves married to an unsuitable husband, they should elope with some other man who scorned the rigid conventions of the Victorian era. There seems no reason to doubt that, in writing these two novels, Allen's intention was to ease the lot of women. However, their message could equally well be read as promoting a general libertarianism, which would favour licentious men just as much, if not more, than downtrodden women.

Religion

Religion, and the conflicts that it engenders, dominated the life of most Victorians in a way that it failed to do in both the preceding and the following centuries. In the first half of the nineteenth century, the Anglican Church had been deeply divided into Evangelical Low and Anglo-Catholic High Churches. Towards the end of the century, this particular issue, though by no means extinct, began to seem less important, as others emerged to perplex churchmen and their flocks. A Broad Church had arisen, more concerned with social matters than with church ritual, and rejecting the doctrine of hellfire. The new biblical criticism raised questions about the literal interpretation of the sacred text, and was causing unease among the faithful. Above all, the rapid progress of science was creating doubts about the validity of the very foundations of Christian doctrine, in particular the authenticity of the biblical account of the Creation. Not many were prepared to discard the Christian God altogether, but – like Mrs Humphry Ward's character Robert Elsmere – many questioned whether He could be quite the sort of person portrayed by the Church, or if He could not be honoured without elaborate ritual. Even those who were not happy with the notion of a personal deity often still clung to the idea of a supernatural agency. Likewise, those who accepted the picture, gradually evolving from the progress of science, of a universe which operated on exclusively rational principles, often also felt the need to believe in some sort of supernatural presence. Thinking people could therefore choose from a wide spectrum of sentiments, ranging from the total scepticism of the atheists to the total commitment of fervent Christians. But atheist and believer alike recognised that these were serious and important issues. The Hilltop Writers mirrored this range of beliefs, but none treated religious issues as matters of no great consequence, as so many do today.

At one extreme were the atheists such as Grant Allen, who dismissed the immaterial world with bleak assurance. He insisted that he was not an agnostic, for agnostics merely say 'I don't know' whereas true atheists, like himself say 'There is nothing to be known.'[49] But this was not a sign of indifference to religious issues: his book, *The Evolution of the Idea of God* (1897) testifies to the deep thought he had given to such matters. Richard Carrington, the astronomer, who stipulated in his will that he should be buried without religious ceremony in his own garden, can also be confidently assumed to have been an atheist. So, too, could G.H. Lewes.[50]

Brookbank, where George Eliot and GH Lewes stayed in 1871

Most categorical of all was Lewes's partner, George Eliot, whose majestic statement of the position of an uncompromising atheist made such an impression on F.W.H. Myers (1843-1901). Myers, a Cambridge poet and essayist, recorded the scene and the effect it had on his own wavering faith:

> I remember how, at Cambridge, I walked with her once on the Fellows' Garden of Trinity, on an evening of rainy May; and she, stirred somewhat beyond her wont, and taking as her text the three words which have been used so often as the inspiring trumpet-call of men – the words God, Immortality, Duty – pronounced, with terrible earnestness, how inconceivable was the *first*, how unbelievable the *second*, and yet how peremptory and absolute the *third*. I listened, and night fell; her grave, majestic countenance turned towards me like a Sybil's in the gloom; it was as though she withdrew from my grasp, one by one, the two scrolls of promise, and

left me the third scroll only, awful with inevitable fates. And when we stood at length and parted, amid that columnar circuit of the forest-trees, beneath the last twilight of starless skies, I seemed to be gazing, like Titus at Jerusalem, on vacant seats and empty halls – on a sanctuary with no Presence to hallow it, and heaven left lonely of a God.[51]

In another memorable passage, Bertrand Russell set out the tenets of his own equally bleak creed:

That man is the product of causes which had no prevision of the end they were achieving; that his origin, his growth, his hopes and fears, his loves and his beliefs, are but the outcome of accidental collocations of atoms; that no fire, no heroism, no intensity of thought and feeling, can preserve an individual life beyond the grave; that all the labours of the ages, all the devotion, all the inspiration, all the noonday brightness of human genius, are destined to extinction in the vast death of the solar system, and that the whole of Man's achievement must inevitably be buried beneath the debris of a universe in ruins – all these things, if not quite beyond dispute, are yet so nearly certain, that no philosophy which rejects them can hope to stand.[52]

The sense of high drama conveyed by these two pieces of impassioned prose bears out the point made by Elizabeth Jay about the difference between the fervent, even passionate atheism of the late nineteenth century, and the indifference to the whole subject of religion, more characteristic of the late twentieth century. As Jay points out, the 'religious' fervour which characterised Victorian atheism is also revealed by the doubts which sometimes assailed the atheists themselves, leading them on occasion, like Browning's sceptical Bishop Blougram, to suspect that there might, after all, be something in this God business.[53]

John Tyndall, the great Victorian scientist, was quite prepared to proclaim publicly that he was an atheist. His address to the British Association at its Belfast meeting in 1874 was a defence of science against all-comers, and was assumed to be a statement of the hard-line mechanistic view of the universe. Hence it was strongly attacked by the clergy. Yet the printed version of this celebrated address gives a rather different impression. While not denying his own atheism, Tyndall acknowledged the existence of a 'deep-set feeling, which, since the earliest dawn of history, and probably for ages prior to all history, incorporated itself in the religions of the world,' and concluded 'no atheistic reasoning can, I hold, dislodge religion from the human heart'. He does not say anywhere that he has experienced this religious feeling himself, but passages like the above seem to hint that he may well have done so on occasion. Tyndall certainly has to be described as an atheist, but his scepticism may at times have been liable to give way to something more akin to mysticism, as when he quoted with approval Goethe's saying that 'matter is the garment of God'.[54] His friend, Frederick Pollock, in a memorial address to the Haslemere Microscope and Natural History Society on 30th December 1895, said emphatically: 'Tyndall was no vulgar materialist.' According to Thomas Wright, 'Tyndall's knowledge of scripture was marvellous. He would often quote the Psalms, especially the 8th, and he was very fond of the parables of our Lord.'[55]

Francis Galton, another great scientist, had discarded the last shreds of a Christian upbringing 'as if it had been a nightmare' after reading his cousin, Charles Darwin's, *Origin of Species*. Galton's agnosticism – or more properly, atheism – was fortified by his own studies which seemed to show that prayer had no effect. Yet even he felt that the inhabitants of his eugenic paradise 'Kantsaywhere' needed a belief in a spirit world, allied to ancestor worship. And he himself welcomed the custom of family prayers, because it afforded 'a few minutes of daily companionship in reverent thought and ritual'.[56] So he, too, may not have been without an occasional hankering after something outside the material world of science.

Most nearly related to the atheists were those who rejected the idea of any sort of personal deity, yet felt that something intangible lay behind that material world, and that this abstraction in some way helped them to understand the purpose of their own lives, and their place on the Universe. Annette Beveridge had this sort of faith: 'I do believe in a great unknown which through us makes for righteousness. I do not care what it is called.' Hubert Wales, novelist and Hilltop Writer, likewise could get no nearer to it than 'there must always have been Something – an unbeginning to eternal Something – and that Something is your Self'.[57]

Then there were the true agnostics. This word is often used loosely as a rather less compromising term to apply to those who were really simple atheists. But one author who was a genuine agnostic – in the strict sense that he really did not know what to believe – was Gilbert Murray). Murray pondered deeply about religion throughout his life, without ever coming to a final conclusion. He was born of a Catholic father and a Protestant mother; and although he was baptised a Catholic, both parents were easygoing in the matter of religion. His father wrote in his will: 'It has been throughout my object to impress the broad principles of Christianity on the minds of my children, and to keep them free from the narrow sectarian prejudices which in all ages have done so much mischief in society.' This tolerant attitude left Gilbert free to make up his own mind. Quite early in childhood his innate softheartedness compelled him to discard Christianity. As he recorded in his autobiography, 'it was the miracle of the Gadarene Swine that first shocked me … so monstrously cruel to drive a lot of unoffending pigs over a precipice.'[58] Having eliminated Christianity on account of its mistreatment of pigs, Murray spent the rest of his life looking for a substitute. In his youth, he flirted briefly with Positivism, attending services at the chapel in London; then with Buddhism – 'the best of religions' – but that lasted only one term at Oxford. At the end of his life, Murray wrote that he was 'more conscious in the sphere of religion of the impenetrable mystery that surrounds our little island of knowledge'. A fine passage in his *Five Stages of Greek Religion* (1935), portrays the attempts of a man of great integrity and sensibility to come to terms with the mysteries that beset us:

> The Uncharted surrounds us on every side and we must needs have some relation to it, a relation which will depend on the general discipline of a man's mind and the bias of his whole character. As far as knowledge and conscious reason go, we should follow resolutely their austere guidance. When they cease, as cease they must, we must use as best we can these fainter powers of apprehension, surmise and sensitiveness by which, after all, most high truth has been reached, as well as most high art and poetry; careful always to seek for truth and not for our emotional satisfaction, careful not to neglect the real needs of men and women through basing our life on dreams; and remembering above all to walk gently in a world where lights are dim and the very stars wander.[59]

George Bernard Shaw felt that both religion and science failed to provide an adequate account of the world, and set about knocking their heads together, in his usual robust fashion, in a lengthy Preface to *Back to Methuselah* (1921). He began by explaining why he could not accept the teachings of conventional religion. 'It is,' he wrote, 'the adulteration of religion by the romance of miracles and paradises and torture chambers that makes it reel at the impact of every advance in science, instead of being clarified by it.' But the science which Shaw thought should illuminate religion was an idiosyncratic, Shavian science which rejected Darwin's evolution by natural selection for Lamarck's earlier theory of the inheritance of acquired characteristics. At the time Lamarckianism was already beginning to be considered disreputable in scientific circles, but that did not deter Shaw. His solution was what he called 'creative evolution', an idea which he had picked up from Samuel Butler – also an admirer of Lamarck. In 1887, Shaw had been sent Butler's *Luck or Cunning?* to review, and was impressed. 'From this time on,' he wrote, 'I was acquainted with Butler's view of evolution, though I do not think I grasped its full significance until years afterwards when I had arrived at it in my own way.' The idea behind 'creative evolution' seems to be that it is a process which is continually being modified by an input from the experience of countless individual human beings. Hence the dead can be said to achieve a sort of immortality. Shaw considered it to be 'the genuinely scientific religion for which all wise men are now anxiously looking'. In this respect, he proved to be mistaken, but he evidently derived some personal consolation from his queer religion. In the week before he died, he told his former secretary: 'I believe in life everlasting, but not for the individual.'[60]

Another sect whose deity was an abstract entity were the Positivists, who worshipped 'Humanity'.[61] Positivism appealed to those who accepted the scientific evidence which seemed to show that there was no rational need to postulate a personal deity, yet who felt the need for some sort of spiritual support in an otherwise bleak and indifferent universe. It was too patently artificial a religion to gather more than a modest following during the last decades of the nineteenth century and the early years of the twentieth. Positivists were represented among the Surrey hills by their leader, Frederic Harrison, by Rayner Storr and – although a visitor rather than a resident – by F.W. Bockett. Storr's friend, S.H. Swinny, editor of the *Positivist Review*, also stayed with him in Hindhead in 1907.

Rayner Storr, photographed by George Bernard Shaw

Positivists worshipped at solemn ceremonies derived from Christianity, at their meeting-houses in London, at Chapel Street, and in Newton Hall, near Fleet Street. The sect was originated by Auguste Comte (1798–1857), the French philosopher who wrote the six-volume *Cours de philosophie positive*. Positivism was introduced into England by Richard Congreve, an Oxford don who gave up his fellowship at Wadham to propagate the new doctrine. One of his pupils was Frederic Harrison, who came up to Oxford as an Anglo-Catholic, but was converted to Positivism by Congreve. Harrison was a founder member of the Positivist Society in 1867, and when a split developed between his followers and those of Congreve in 1880, he became president of the English Positivist Committee, and soon the recognised leader of the English movement.

The beliefs and practices of the cult are succinctly summarised, in a little booklet, *The Positivist Calendar*, edited by H. Gordon Jones and published in 1905. This was based on earlier versions by Congreve and Harrison, and contains an explanation of the Calendar by the latter. The Calendar, which was devised by Comte in 1849, divides the year into thirteen months, each of precisely four weeks, with one additional day, dedicated to 'All the Dead' at the end of the year, plus another, to 'Illustrious Women' in leap years. The months, weeks and days are named after past worthies representing Religion, Poetry, Philosophy, War, Statesmanship, Industry and Science, those thought to be most important being assigned to months, a lesser grade getting weeks, and the lowliest merely days. Thus the year begins with a month dedicated to Moses, and Theocratic Civilisation. The first week goes to Numa, the legendary King of Rome, who is said to have founded most of the religious institutions of the city; while Prometheus gets New Year's Day. The second month, starting on 29th January, belongs to Homer, and Ancient Poetry, with a first week of Aeschylus, and a first day of Hesiod. And so on through the year, with the named heroes getting progressively more modern. The thirteenth month is assigned to Bichat and Modern Science. It is not obvious why Bichat (1771–1802), a French anatomist, is preferred to Galileo, Newton and Lavoisier, who merely get a week each, or Copernicus, who only gets a day. A preamble explains that the names are drawn from what is described as 'the Western Republic ... formed by the free cohesion of the five leading populations – the French, Italian, Spanish, British and German', an apparent anticipation of the European Union.

Positivism, Comte insisted, was a state and not a creed. As such, it embraced both science and religion, but was based on the material world of scientifically verifiable facts. However, at the same time it claimed to be 'the crown and fulfilment of all the religions that have gone before'. 'The whole human problem,' according to Comte, 'consists in establishing Unity, personal and social, by the constant subordination of Egoism to Altruism.' Positivism was indeed all-embracing: while firmly based on scientific facts, it also acknowledged the power of mysticism, and valued highly such moral qualities as unselfishness, devotion and love of beauty. Its services were simple ceremonies, consisting mainly of hymn-singing and a thoughtful address. There were no less than nine 'Social Sacraments' to mark rites of passage: 'Presentation' at one year; 'Initiation' at 14; 'Admission' at 21; 'Destination' at 28; 'Marriage' 21–28 for women, 28–35 for men; 'Maturity' at 42; 'Retirement' at 63; 'Transformation' at death; 'Incorporation' at seven years after death. As with the early Nonconformists, Positivist services centred on the address, but its content was of course very different and very varied, as can be seen by taking at random the titles of some of the addresses offered at the regular services at 11.15 a.m. and 7 p.m. every Sunday at the Chapel Street meeting-house: 'The History of Physics', 'Modern Banking Theories', 'Art and Humanity', 'Man and his Universe', 'A Century of Railway Development'. No doubt some of these addresses were rather more gripping than the average Anglican sermon; but it is not easy to see how the contemplation of railway development, or even banking theories, could inspire the mystical feelings and high moral tone which Positivists valued so deeply.

Despite the seemingly materialistic trappings, there was also a pronounced mystical element in Positivism, shown most clearly in the admiration and respect felt for Thomas à Kempis's *Imitation of Christ*. Positivists seem to have been able to appreciate the beauty and purity of its sentiments, while treating as an irrelevancy any mention of the Deity. Positivism appears to have combined an austere respect for objective truth, with an impeccable moral code, a rather ludicrous mock-Christian ritual and a generous dash of mysticism. It appealed to some of the deeply serious, male-dominated late-

Victorian intelligentsia, but much less to women, who tended to be repelled by the austerity of the services and never came in any numbers.[62] In the 1880s, Beatrice Webb often attended services at Newton Hall, and at one time contemplated becoming a Positivist. However, she finally came to the conclusion that their rites and observances did not amount to more than 'a valiant effort to make a religion out of nothing, a pitiful attempt by poor Humanity to turn its head round to worship its tail'.[63]

Highcombe Edge, home of Rayner Storr at Hindhead

Soon after Frederic Harrison's own death in 1923, Positivism, too, quietly died, without anyone taking much notice.

Then there were those, usually described as 'deists', who believed in 'Somebody', as opposed to 'Something', yet could not quite bring themselves to identify this person with the Christian God. The deist position was most clearly stated by William Allingham, the poet and diarist. On a summer's day in 1882 he had been talking to William Morris as they walked through the streets of Bloomsbury. Before they parted, Morris had dismissed the whole God business as unimportant. This led Allingham to think over his own position, and to confide his thoughts to his diary, in what is a lucid account of the deist position:

> I will have nothing to do with the Church of Rome, or indeed with any form of Christianity, in spite of all the beauty and power, all the comforting and controlling influences, because I know the structure is built on false dogmas. No verbal Revelation of any date, in any tongue, has the least authority with me. Nor do I want a puppet God constructed or kept up because it may scare some from robbery and

revolution, murder and suicide; and it seems to me that whoever goes about to describe or define the Deity, sets up an idol or puppet, a man's work, whether it be mean as African fetish or majestic as the Jupiter of Pheidias. We cannot in the least describe, or comprehend, or even think Deity. And yet we can believe in Deity, and that belief is not fantastic, but natural, sound, and reasonable. There is to me no conception of the universe possible save as the dominion of Power and Wisdom, unfathomably great, yet in sympathy with my own intelligent nature; a Greatness presenting itself to me (when I dare at all to shape it) as a true Personality, comprising all that man at his best in measured degree feels, thinks, and is; and much more. *Almighty God* – to whom turns my soul, sharing, I know not how, the mystic divine nature; whose reality is indubitable, whose quality is incomprehensible, whose plans are inscrutable. This conception is in harmony with my whole moral, reasonable and imaginative being. It bears little talking about, and that only in the choicest moments. Logic has no hold here. Rhetoric is out of place. I do not know that I am bound to turn my mind towards the problem of the universe, or that anyone is bound to send his thoughts outside of his daily life and business. But my mind does naturally so turn, and when it does so turn it finds before it the idea of *God*, and therefore receives a sense of strength and serenity.[64]

It is not always possible to make a clear distinction between deists and those Christians who reject a large part of the church's teaching, while retaining their belief in God. Richard Le Gallienne, novelist and poet, for example, brushed aside all talk of life after death: 'we can do without the hereafter'. He considered that organised Christianity is not the religion of Christ, that Walt Whitman's *Leaves of Grass* was more helpful than the New Testament, and that the dogma of the religion of the future would be 'Love, Beauty, Purity and Strength'. Le Gallienne thought of his own religion as a modified form of Christianity, calling it 'essential Christianity; a religion for *this* world, and *this* life'.[65] But so considerable is the modification that it is not easy to distinguish his position from that of a simple deist like Allingham.

Mrs Humphry Ward was another who sincerely accepted Christianity, but wanted to have it on her own terms. She longed for Holy Communion, but for much of her life she was regarded as unfit to take it because of her scepticism about doctrines such as the Virgin Birth and the Ascension. She was tempted at one time to join the Roman Catholic Church, as her father had. She was attracted by its rituals but repelled by some of its doctrines, and by the practice of confession. However, after she became a national figure and a member of the county Establishment, it became incumbent upon her to attend services in the local Anglican church, where her large country house, Stocks, had its own pew.[66]

Another of the Hilltop Writers who favoured a greatly modified Christianity was Jonathan Hutchinson, the surgeon and founder of the Haslemere Museum. He had been brought up as a Quaker, but ended with an odd mixture of beliefs, largely of his own devising. He called this brew 'Planetarianism', to indicate that it was – like Positivism – entirely concerned with life on this planet. So there was no heaven and hell, and no place to go to when life ended. However, to make up for this deficiency, he devised an ingenious arrangement for the survival of the soul after death. Although a great admirer of Darwin, he accepted the Lamarckian doctrine of the inheritance of acquired characteristics. So when a child was born, it was endowed, through its genes, with the characteristics of its parents at the time of its conception, including those they had acquired as well as those they were born with. This, he thought, was the equivalent of the survival of the soul, as conceived by orthodox Christianity.[67]

Those of the Hilltop Writers who have left no written record of their religious affiliations were probably nominal Anglicans who dutifully attended church on Sundays, without letting religion interfere too much with their daily lives. But many followed the example of the amiable and tolerant Broad Church Rector of Haslemere, Reverend George Herbert Aitken. He believed that all human activities came within the province of the Church: 'nothing is secular except sin' was his favourite saying. A close friend of Jonathan Hutchinson, he was active in the Museum and the Natural History Society, and held study circles and amateur dramatics on the rectory lawn. (Indeed, so prolific were his activities that one despairing parishioner was heard to complain: 'There is no home life left in Haslemere since Mr Aitken came.')

George Herbert Aitken, Rector of Haslemere

The novelist Bernard Hamilton, on the other hand, reverted to the intolerant type of Evangelical Anglicanism common in the earlier part of the nineteenth century, for he was vehemently opposed to High Church practices, and worried by the spread of Roman Catholicism. At the same time, he wanted to introduce what he called 'commonsense principles' into the Church of England, which seems to imply an affinity with the Broad Church. He set out his views in his novel, *The Light?* (1898), a weird mixture of fiction, history and religious propaganda. He described it as 'a romance of a man who went to seek the Light – for himself. His strange adventures are here set forth.' The narrative starts in ancient Egypt, ending in the 1870s, and is interlarded with long religious essays. Mercifully, these are indicated by markers, so that they may be omitted by readers who are 'not interested in matters of religious moment'. It is a long work, and I cannot claim to have read it; but I have studied the Preface, and also an Appendix in which the author sets out what he thinks should be done about the Church of England. Both are written in an excitable and at times incoherent style, so that it is not always easy to make out what he is driving at. He does, however, conclude with a list of concrete proposals, including abolition of the Thirty-nine Articles, which, he thinks, 'might with advantage be nailed to the door of Westminster Abbey'.[68]

The Low Church Anglicanism of Agnes Weston, the founder of Sailors' Rests, was sincerely held, and entirely orthodox. Although always eager for converts, she was however willing to dispense tea and a hot meal to even the most sceptical tar. The faith of the Haslemere Congregationalists, the Whymper family and Joseph King, was equally unshakeable.

But in no case was the faith of any of these tested in the fire, as Margaret Oliphant's was. All her life she was battered by misfortune, and obliged to work herself to the bone to support by her writing a crowd of feckless relatives. But by far the greatest of her trials was the death of her beloved daughter Maggie. Yet even that did not shake her belief. In a most moving passage in her *Autobiography*, she described her feelings at that time:

> I used to think faith meant only believing in our Saviour which is but the dearest easiest beginning. It never was any difficulty to me to believe in Him. Does He not prove himself above all criticisms and questions? – I cannot but think so. In Him, the one thing certain in this terrible problem of human existence, I believe, as in the only light which throws a little illumination on the darkness. That is not the agonizing faith that God demands of me. It is to believe in the face of all appearance to the contrary, in opposition to my knowledge of myself, against the aching and yearning of my heart, that in this and all He does He has done well. It is to trust Him that it has not been done unadvisedly, that there is a reason for it greater than all the manifest human reasons which were against it.[69]

Margaret had been brought up in the Church of Scotland, and in the 1843 'Disruption' she went with the radical Free Church of Scotland. The English equivalent was the Presbyterian Church, and this is where she worshipped when in England.

Manley Hopkins was an Anglo-Catholic, and remained so after the conversion of his poet son Gerard to Roman Catholicism. So, too, was Christina Rossetti, despite the influence of her two atheist brothers. She testified to the depth of her faith in a long series of poems and prose essays. Her brother William, who appreciated the sincerity of Christina's beliefs though he did not share them, wrote in his Memoir of her:

> Her religion was far more a thing of the heart than of the mind; she clung to and loved the Christian creed because she loved Jesus

Christ. 'Christ is God' was her one dominant idea. Faith with her was faith pure and absolute; an entire acceptance of a thing revealed – not a quest for any confirmation or demonstrative proof … Her attitude of mind was: 'I believe because I am told to believe, and I know that the authority which tells me to believe is the only real authority extant, God.' To press her, 'How do you know that it is God?' would have been no use; the ultimate response could only have come to this – 'My faith is faith; it is not evolved out of argumentation, nor does it seek the aid of that.'[70]

Hill Farm, Camelsdale, home of Joseph and Maude King in the 1920s

William had 'often thought that Christina's proper place was in the Roman Catholic Church, yet I never traced any inclination in her to join it'. Her faith was expressed in a large collection of religious verse, of which the best known and loved is the Christmas carol, *In the bleak mid-winter*. The last verse effectively conveys the beautiful simplicity and modesty of her faith:

> What can I give Him,
>   Poor as I am?
> If I were a shepherd
>   I would bring a lamb,
> If I were a Wise Man
>   I would do my part,
> What I can I give Him?
>   Give Him my heart.[71]

The only Roman Catholic among the Hilltop Writers was Frank Costelloe, who had been brought up in a Catholic family in southern Ireland. He took his faith seriously, writing three books on religious subjects. Flora Thompson, who would later contribute many stories and articles to *The Catholic Fireside*, also became deeply sympathetic to Catholicism, but could not bring herself to desert the Anglicanism in which she was brought up. In 1932, she wrote to her sister May, who had recently become a Catholic:

> I have always had a great love for the Catholic religion from a child ... I am fairly well instructed in the faith, as I have read many books on it, and of course have attended many services at different times, but I do not suppose I shall ever take the great step you have taken as there are family and other obstacles.[72]

There remain to be discussed two writers who do not fit comfortably into the wider scheme outlined above. They are Arthur Conan Doyle and Alfred Tennyson.

Conan Doyle was a special case. His father was a convinced Roman Catholic, but his mother was more dubious. So, when he was despatched to Hodder, the preparatory school for Stonyhurst (the Catholic public school) his mother's advice was 'Wear flannel next to your skin, my dear boy, and *never* believe in eternal punishment.'[73] He may well have scorned the first part of this advice, but he certainly took note of the second, and by the time he had finished his medical studies in 1882, Doyle had become a convinced materialist. 'I thought,' he said later, 'that when the candle is burned out the light is gone. 'His materialism was, however, modified by a belief that 'Somebody' must have made the immutable laws he had learnt about in his scientific studies. He then discovered spiritualism, and from then on, for the rest of his life, that became his sole religion. He did not actually reject Christianity – he believed that Christ himself was 'endowed with an intense psychic power' – but simply ceased to think much about it. He did not need to, since spiritualism told him all he wanted to know about life after death. The death of his son in the Great War intensified his belief in spiritualism; he felt the need to spread this particular gospel, and undertook world-wide missionary tours. Although he had to put up with a fair amount of scepticism and ridicule, his commitment to spiritualism remained total. His credulity even extended to a belief in fairies. He had heard about two little Yorkshire girls who claimed to have taken photographs of fairies with a small box camera. Doyle investigated, and found that 'there is no flaw at all in the evidence'. He went so far as to write a book about it, *The Coming of the Fairies* (1922). Other, more sceptical observers noted that the 'fairies', who were clad in the latest Paris fashions, closely resembled some female figures used by Messrs Price and Sons to illustrate advertisements for their candles. The experience encouraged Doyle to experiment with photographing the spirits who materialised during his séances, in the hope of convincing his friends that the smudges on his plates represented ectoplasm.[74]

Many others in this period – notably Tennyson – had dabbled with spiritualism, by way of sampling a novel experience, but that was very different from Doyle's total commitment. It is indeed astonishing that this bluff, genial, athletic giant, with his robust patriotism and love of adventure, and yet also with the ability and astuteness to create Sherlock Holmes, epitome of acute observation and subtle inference, should have been so credulous as to be fooled by a photograph of fairies taken by two schoolgirls with a cheap camera.

Tennyson is not so much a special case as an enigma. In view of the deep respect in which he was held by the public, he could no more have admitted to being either an atheist, or a Roman Catholic, than the Queen herself. In fact, his faith lay somewhere in between these two extremes, but it is difficult to say just where. What can be said is that he was deeply religious, in the sense that he took the great issues of human existence, and its aftermath, a lot more seriously than most. All his life he had worried about such things; particularly, about what happens after death. But the conclusions he came to, and the firmness with which he held them, remain a mystery, and probably fluctuated from time to time. The vehemence with which he rejected Positivism – telling Frederic Harrison 'If I thought as you do, I' d go and hang myself' – seems to indicate belief in a personal deity.[75] Nominally, he remained an Anglican (in his exalted position, he could scarcely have done otherwise), but he seldom attended church services. He had been put off by the narrow-minded parson at Freshwater, he told Mangles. He also mentioned an occasion, during his walking tour of Wales, when he would have attended service in Chester Cathedral, if his trousers had not been torn.[76] There were certainly times when he had serious doubts about Christian doctrine; his brief flirtation with spiritualism after the death of his son Lionel in 1886 indicates that he was not too confident about the Christian vision of life after death. T.S. Eliot said of Tennyson's great masterpiece, *In Memoriam*, that 'It is not religious because of the quality of its faith, but because of the quality of its doubt,' though the poem is surely a finely expressed mixture of both faith and doubt. But whatever the ups and downs in Tennyson's turbulent mind, his final testament, in the serenely beautiful *Crossing the Bar*, appears to show that his doubts had in the end been resolved. Yet, even as he prepared to meet his Maker face to face, there seems to be a hint that he might really have preferred to make his exit in the old pagan style, on the deck of a longship, or perhaps an Arthurian barge:

> When that which drew from out the boundless deep
> Turns again home,

rather than beneath the cold stones of Westminster Abbey.

Summary of Section Two

It is probably rash to make any generalisations about a group of individuals. Yet in choosing the Surrey hills as a place to live these writers showed a common desire to escape from both the feverish search for novelty and the brash imperialism which – as well as the murky atmosphere – characterised the capital at this period. At the same time, they were not loners, seeking solitude, and had no desire to cut themselves off from the amenities of civilised life. So we can expect to find them collectively – there will of course be exceptions – conservative in their outlook, dignified in their behaviour, co-operative and sociable, and with a deep respect for the accumulated knowledge of the past, of whatever nature it might be.

Haslemere Town Hall, when used as a 'lock-up'

And if they were conservative in their outlook, for the most part they were not Conservative in their politics. Equally, they were not by nature Radicals. The minority who were involved in politics tended to support – with the notable exception of Tennyson – the Liberal position, as defined by Gladstone. On specific issues, not many had strong views on what to do about Ireland, and opinions were probably fairly evenly split for and against Gladstone's proposal for Irish independence. But at the time of the South

African War, there seems to have been substantially more sympathy for the cause of the Boers among the hilltop community than would be found in the country generally, or indeed among the native population of those hills.

As regards social issues, the problem of 'degeneration' among slum-dwellers did not excite much interest until after 1900. But the 'woman question' concerned everyone, and was gathering force throughout the 1890s. A puzzling feature is the surprising number of able and successful women writers who fervently believed that females were constitutionally incapable of so simple a task as registering a vote.

The topic which roused the deepest feeling was religion – and this applied as much to the atheists as to the committed believers. The perplexity caused by the new discoveries of science, which increasingly portrayed a universe governed by impersonal laws, caused all thinking people to reflect deeply on the nature of the cosmos, and their own relations to it. The position of truly committed Christians, and of complete materialists, was clear enough. But the tenets of the majority hovered somewhere in between, as they tried to reconcile the two extreme positions. They were reluctant to abandon either the faith in which they had been brought up, or the belief in the power of the human intellect, which they had later acquired. For some, this involved a series of sometimes rather desperate proposals – such as Harrison's Positivism, Doyle's spiritualism, Shaw's and Hutchinson's contrivances with Lamarckianism – and a series of deistic modifications of Christianity which left it barely recognisable. The majority probably arrived at a compromise, acceptable to the ever-accommodating Anglican communion, whereby some of its more distasteful doctrines, such as the everlasting torture of the damned, were quietly forgotten.

Footnotes to Section Two

[1] Fenn, Alice Maud, *Century Magazine*, 'The Borderlands of Surrey', 1882, p. 487.
[2] Wilson, Duncan, *Gilbert Murray, O.M.*, p. 71.
[3] Sutherland, John, *Mrs Humphry Ward: Eminent Victorian, Pre-eminent Edwardian*, pp. 266, 310.
[4] Nevill, Lady Dorothy, *The Reminiscences of Lady Dorothy Nevill*, pp. 284–91.
[5] Martin, Robert Bernard, *Tennyson: The Unquiet Heart*, p. 575.
[6] Sutherland, *Mrs Humphrey Ward*, p. 77.
[7] Nevill, *Reminiscences*, pp. 276–77.
[8] Reported in the *Surrey Times*, 11th November 1899.
[9] Sutherland, p. 197.
[10] Harrison, Austin, *Frederic Harrison: Thoughts and Memories*, p.146.
[11] Kevles, Daniel J., *In The Name of Eugenics*, p. 90.
[12] Harrison, J.F.C., *Late Victorian Britain*, pp. 132–33.

[13] Lankester, Ray, *Degeneration: A Chapter in Darwinism*, p. 30.

[14] Allingham, William, *William Allingham: A Diary*, Introduction by John Julius Norwich, p. 358.

[15] Forrest, D.W., *Francis Galton: The Life and Work of a Victorian Genius*, p. 256.

[16] Russell, Rollo, *Epidemics Plagues and Fevers: Their Causes and Prevention.*

[17] Russell, Rollo, *First Conditions of Human Prosperity.*

[18] Russell, Rollo, *The Distribution of Land.*

[19] Lindsay, Gillian, *Flora Thompson: The Story of the Lark Rise Writer*, p.90.

[20] Rubinstein, David, *Before the Suffragettes: Women's Emancipation in the 1890s.*

[21] Rubinstein, p. 5.

[22] Darley, Gillian, *Octavia Hill: A Life*, p. 132.

[23] Bellringer, Alan W., *George Eliot*, pp. 11–15.

[24] Jay, Elizabeth (ed.), *The Autobiography of Margaret Oliphant*, p. 15.

[25] Williams, Merryn, *Margaret Oliphant: A Critical Biography*, p.117.

[26] In *Blackwood's Magazine*, 1896, vol. 159, pp. 135–49.

[27] Coghill, Mrs Harry (ed.), *Autobiography and Letters of Mrs Margaret Oliphant*, with an Introduction by Q.D. Leavis, p. 15.

[28] Steevens, Mrs Christina, *A Motley Crew: Reminiscences, Observations and Attempts at Play-writing*, 1901, pp. 142–43.

[29] In *Nineteenth Century*, June 1889, vol. 148, pp. 781–88.

[30] Sutherland, *Mrs Humphrey Ward*, pp. 198–200.

[31] Jones, Kathleen, *Learning Not to be First: The Life of Christina Rossetti*, p. 140.

[32] Jones, Kathleen, p. 193.

[33] Strachey, Barbara, *Remarkable Relations: The Story of the Pearsall Smith Family*, p. 93.

[34] Strachey, B., *Remarkable Relations*, p. 165.

[35] *Nineteenth Century*, June 1894, vol. 35, pp. 443–50; see also Rubinstein, p. 14 & p. 21, note 6.

[36] *Fortnightly Review*, 1889, vol. 46, pp. 123–39.

[37] Webb, Beatrice, *My Apprenticeship*, p. 10.

[38] MacKensie, Norman and MacKensie, Jean (eds.), *The Diaries of Beatrice Webb*, vol. 1, p. 111.

[39] Webb, pp. 254–55.

[40] Jones, Raymond A., *Arthur Ponsonby: The Politics of Life*, p. 65.

[41] Holroyd, Michael, *Bernard Shaw*, vol. 2, p. 255.

[42] Vogeler, Martha S., *Frederic Harrison: The Vocations of a Positivist*, p.267.

[43] Tennyson, Hallam, *Alfred Lord Tennyson: A memoir*, vol. 1, p. 249.

[44] Wilson, pp. 145–46; 180–84.

[45] Allen, Grant, *Fortnightly Review*, 'Plain Words on the Woman Question', vol. 46, 1889, pp. 448–458.

[46] Quoted in the *Contemporary Review*, vol. 67, 1895, pp. 625–31.

[47] Quoted from Allen's *Fortnightly Review* article.

[48] Wells, H.G., *Experiment in Autobiography*, pp. 549–51.

[49] Clodd, Edward, *Grant Allen: A Memoir*, pp. 192–93.

[50] Ashton, Rosemary, G.H. *Lewes: A Life*, pp. 16, 106.
[51] May, J. Lewis, *George Eliot: A Study*, p. 258; also Harrison, pp. 123–24 (first published in *The Century Magazine* in 1881).
[52] Quoted from Clark, Ronald W ., *The Life of Bertrand Russell*, p. 94 (first published as 'The Free Man's Worship' in *Independent Review*, 1903).
[53] Jay, Elizabeth (ed.), *Faith and Doubt in Victorian Britain*, pp. 101–02.
[54] Tyndall, John, *Fragments of Science*, vol. 2, 1892, pp. 196–205.
[55] Wright, T., *Hindhead, or the English Switzerland*, p. 101.
[56] Forrest, pp. 84, 269 and 286.
[57] Wales Hubert, *The Purpose: Reflections and Digressions*.
[58] Wilson, p. 5.
[59] Wilson, p. 409.
[60] Holroyd, Michael, *Bernard Shaw*, vol. 3, pp. 36–42 and 513.
[61] Wright, T.R. *The Religion of Humanity*.
[62] Harrison, A., p. 190.
[63] MacKensie's, *The Diaries of Beatrice Webb*, vol. 2, p. 211.
[64] Allingham, pp. 317–18.
[65] Quoted in Le Gallienne, R., *The Religion of a Literary Man*.
[66] See Sutherland, *Mrs Humphreys Ward*, pp. 192–96.
[67] See Hutchinson, Herbert, *Jonathan Hutchinson: Life and Letters*.
[68] Hamilton, Bernard, *The Light? A Romance*, p. 518.
[69] Quoted in Jay, *The Autobiography of Margaret Oliphant*, pp. 7–8.
[70] Rossetti, William Michael (ed.), *The Poetical Works of Christina Georgina Rossetti, with Memoir and Notes*, p. liv.
[71] Quoted in Rossetti, p. 246.
[72] Lindsay, p. 133.
[73] Quoted in Martin, Robert Bernard, *Gerard Manley Hopkins: A Very Private Life*, p. 201.
[74] Orel, Harold (ed.), *Sir Arthur Conan Doyle: Interviews and Recollections*, p. 225–268.
[75] Quoted in Le Gallienne, *The Romantic '90s*, p. 49.
[76] Knies, Earl A., *Tennyson at Aldworth: The Diary of James Henry Mangles*, pp. 68, 84.

Section Three:
Biographical Notes

[The main sources consulted are given in square brackets after each entry. 'DNB' = Dictionary of National Biography.]

ALLEN, (Charles) Grant (Blairfindie) (1848–1899): novelist, naturalist and writer on popular science.

Although now virtually forgotten, Allen was a well-known literary figure in his day, a friend of George Meredith, Algernon Swinburne, R.L. Stevenson and H.G. Wells, and a key figure in the establishment of the Hilltop Writers on Hindhead. From 1881 to 1893 he had been living in Dorking, at a house called The Nook. Then he discovered the 'wild and romantic beauty of Hindhead, and returned to Dorking declaring that not a day must be lost, that he must buy some land on the side of the Punch Bowl and build a house'.[1] So in 1893, with Edward May as his architect, he built a house called The Croft (now Forest House), situated just off the

Grant Allen

Tilford Road, on the rim of the Devil's Punch Bowl and exposed to the full force of the north-east wind. If it was fresh air he wanted, he certainly got plenty of it. It was a drastic treatment, but it seems to have done him good. While he was living at Dorking, he had had to go abroad to Antibes, Algiers or Egypt each winter for the sake of his health, but so beneficent was the Hindhead air that he found he was able to stay there throughout the winter months.

Born in Canada of mixed Irish and French-Canadian ancestry, Allen received a cosmopolitan education in America, France and England, ending with an Oxford degree in classics in 1871. While at Oxford, he married a young girl who was already in poor health; she became paralysed, and died two years later. In 1873 he married his second wife, Ellen Jerrard ('Nellie'). It was a happy and lasting union, resulting in the birth of one son. After leaving Oxford, Allen had hoped to make a living by writing on scientific subjects, but he soon found that this was not possible. So, reluctantly, he had to take to schoolmastering. But in 1873, he applied successfully for the post of Professor of Mental and Moral Philosophy at a newly-founded college in Jamaica, and this gave him just sufficient funds to embark on marriage. Immediately afterwards the newly-married couple set sail for Jamaica.

The college, however, was not a success; for the first half year there were only three students. Not long after it opened, the Principal died of yellow fever, and Allen was appointed in his place. This left him as the one and only member of the staff, and the whole burden of teaching fell on his shoulders. The college was finally wound up in 1876. While in Jamaica, Allen wrote a long, light-hearted account of his life there, in rhyming couplets, to Franklin Richards (father of his nephew, Grant Richards). The four following lines summed up his activities:

> At ten I depart for the College to lecture,
> On every subject of human conjecture,
> For this being but a one-man-power College,
> I alone must explore the whole circle of knowledge.[2]

His experience in Jamaica obliged Allen to acquire a knowledge of all branches of human learning, and laid the foundation which made him in later life such a remarkable polymath.

On returning to England, Allen still attempted to scratch a living by writing on scientific subjects. But by then there was little market for even well-informed amateur speculations, as scientists were gradually becoming more professional. So the works which Allen regarded as his major contributions to science, *Physiological Aesthetics* (1877) and *Force and Energy* (1888), made little impact. But he must have been gratified when Herbert Spencer – his great hero – praised the first of these as 'highly philosophical in its conception and admirable in its arrangements ... showing great originality and insight'. Allen also received some complimentary letters from Charles Darwin, who thanked him for defending his ideas on sexual selection and for confirming his ideas on the evolution of flowers. He also congratulated Allen on the easy, clear and pleasant style of writing in his *The Evolutionist at Large* (1881). Darwin was also concerned about Allen's health and, in conjunction with Herbert Spencer, raised a fund to enable him to spend the winter at Cap d'Antibes in the South of France.

In *The Evolution of the Idea of God* (1897), Allen took an objective look at the development of the world's religions, based on the early volumes of James Frazer's *The Golden Bough* and on Herbert Spencer's 'ghost theory'. Allen's approach was fairly conventional: he saw religions as developing from polytheism to monotheism to Christianity. However, he claimed two novelties for his interpretation: religion should be completely separated from mythology; and an important feature in most religions was the deliberate manufacture of gods by killing. His ideas were similar to those of his friend – and future biographer – Edward Clodd, whose presidential address to the Folk Lore Society in 1895 caused great offence for suggesting that Christian rites might have evolved from the beliefs of primitive peoples. Allen wrote to congratulate him on the address: 'What a capital paper! So clear, so learned, so bold, so cogent!'[3]

H.G. Wells was a friend of Allen's, and understood his position well, for it resembled his own:

> Like myself, Grant Allen had never found a footing in the profes-
> sional scientific world and he had none of the patience, deliberation
> – and discretion – of the established scientific worker, who must
> live with a wholesome fear of the Royal Society and its inhibitions
> before his eyes. Grant Allen's semi-popular original scientific
> works such as his *Origin of the Idea of God* (1897) and his
> *Physiological Aesthetics* (1877) were at once bold and sketchy,
> unsupported by properly verified quotations and collated refer-
> ences, and regardless or manifestly ignorant of much other contem-
> porary work. They were too original to be fair popularization and
> too unsubstantiated to be taken seriously by serious specialists, and
> what was good in them has long been appropriated, generally with-
> out acknowledgement, by sounder workers, while the flimsy bulk
> of them moulders on a few dusty and forgotten shelves.[4]

So, reluctantly and without much hope, Allen took to writing fiction. He found, rather to his surprise, that it was something he could do with a fair degree of facility. In 1880 he started to write short stories (under various pseudonyms, lest his friends should discover the depths of ignominy to which he had descended). A collection of these, *Strange Stories*, was published in 1884, and so also was his first novel, *Philistia* – still anonymously, as 'Cecil Power'. Some thirty novels followed, written for the most part in accordance with the conventions of the time, and so for the most part they were modestly successful. While many of them have ingenious plots, Allen lacked the born novelist's ability to make his characters come alive. In his Introduction to *Twelve Tales*, a selection of the short stories which he considered 'to possess most permanent value', Allen describes how it was that he came to write fiction. 'About the year 1880 (if I recollect aright), wishing to contribute an article to *Belgravia* on the improbability of a man's being able to recognise a ghost as such, even if he saw one … I ventured for the better development of my subject to throw the argument into the form of a narrative. I did not regard this narrative as a story; I looked upon it merely as a convenient method of displaying a scientific truth. However, the gods and Mr Chatto thought otherwise. For, a month or two later, Mr Chatto wrote to ask me if I could supply *Belgravia* with "another story".[5] All of the twelve stories in this volume have original plots, but the only truly vibrant characters live in foreign parts: Zelie, the French cook, and her illegitimate daughter; Cecca, the Neapolitan servant girl, and her fisherman lover; Clemmy, the mulatto girl living in rural Jamaica.

All these works of fiction were in truth no more than pot-boilers, designed to please an undemanding, but paying, public. The winds of Hindhead seem, however, to have stimulated him to attempt something more profound, and he wrote two novels which, he hoped, would induce public opinion to accept some of his radical ideas about the institution of marriage. He called these two books his Hilltop Novels, *The Woman who Did* (1895) and *The British Barbarians* (1895). 'I propose in future,' he wrote in the Introduction to the second of these, 'to add the words "A Hilltop Novel" to every one of my stories which I write of my own accord, simply and solely for the sake of embodying and enforcing my own opinions.' In fact, Allen's premature death in 1899 did not permit him to write any more than these two. Both are really tracts, dressed up as novels, in which the thoroughly wooden characters express Allen's own views in a series of homilies. The general theme of both books is the iniquity of the existing social and legal system, which kept wives subject to the whims of their husbands. It is not apparent that anything in Allen's own experience had led him to feel so very strongly on the subjection of married women, and the first of his controversial novels is dedicated affectionately to his second wife Nellie, 'with whom I have passed my twenty happiest years'.

The Woman who Did was about an early feminist, Herminia Barton, who regards marriage as a barbarous convention, used to trap women into subjection, which she is determined to avoid. So although she is in love with Alan Merrick, and is glad to bear his child, she refuses to marry him, although fully aware of the social ostracism which will inevitably result. The child is duly born, Alan unhappily dies of typhoid, and Herminia is left as a single parent, disowned by her stern clerical father. Being a resolute girl, she manages to survive, and successfully rears her daughter, Dolores. Herminia's intention was that Dolores should be brought up free from the conventions which she herself had found so constricting. But Dolores turns out to want nothing more than a conventional marriage. When it seems that this may be thwarted by her mother's irregular lifestyle, Herminia nobly removes herself from the scene with a large dose of prussic acid. As the author defiantly ended his narrative, her 'stainless soul had ceased to exist for ever'.

The Woman Who Did might have been taken as showing the dreadful fate which befalls anyone who defies the conventional view of marriage, but in fact it was generally regarded, even by feminists, as an attack on Christian morality. As has been discussed in the section on the 'woman question',

Allen's two Hilltop Novels left him in the curious position of being reviled both by the strict conventionalists and by the feminists, although like him they were also engaged in the fight for women's rights in marriage. Not surprisingly, Allen had some difficulty in finding a publisher for this daring work, but his nephew, Grant Richards, managed eventually to persuade John Lane to undertake it. When he did, the resulting uproar was considerable. Bookshops in Ireland refused to sell it, and a clergyman wrote to Allen to say he could no longer ask him to his house, 'while you treat my Divine Master as you are doing'. Allen replied in a dignified letter, saying that he respected the clergyman's motives, and setting out his own position.

The scandal caused by *The Woman Who Did* very nearly deprived Allen of the presidency of the Haslemere Microscope and Natural History Society. When Hutchinson resigned from that post in 1896, the Committee proposed Allen as their preferred candidate to succeed him. But at the meeting of the Society for the election, there was considerable opposition, led – very politely – by the then Rector, Revd S. Etheridge. As the *Surrey Advertiser* pointed out, 'But for the existence of a certain book, which has attained a consider-able notoriety, the election would have been unanimous.' In the event, Allen just won, by 30 votes to 28. Afterwards, Allen wrote another long concilia-tory letter to the Rector.

H.G. Wells sympathised with Allen's attempt 'to change himself over from a regularly selling, proper English "purveyor of fiction" to the novelist with ideas and initiative and so contribute materially to vital literature'. He had similar inclinations himself, later expressed in such novels as *Ann Veronica* and *The New Machiavelli*. But he perceived that *The Woman Who Did* was poorly executed. He felt that 'this hasty, headlong, incompetent book seemed like a treason to a great cause', and slated it unmercifully in a long and trenchant review. Such was Allen's benign and forgiving nature that this resulted in an invitation to lunch at Hindhead for a friendly discussion.[6]

For about a year after the publication of *The Woman Who Did* there was a slump in the sales of all Allen's books. Eventually though, it sold far better than any of his other works, going through nineteen editions in a year.

The second Hilltop Novel, *The British Barbarians*, was also a protest against marriage and the power it gave to overbearing husbands. But the book also took a more general swipe at current conventions, or taboos, as the hero, Bertram Ingledew, persists in calling them. He was no ordinary hero, but a being from the twenty-fifth century, who had suddenly materialised in a respectable suburban street. He was making a world tour, in order to study and compare the customs and mores of the people living in various parts. His studies were interrupted by an affair with the heroine, Frida Monteith, wife of a dour, thoroughly conventional businessman. Bertram and Frida fall in love, and elope to what is clearly Hindhead. The brutal husband catches up with them on the edge of the 'Devil's Saucepan'. He draws a revolver and shoots Bertram, who then vanishes in a puff of blue smoke. Frida captures the revolver and walks off with it by herself, with the apparent intention of following Bertram into the twenty-fifth century.

Allen's reputation with the public at that time was summed up in a limerick in the *Sketch* for 11th August 1897:

> G is for Mr Grant Allen,
> Who pours out his views by the gallon
> His books are improper,
> But he's a Hill-Topper,
> So he fears not the critic's sharp talon.[7]

Allen gave three addresses to the Haslemere Microscope and Natural History Society. They illustrate two of his multifarious interests: natural history and Italian art. On 21st December 1894 he talked about 'Swallows and House Martins', eruditely beginning his remarks with an apposite quotation from the Talmud. He tried to look at the martins who had colonised his Hindhead house, even before it was ready for human occupation, from their point of view, and imagined them saying, as the Allens moved in: 'How terribly inconvenient! here are some of those great nasty creatures that walk so awkwardly erect ... how they'll frighten the children!' Allen's next talk, on 5th February 1897, was entitled 'How a Picture Grew'. Human workmanship, he maintained, should be treated as a branch of natural history, and its development paralleled the evolution of living creatures. He illustrated his thesis with lantern slides showing how the story of Our Lady giving the girdle to St Thomas had been subtly modified by a succession of painters from medieval times onwards, culminating in the version by the Florentine artist Granacci (1477–1543). His third lecture, on 4th February 1898, had a similar theme: 'A Life History: being a comparative examination of pictures and sculpture, illustrative of the Adoration of the Magi'.

Grant Allen was described by his nephew, the publisher Grant Richards, as 'a tall, rather gaunt, beak-nosed, red-bearded man'. His niece, the novelist Netta Syrett, who had stayed with him on several occasions, both at Dorking and at Hindhead, called him 'tall, thin, long-faced, and occasionally, at least to me, disconcerting'. She was then in her early twenties, and was embarrassed by Allen's frank talk on sexual topics: 'I think sex was something of an obsession with Grant.' None-the-less, she found him 'a gentle-mannered man, deeply moved by the suffering and injustice in the world, and as a great upholder of freedom in every aspect of life, he wanted to see it extended to the relationship between the sexes'.[8]

Allen was frequently ill, possibly with consumption – when Grant Richards used to visit him as a child, he was impressed by his uncle's invalid diet, which appeared to him to consist solely of 'oysters and Benger's Food'. Allen was a sympathetic uncle to Richards, and helped to start him on his publishing career. A kindly man, he detested war; at a 'peace campaign' meeting at Hindhead Hall in 1899, Allen and Bernard Shaw were the principal speakers. Allen was also a close friend of his neighbour Conan Doyle. When he knew he was dying, he asked Doyle to write the last two numbers of his novel *Hilda Wade*, which was then being serialised in the *Strand* magazine.

Charles Darwin and Herbert Spencer were Allen's great heroes throughout his life (it may have been some consolation to him for his lack of recognition by the scientific community, that he possessed a microscope given to him by Charles Darwin). In his opinion, Darwin and Spencer had superseded Comte and his Positivism, though he remained a friend of Frederic Harrison, the Positivist guru, who gave the address at Allen's funeral. Like Spencer, Allen has been largely forgotten by subsequent generations. Considering his talents, he has to be considered a failure. He would have liked, most of all, to have been remembered as a scientist; as that proved impossible, he had to settle for the status of a second-rate novelist, and a writer on miscellaneous topics. The most impressive thing about him was the extent and depth of his knowledge and learning. His biographer Edward Clodd described him, with justice, as 'naturalist, anthropologist, physicist, historian, poet, novelist, essayist, critic'.[9] He could have added art historian to the list. Despite his failure to make a lasting impact, Allen was a staunch upholder of the cause of learning, and an interesting personality, deserving of a more informative biography than he got.

Allen died as learnedly as he had lived. His friend Conan Doyle was at his bedside during the final illness. Despite paroxysms of severe pain, Allen, 'his long thin nose and reddish-grey goatee projecting over the sheet' gave, 'in his curious high nasal voice' a lucid account of 'the four phases of Byzantine art'.[10]

[DNB; Sutherland, 1988; Clodd, 1900; Richards, 1932; Syrett 1939.]

ALLINGHAM, William (1824–1889): poet and diarist.

Allingham was born and brought up in a middle-class Protestant family in Ballyshannon, Co. Donegal, Ireland, and obtained a job there as a Customs Officer. In his spare time, of which there was plenty, he wrote poetry. His first volume of poems was published in 1850. He made frequent visits to London, and became well known in literary circles there. In 1863 he transferred to Lymington in Hampshire, where he was the sole Customs Officer. He retired from the Civil Service in 1870, with some relief: he could never, he said, 'attain a true *official manner*, which is highly artificial and handles trifles with ludicrously disproportionate gravity'. For the next ten years he lived in London, becoming sub-editor, and then editor, of *Fraser's Magazine*, until it ceased publication in 1876. In 1874 he married Helen Paterson – soon

ALLINGHAM

to become celebrated as a water-colour artist. After his death, she edited the early beginnings of an autobiography, never completed, which dealt with his youth in Ireland, and the diary, which took over from the autobiography in 1847 and continued with only brief interruptions until a month before Allingham's death.

As a poet, Allingham has to be classed as somewhat of a lightweight; indeed he more or less admitted as much, in the modest introductory poem to his 1884 volume: 'These little Songs, /Found here and there, Floating in air ... /Have come together /How, I cannot tell.' But he was an agile versifier and was capable of sudden illuminating glimpses, though perhaps not of any more sustained vision. One of the most pleasing of these glimpses was published in 1882, and may have been written at either Haslemere or Witley:

> Four ducks on a pond,
> A grass-bank beyond,
> A blue sky of spring,
> White clouds on the wing;
> What a little thing
> To remember for years –
> To remember with tears!

Allingham himself considered his greatest work to be *Laurence Bloomfield* (published in 1864), a long poem in heroic couplets describing the efforts of a landlord to improve the sorry condition of his Irish estate. It was praised by Tennyson, quoted by Gladstone in the House of Commons, and helped Turgenev 'to understand Ireland'; but it was not a success with the reading public.

It is for his diary, rather than his poetry, that Allingham is remembered. He derived evident pleasure from mixing with the great literary figures of the day, and used the diary to record their remarks, whether profound or trivial. As with other great diary writers, it was his readiness to record apparent trivialities which gives life to the narrative, and often provides insights into the personalities of some of the great Victorians which have eluded the authors of their massive biographies. In the present context, its principal interest derives from the numerous glimpses it provides of Tennyson in his various homes.

Allingham's two great heroes were Carlyle and Tennyson, and both feature prominently in the diary. The first mention of Tennyson is an account of how, while Allingham was training to be a Customs Officer in Belfast in 1846, he used to recite *Locksley Hall* to his astonished fellow clerks. His first meeting with its author was arranged by Coventry Patmore in 1851. Tennyson was then living in a terraced house at Twickenham. Allingham was struck by his hollow cheeks and sallow skin – 'a strange and almost spectral figure' – but deeply impressed by his personality. He was very encouraging about Allingham's verses, some of which he read aloud in a 'rich solemn chant'. From then on Allingham became a staunch devotee of the Tennyson cult.

When living at Lymington between 1863 and 1870, Allingham took every opportunity to pop over to the Isle of Wight and call on Tennyson at Farringford. He was a welcome visitor; Tennyson was not one to turn away an adulatory disciple. Allingham's admiration at times bordered on servility, as, for example, in the small incident of the Farringford fig-tree. Thinking perhaps to impress the great man with his poetic imagination, he compared the 'large tangled fig-tree' to 'a breaking wave'. The unlikely simile was brusquely dismissed. 'Not in the least,' replied Tennyson. Others might have been offended by such an abrupt rejection, but Allingham recorded with humility that 'such contradictions, *from him*, are noway disagreeable.' He would probably have felt flattered, rather than annoyed, had he known that Tennyson would later make use of the same simile himself – without acknowledgement – as he led visitors past the tree.

William Allingham

In October 1869, Allingham visited Aldworth, the Tennysons' new house on Blackdown. They had only moved in that July, so he must have been one of the first visitors. He noted: 'kind reception, magnificent prospect'. We get a more extended view of life at Aldworth in 1880, when the Allinghams spent the spring and summer in Haslemere. For most of the time, they lived in a house in the High Street belonging to Cecil Lawson, the landscape artist, but in September they moved to 'a house under Courts Hill'. Tennyson called on them in both these houses; in the first, he praised the house, and liked the steps in the garden, 'done by an artist – that accounts for it'. In the second, he admired the up-hill garden, remarking that it reminded him of one at Florence. Allingham's diary records seven visits to Aldworth between August and October.[11] Usually they walked up, sometimes returning at night by lantern-light 'on the heath and down the shady lane to Haslemere'. Most of the numerous conversations were about literary matters and other weighty topics, but the last visit by the Allinghams during their time at Haslemere ended on a more rumbustious note, with Tennyson and his son Hallam singing *John Brown's Body*, Tennyson thumping time with his fist on a table, and exclaiming 'I like it, I like it.'

In June 1881, the Allinghams bought a house at Sandhills, near Witley, on a sandstone ridge similar to the hills round Haslemere, though not quite so high. From there they had a good view of both Blackdown and Hindhead, and of the South Downs. They stayed there until 1889, when they moved to London, where William died. The Witley house was then bought by Graham Robertson, artist and author, who spent the next forty years there, during which the house remained as it had been in Allingham's day – without electricity, telephone, bathroom or even a name.[12] From Witley, William and Helen made frequent excursions by train to Haslemere, mostly going on to the Tennysons at Aldworth, but sometimes visiting other friends, such as Lady Agatha Russell at Hindhead and Mrs Mangles at Valewood. Allingham's last sight of Tennyson was on 3rd November 1888. He had come by train to Haslemere, and walked up to Aldworth. Tennyson was in his study, suffering from gout, with his feet resting on a chair. 'He wore a black skull-cap, his long Don Quixote nose was sharply outlined, his moustache looked dark and full. One might have guessed him seventy rather than eighty.'

One year later, William Allingham died at Hampstead. His last words, 'I see such things as you cannot dream of', were a source of great comfort to Tennyson, who often repeated them for his own consolation.[13]

[DNB; Allingham, 1985, with Introduction by John Julius Norwich.]

BARING-GOULD, Revd Sabine (1834–1924): clergyman; author of books on religion, mythology, Devonshire life, and many novels.

Baring-Gould was the rector, and a large landowner, at Lew Trenchard, Devon, where he wrote most of his many books. He is best remembered as the author of the hymn *Onward Christian Soldiers*. In the early 1890s he stayed for a time with Revd F.H. Gooch at Thursley vicarage, in the midst of wild heathlands, inhabited only by a scattering of 'broom-squires' (makers of birch and heather besoms), who lived in primitive huts. Baring-Gould had been one of the first authors to support Algernon Stedman – later Methuen – in his new publishing venture, and now Stedman, who was familiar with the ways of the hilltop country, suggested to him that the broom-squires of the Hindhead heathlands might provide the subject for a novel.[14] Baring-Gould decided to combine a tale about these figures with the well-known local story of the sailor who was murdered at the Hindhead Punch Bowl. The result was *The Broom Squire* (1896), a melodramatic and not altogether convincing story, which nevertheless gives a striking and quite plausible picture of the wild and lawless heathlands round Thursley and Hindhead, and their inhabitants, as they might have appeared in the earlier years of the nineteenth century.

[ONB; Drabble; Sutherland.]

BEVERIDGE, Annette Susannah, née Akroyd (1842–1929): oriental scholar.

Annette Akroyd was one of the first students at Bedford College, London. In 1867 she passed the equivalent of the London University BA in Latin, but women were not then permitted to take the degree. When she was twenty-eight, and living in London, she came under the spell of an Indian guru, and decided to go to India to improve the lot of Indian women. There she met Henry Beveridge, a District Judge who took an unusual interest in Indian culture and welfare, and they married in 1875. Henry was due to retire in 1892, and Annette returned to England in 1890 in order to look for a house. Her quest brought her to Grayshott, the hilltop village just over the border in Hampshire, where her sister, Mrs Fanny Louise Mowatt, had been living since 1887. Mrs Mowatt, like her sister, was a scholarly lady, and had translated an Anglo-Norman account of a perambulation of Woolmer and Alice Holt Forests. In 1893 Henry Beveridge finally retired, and while he and his wife were searching for a house, they suddenly received a telegram from Mrs Mowatt, saying that a house nearby was on the market. Two days later, the Beveridges signed a contract for the purchase of Pitfold House on Woolmer Hill, just below Hindhead.

Pitfold House had begun in 1792 as little more than a cottage, but a front and a turret had been added to the design of a local hairdresser. Three years after the arrival of the Beveridges, Annette and her sister quarrelled about an Oxford scholarship for which their respective sons were competing – William Beveridge won – and they never spoke to each other again. In the summer of 1898, the Beveridges decided to go elsewhere for a change, and let the house to Bernard Shaw and his bride for their honeymoon. In the following year Henry Beveridge went on a long nostalgic visit to India. Annette stayed at home and supervised a radical re-building of the house – in effect, the addition of a new wing which was itself much larger than the original building, making it a substantial mansion of eighteen principal rooms. She and her husband remained in Pitfold House until they both died in 1929. The Beveridges created a fine garden in the ten-acre grounds, with an entrance flanked by two statues of Buddha which they had brought back from India.

During her time at Pitfold, Annette looked for some way to occupy her quite considerable intellect. (Bernard Shaw once presented her with a copy of *The Perfect Wagnerite*, inscribed to 'perhaps the cleverest lady and the wickedest in her opinions that I have ever met' – possibly because she had formed a local branch of the National Women's League Against Women's Suffrage.) Well into her fifties, although handicapped by lifelong deafness which by then had become total, and later by cataracts, she settled down to a serious study of Persian and Turki, translating and editing the two volumes

BLOUNT

which made her reputation as an oriental scholar.

Annette translated the *Humayun-Nama* from the Persian, and edited it as *The History of Humayun* (1902). Humayun was the son of Bábur, the Mogul conqueror of India. She then went on to her most important and laborious task, the translation from Turki of *The Bábar-Náma*. This huge work is an autobiography written by Bábur himself; its translation and editing took twenty years. It was published in parts from 1912 to 1921, and was highly regarded by oriental scholars. Annette also translated *The Key to the Hearts of Beginners*, a collection of stories in Persian for children. In 1904, she contributed a story, 'What the Rose did to the Cypress' to Andrew Lang's *Brown Fairy Book* (1904).

Annette was the mother of William Henry, later Lord Beveridge (1879–1963), author of the Reports on *Social Insurance and Allied Services* in 1942, and on *Full Employment in a Free Society* in 1944, which are generally regarded as having laid the foundation of the Welfare State.

William was educated at Charterhouse and Oxford. Soon afterwards, he rejected a legal career in favour of social work at Toynbee Hall, where he came under the influence of Sidney and Beatrice Webb. Although he had a small flat in London, Pitfold House remained his main base, and it was there that he wrote his first book, *Unemployment: A Problem of Industry* (1909). William Beveridge also found congenial occupation in Haslemere. Here he became a member of a committee, formed in 1909 under the chairmanship of Sir Algernon Methuen, to deal with the local problem of unemployment, both by finding work for those already unemployed, and by initiating an insurance scheme for those in work. This must have been a useful preparation for young Beveridge for his later work in the national arena.

[Beveridge, 1947; Harris, 1977; *The Times*, obituary notice, 6 April 1929.]

BLOUNT, Godfrey (1859–1937), and Ethel, née Hine (d.1943): exponents of Peasant Arts.

Godfrey and Ethel Blount worked as a united team in the pursuit of Arts and Crafts, and the Simple Life, and collaborated with Joseph and Maude King in these endeavours. Ethel, like Maude King, was a daughter of Henry Hine, the landscape artist. Godfrey, who was born not far away at Bagshot, married Ethel in 1887.

The Blounts came to Haslemere in 1896, and lived at Foundry Cottage, King's Road, until 1902. They moved then to St Cross, Weydown Road, where they built a house. Therese La Chard, who was the schoolmistress at the elementary school at Anstead Brook in 1904, and later wrote a lively account of her experiences, saw the Blount ménage at close quarters, for she rented a small bungalow, previously used as a studio, in the grounds of their house in Weydown Road. Because of this association, Therese became accepted as 'one of the cranks', and was able to observe their way of life at first hand. Her neighbours were two women 'with an unswerving faith in handweaving' who 'almost squeezed themselves out of their homes by the number of handlooms they had installed'. She herself was often invited to the Blounts' 'new barnlike house with its open roof'. As one entered, an inscription on one of the beams commanded cryptically: 'Be in league with the toad and the stone.' Meals consisted of 'salads and haricot beans eaten with horn spoons'.

Together with Joseph and Maude King, Godfrey and Ethel Blount started the Peasant Arts movement. It flourished in Haslemere in the early twentieth century, but withered in the 1920s and 1930s, leaving as its only memento a gallery in Haslemere Museum. Godfrey Blount became a leading figure in the Arts and Crafts movement: Chairman of the English Handicraft Society, Honorary Treasurer of the Peasant Arts Museum, Master of the Guild of Country Players, Warden and Founder of the Country Church of the New Crusade. He was also a founder of the Supernatural Society.

Godfrey Blount

The Weaving House in King's Road, Haslemere, had opened for business in 1899, and a band of enthusiasts, led by the Blounts and Maude King, was soon busy there spinning, weaving and embroidering; appliqué work was a particular feature. Godfrey was responsible for most of the designs of the embroideries, which included portières, hangings, bedspreads and banners. The Haslemere Peasant Arts movement was praised for the quality of its work, and was said to 'compare with anything of the kind in the country ... it also produced pottery, hand-made furniture, baskets, repoussé copper-work and leather-work'.[15]

Both the Blounts wrote books. Godfrey's were: *The Song of the Sower* (1898); *Arbor Vitae* (1899); *The Blood of the Poor* (1911); Ethel wrote *The Story of the Homespun Web – a Simple Guide to Spinning and Weaving*, and also helped to start the Vineyard Press.

[La Chard, 1967; Callen, 1979.]

BROWN, George Douglas (1869–1902): novelist.

The illegitimate son of a Scottish farmer, Brown was educated successively at the local school, Glasgow University and Balliol College, Oxford. He moved to London, existing precariously as a publisher's reader, and by writing short stories and a boys' adventure novel. Then, in the autumn of 1900, he rented Briar Cottage at Hindhead, and moved in with his dog Cloigh and a plentiful supply of large, black-covered exercise books. There he settled down to write – under the pseudonym George Douglas – his novel, *The House with the Green Shutters* (1901). It is a grimly realistic story, intended to counteract the prevailing Scottish 'kailyard' school of sentimental novels. It concerns a small Scottish town, dominated by a saturnine and tyrannical character, John Gourlay. He is the town carrier, and when the railway comes, his business is ruined. His anger at his loss is taken out on his unfortunate family. He strikes his wife and torments his feeble son, until the latter can stand it no longer and dispatches his father with a blow on the head from an outsize poker. Overcome by remorse, the son then poisons himself. Not long afterwards his mother goes mad, and kills herself and her daughter.

Despite the depressing finale, Brown's novel was widely acclaimed; J.B. Priestley called it a masterpiece, and Sutherland regards it as the best realistic novel about life in a small Scottish town, and worthy of comparison with Hardy's tales of country life. After this success, Brown started work on a metaphysical study of *Hamlet*. It was never completed, for he developed what was probably 'galloping consumption', and died while on a visit to Muswell Hill, in August 1902.

[DNB; Drabble; Sutherland; Veitch, 1952.

BUCKTON, George Bowdler, FRS (1818–1905): eclectic scientist.

Buckton was crippled for life by an accident at the age of five. Nevertheless, he managed to pursue careers in no fewer than three branches of science. The first of these began in 1848 when he became a student, and then research assistant, to A.W. Hoffman at the Royal College of Chemistry. His major work, on the isolation and identification of methyl mercuric compounds, was published in a series of important papers.

Buckton abandoned chemistry in 1865, married Mary Ann Odling and moved to Haslemere. There he bought 'the estate of Weycombe, on the slopes of Hindhead', and built a house of his own design (Weycombe House), with an adjoining astronomical observatory. His astronomical career ended in 1882, when he fell while trying to close the roof shutter in the observatory, and broke his leg.

Meanwhile he had embarked on what was probably the most important of his scientific careers, this time in entomology. This resulted in monographs on *British Aphides* (4 vols. 1876–83), and on *British Cicadae or Tettigiidae* (2 vols. 1890–1); and *The Natural History of Eristalis tenax, or the Drone Fly* (1895).

George Bowdler Buckton

Buckton also took an interest in electricity, leading him to construct a Wimshurst machine.[16] He was also the first Chairman of the Haslemere Gas Company. William Allingham encountered him at Aldworth in November 1885, doing his best to answer Tennyson, who wanted to know: 'How can Evolution account for the ant?' Buckton replied cautiously that 'the theory presents many difficulties.'[17]

The Bucktons' daughter, Alys Mary (c.1867–1944), also merits notice, as poet, playwright and educationalist.

As a small child, Alys was a favourite of Tennyson, and once spent a whole day with him, holding a candle for him to read by, walking with him through the fields, and sitting on his knee while he chanted his poems – I have never heard such a wonderful voice.' He told her of his belief in the immortality of the soul, and his puzzlement about matter: 'Spirit is everywhere; it is Matter that bothers me.' She related this anecdote, together with other reminiscences of Tennyson, when the Gaekwar of Baroda – the then-owner – invited the Poetry Society to a large gathering at Aldworth in 1925.[18]

Alys's first book of poems, *Through Human Eyes* (1901), though only a small, privately-printed volume of 130 copies, had the distinction of including an introductory poem by Robert Bridges. Others were: *The Burden of Engela*; *A Ballad Epic* (1904); *Masques and Dances* (1907); *Songs of Joy* (1908). Her first dramatic work, *Eager Heart, A Christmas Mystery Play* (1904), was her greatest success. It was produced in Haslemere in 1905, and later in London and elsewhere, while the book ran into eighteen impressions. She also wrote: *Kings in Babylon; A Drama* (1906); *The Coming of Bride; A Pageant Play* (1914).

As well as her poetry and her plays, Alys took a great interest in educational matters; at the South-Eastern Congress at Haslemere in 1901 she read a paper on the place of nature study in the education of children, mentioned in

BURROUGHS

the *Surrey Advertiser*, June 1901.

[DNB; the copy of Buckton's monograph on the Drone Fly in Haslemere Museum contains two anonymous obituary notices; for Alys, see Sillick archives, p. 4 and 18.]

BURROUGHS, John (1837–1921): American author and naturalist.

Burroughs led a Thoreau-like existence on a farm in the Catskill Mountains of New York State, where he observed and wrote about natural history in a number of highly regarded books. He was a friend – and subsequently biographer – of Walt Whitman, and through him met, and admired, Anne Gilchrist during her stay in Philadelphia of 1876–79. In her turn, Anne was enthusiastic about Burroughs' book, *Birds and Poets*. He is described as 'an erect, substantial figure, with a long rustic beard and a pervasive air of repose'.

Burroughs spent the summer of 1882 in Scotland and England, and wrote *Fresh Fields* (1885) about his experiences. After landing in Glasgow and exploring Scotland, he came to London, and paid two visits to Anne Gilchrist, who was then living in Hampstead with her daughter Grace. One of his main objects in coming to England was to hear the nightingale. It must have been Anne who suggested that the Surrey hills would be a suitable hunting-ground for this purpose, and gave him the name of a farm at Shottermill where he could stay. He duly spent some days there, and described his adventures in a chapter of his book, of thirty-eight pages, entitled 'A Hunt for the Nightingale'. The farm is not named. Despite the shortness of his stay, the vivid style of Burroughs's detailed account of his adventures in the search for the nightingale seemed to justify his inclusion as a Hilltop Writer. His rendering of the local dialect is particularly impressive, considering that this must have been his first encounter with it.

Burroughs came to Shottermill on 17th June, and almost immediately realised, to his great dismay, that it was a little too late in the season for the bird to be in full song. However, as the result of considerable exertions he was in the end able to catch at least a few snatches. He set out on the afternoon of his arrival to explore the countryside, which he found 'quite wild and irregular, full of bushy fields and overgrown hedgerows, and looked to me very nightingaly'. He sought news of the bird from everyone he met, but was usually told 'She be about done singing now, sir'; or else that the speaker had heard one a few days, or hours, before. He spent some hours that evening squatting in a damp copse, clad in a 'rubber waterproof', which he had prudently reinforced with layers of newspaper against the unaccustomed chill of an English June. However, he heard no nightingales. He was up again at four o'clock the next morning and wandered about for two miles, but once more he was disappointed.

After breakfast he was again roaming around, and this time encountered a man with a stove-pipe hat who turned out to be a barber – and tailor and painter – from Haslemere. He claimed that he could call up nightingales at will by imitating their song. Burroughs arranged to meet him that evening at eight o'clock. Meanwhile he met a boy who said he had heard a nightingale only fifteen minutes ago, 'on Polecat Hill, sir'. Burroughs hurried there, but heard nothing. Next he called on 'the village squire' – James Simmons of Cherrimans, Shottermill – who gave him the name of a taxidermist in Godalming, who might be able to help.[19] Meanwhile, Burroughs kept his appointment with the stove-pipe-hatted Haslemere barber, and they set off on a long cross-country tramp, which took them to a 'wild and picturesque spot' where his guide, placing a blade of grass between his teeth, repeatedly blew his shrill call.' Twice he called out, 'There! I believe I 'erd 'er', but he was mistaken.

Next day, Burroughs set out by train to Godalming. There he met the taxidermist, who arranged for the lad who worked for him to take Burroughs on a long walk to Eashing and Shackleford. Unfortunately, the boy turned out to be 'full of duplicity', and tried to persuade Burroughs that a passing swallow was a nightingale. When they got to Shackleford, he dismissed the boy with a shilling, and after several encounters with locals, found a labourer whom he felt he could trust. The latter agreed to meet Burroughs later that afternoon, and lead him to a spot where he had heard the nightingale the previous evening. By this time, Burroughs was getting hungry, and called at the local pub. There, as on several other occasions, he discovered that 'these back-country English inns' were no more than beer-shops, and he was lucky to get some 'rye-bread and cheese ... and a glass of home-brewed beer'. His guide then took him to a small wood where he had previously heard the bird, and Burroughs settled down to wait for nightfall among some 'tall ferns under a pine-tree'. There at last he heard the call he was hoping for; but it ceased after only a few notes. A man and a boy passing by confirmed that it was indeed a nightingale, and the guide cried: 'Now she's on, sir; now she's on. Ah! but she don't stick.' Burroughs waited a long time, but she never did stick.

Then he had to think about a bed for the night. He tried in vain at three inns, and eventually got a lift in a trap to Godalming, where he arrived at one o'clock, and was lucky to be admitted. He was up again at five the next morning, walked back to Shackleford, and once more heard only a few bars of song. After trying unsuccessfully to get breakfast at an inn at Eashing, he returned to Godalming and then Shottermill. The same afternoon he walked with his belongings to Liphook. The path took him through 'Leechmeer [Linchmere] bottom', where he admired the furze and heather sweeping up over the hills 'like sable mantles'. On his way he tested the reliability of some local youths by asking them which, out of a jumble of bird-song, was the nightingale's; they usually picked out the robin's. He spent the night at an inn at Liphook, and was off again at five next morning. He walked to Selborne, where he spent two rainy days, then on to Alton and back to London by train.

Despite having had so little reward for his great efforts, Burroughs was not entirely dissatisfied with his visit: 'Although I heard the bird less than five minutes, and only a few bars of its song, but enough to satisfy me of the surprising quality of the strain. It had the master tone as clearly as Tennyson or any great prima donna or famous orator has it.'

Burroughs never returned to Haslemere, and there are no indications of any further meetings with Anne Gilchrist during his stay in England. But he had certainly not forgotten her, for when the news of her death reached him on 18th December 1885, he noted in his journal: 'Just now I can see or think of no one in England but her. She is the principal fact over there, and she is gone. The only woman I ever met to whose mind and character I instinctively bowed. She was a rare person, a person of rare intelligence.'

[Dictionary of American Biography; Alcaro, 1991; Barrus, 1925.]

CARRINGTON, Richard Christopher (1826–1875), FRS: astronomer.

Richard Carrington is noteworthy, not merely for his observations of the stars and the sun, which were highly thought of by his fellow astronomers, but even more for his eccentricity, for the remarkable observatory he built on one of The Devil's Jumps at Churt, and for the tragic events which ensued.

Carrington started his career as an astronomer at the University of Durham, but becoming discontented with the poor facilities there, he came south and set up his own observatory at Redhill. He was able to do this because his father was the owner of a large brewery at Brentford, which Carrington inherited in 1858. At Redhill, he did most of his best work – on circumpolar stars and sunspots – and it was there that he wrote his two major works: *A Catalogue of 3735 Circumpolar Stars* (1857), and *Observations on the Spots on the Sun* (1863). These books, and his numerous articles, earned him a considerable reputation in astronomical circles. He was Secretary to the Royal Astronomical Society 1857–62, and became a Fellow of the Royal Society in 1860. This phase ended with a severe illness in 1865, which lingered on for several years. When he had recovered, Carrington sold the brewery, and bought nineteen acres of land at Churt (just north of Hindhead), probably in early 1869. This included the middle of the three small conical hills known as The Devil's Jumps – probably part of the same property that Tennyson considered buying in 1866. On this hill Carrington built an observatory, and at its base Jumps House.

The small conical hill, sixty feet high, suited Carrington's purpose admirably as a site for his unique subterranean observatory. He described it in *Monthly Notices of the Royal Astronomical Society* for 10th December 1869: 'Being on a hill I did not want elevation, so I have sunk the Observatory below ground, just peeping out over the soil. But I have further sunk a dry well, six feet in diameter, to the depth of forty feet from the centre of the observatory, and with a horizontal shaft communicating with the south side of the hill, 166 feet in length, closed with three doorways. This is principally intended for the clock, for I am determined that one clock at least shall be properly mounted, at a position of invariable temperature and in an air-tight case. I propose to reduce the pressure to twenty-seven inches of mercury ... I hope I shall shortly have the most perfect clock in England, perhaps in the world.' He went on to describe his azimuth, 'constructed on a new principle'. When Thomas Wright visited the site in 1897, a contemporary witness told him that the observatory had been protected by a semi-spherical cover made of match-boarding covered with felt, which 'revolved on globes which looked like cannonballs'. Both house and observatory are depicted in an engraving in the *Illustrated London News* for 16th September 1871:—

Jumps House and Carrington's observatory in 1871

Before his illness, Carrington had been a prolific author of astronomical papers. Once his new observatory was completed, he gradually resumed his publications in *Monthly Notices of the Royal Astronomical Society*. The first of these was the 1869 account, already quoted, of his new observatory. This was followed in 1870–71 by a note on a 'Solar Fog-bow', and in 1872–73 by further descriptions of his new clock and azimuth. By 1873–4, he was back in business, with papers on 'Star 515', and on the 'Coaltitude of Ursae Majors'.

On 16th August 1869, shortly after his move to Churt, Carrington married

Rosa Jeffries. According to the account by A.H.M. Brice, he had noticed her while walking down Regent Street. Struck by her beauty, he made himself acquainted, and very soon persuaded her to marry him. We do not know a lot about Rose – as she was generally known – but the marriage certificate shows that she was the daughter of a butcher, and quite illiterate (she signed her name with a cross). She was about twenty years younger than Carrington.

It seems that the Devil does not take kindly to people who drill holes in his Jumps, for before long Carrington's patient observations of the heavens were interrupted by a series of domestic tragedies. It appears – from Brice's account – that, at the time of her marriage, Rose was going under the name of 'Rose Rodway' and was probably the common-law wife of William Rodway, a trooper in the Dragoon Guards. Not long after the Carringtons had settled in at Churt, Rodway himself appeared, and found lodgings nearby. He then proceeded to threaten Rose into yielding money, and then sex. Matters came to a head on 18th August 1871, when Rodway appeared on the doorstep of Jumps House. This time he wanted her shawl and her cloak, which she handed over. However, when he demanded that she should also give him her husband's pet dog, Rose refused, whereupon Rodway drew a knife, stabbed her in the arm and back, and ran off. She managed to get to a nearby inn and raise the alarm. Rodway was pursued and caught, and later sentenced to twenty-one years' penal servitude for attempted murder. He died in prison in early 1874.

The wound in Rose's back took some time to mend, and it seems that from then on her health gradually worsened. She developed epileptic fits, and her mental state deteriorated to such an extent that she was about to be removed to an asylum when on the morning of 17th November 1875, she was found dead in her bed. At the inquest, her husband said he had last seen her alive at six o'clock on the previous evening. He had given her her usual dose of ten grains (65 mg) of chloral hydrate, which she took in 'Hungarian wine'. He had slept in the same bed, and had noticed nothing unusual. When he got up at twenty minutes to eight the next morning, he had not looked at her particularly, and assumed she was asleep. But at a little before nine o'clock the same morning a Mrs Marchant entered the room and found Rose lying on her face, dead.

At the inquest (reported in the *Surrey Advertiser* for 29th November 1875), Dr R. Oke Clark, who had been attending Rose, said that 'she had been of unsound mind, and a recurrence of the insanity took place through epileptic fits, of which she had four or five. He had certified her for removal to an asylum, and it was intended that she should be sent away on the morning on which she was found dead.' He did not speculate on the nature of the insanity and fits; both could have been caused by tertiary syphilis, which was then by no means uncommon. Dr Clark carried out a post-mortem, and found evidence in the state of the lungs and heart to suggest that she had died from suffocation. Accordingly, the jury brought in a verdict of death from suffocation, 'but how such suffocation came about there was not sufficient evidence to show'.

This was essentially an open verdict, but it is unlikely that a modern jury, with all the facilities of forensic science at its disposal, would have come to any different conclusion. It could be that Rose, in a deep sleep induced by chloral, had managed to bury her face in the pillow so firmly that she had been unable to breathe. Or she might have had an epileptic fit, with the same result. But other possibilities have also to be considered. She might, without her husband's knowledge, have taken an overdose of chloral, but there were no signs of this at the post-mortem. Finally, there is the possibility that Carrington had murdered her. The *Surrey Advertiser*, in its initial report (20th November 1875), noted that 'We learn on the best authority that the conjugal life of the parties was anything but a happy one.' Carrington was obsessively devoted to his astronomical studies, and would have been intolerant of anything that interfered with them, as his wife's mental disturbance and fits must surely have done. He could have persuaded himself that in her condition it would be a kindness to put her out of her misery, by pressing her face firmly into the pillow while she was in a deep sleep induced by chloral.[20] Yet it seems odd that he should have wanted to dispose of her in this way, just when she was about to be removed to an asylum.

All this is the merest speculation, but the murder hypothesis does get some credence from the fact that it was held with conviction, and indeed passion, by Carrington's own solicitor. Many years after the event he told J. Alfred Eggar, 'there was no doubt but that the astronomer had murdered his wife. He added, with tears in his eyes, that it was the saddest case he had ever experienced; a man who was wonderfully clever and of exceptional ability, but an infidel. He was a God-forsaken man; he repeated this expression two or three times.'[21]

After the inquest on his wife, Carrington disappeared temporarily. He returned on Saturday the fourth of December, and was seen to enter his house – by then empty, as the servants had fled – by the driver of the fly which had brought him from Farnham station. This was the last time Carrington was seen alive. By the following Tuesday, the neighbours had become suspicious. The police were sent for, and forced an entry. Carrington's dead body was discovered in the servants' bedroom, lying on a mattress on the floor. He was dressed in a shirt, underclothes and socks, and a handkerchief tied round his head was keeping in place a poultice of tea-leaves over the left ear. A post-mortem was performed by Dr Oke Clark, who concluded, after what appears to have been a fairly thorough examination, that the deceased had died from 'sanguineous apoplexy' – cerebral haemorrhage – and that he had fallen down in a fit. At the inquest, the jury returned a verdict of 'sudden death from natural causes'.[22] There seems no reason to challenge this verdict – the cerebral haemorrhage could have been caused by degenerative arterial disease, or late syphilis. But mysteries remain: the tea-leaf poultice; and why

COSTELLOE

should Carrington have locked himself in the servants' bedroom, and lain on a mattress on the floor, in his underclothes?

Carrington's will, dated 9th January 1873, stipulated that he should 'be buried at a depth of between ten and twelve feet in the grounds surrounding my own Freehold house at Churt aforesaid at an expence not exceeding Five pounds and without any service being read over my grave or any memorial being erected to my memory and that after my death neither my chin be shaved nor my shirt changed'. He was indeed an eccentric, and also, as his solicitor said, an 'infidel'.

The remains of Carrington's tunnels were noted by Thomas Wright on his 1897 visit to Hindhead, and by Mr R. D. Clarke, of Lower Bourne, Farnham, in 1949. The vertical tunnel has been filled in, but a depression on the top of the Middle Jump still marks its upper opening. The horizontal tunnel is remarkably intact today, though the entrance door is missing. The tunnel, about seven feet high and wide, had been carved out of the solid sandstone, and there are no signs of rock-falls. It is easy to picture Carrington making his way along it with his lighted candle, to attend to the regular maintenance of his special clock.

One further mystery remains. The dramatic events related above were fully reported in the local and national press, and must have been endlessly discussed in pubs and meetings. Yet the story was not picked up or noted by any of the many imaginative writers living in the hills around, only ten to twenty years afterwards. Thomas Wright's *Ianthe of the Devil's Jumps* does feature an astronomer who had an observatory with tunnels like Carrington's on the Middle Jump, but his subsequent career, though melodramatic, was quite different. Nearest to The Devil's Jumps was the classicist Gilbert Murray, who might have been expected to see the element of Greek tragedy in the Carrington saga. And Sherlock Holmes, whose creator was living at nearby Hindhead, surely encountered no stranger case than that which Dr Watson might have recorded as 'The Case of the Eccentric Astronomer' ...

[DNB, and obituary in *Monthly Notices of the Royal Astronomical Society*, 1875–6, vol. 36, p. 137 for accounts of Carrington's astronomical career; for the dramatic events described above, see Melene Barnes: *Journ. Brit. Astro. Ass.* 1973.83.2. pp. 122–4; Eggar, 1924; R.D. Clarke, *Farnham and Haslemere Herald*, November 1949, in which he quotes as an authority an article by A.H.M. Brice, Recorder of Tewkesbury, 'in a Sunday newspaper in 1925' (Mrs Melene Barnes has a typescript copy of what seems to be this article, which she kindly allowed me to see).]

COSTELLOE, Benjamin Francis Conn ('Frank') (1855–1899): writer on social and religious matters; first husband of Mary Pearsall Smith; and STRACHEY, Rachel Conn ('Ray'), née Costelloe: author and suffragist.

Frank Costelloe was born in the little village of Passage East, Co. Waterford, on the estuary of that name in the south of Ireland; his family were Roman Catholics. He graduated at Oxford in 1878 and was called to the Bar at Lincoln's Inn in 1881. In 1884, he crossed the Atlantic to attend the meeting of the British Association in Montreal, and after that the meeting of the American Association for the Advancement of Science in Philadelphia. There he met Mary, daughter of Robert and Hannah Pearsall Smith, then a student at Harvard, and the two fell in love. Back in England, Frank proposed by cable, and was accepted. There was then the problem of securing the approval of Mary's formidable Quaker mother. Hannah Pearsall Smith distrusted men – 'they are *masters*, and wish their wives to be slaves' – and a Catholic man was even worse: 'the horror of his religion grows on me more and more'. In the end, however, she grudgingly accepted the situation, and Frank and Mary were married in Oxford in 1885. The reception was held in Frank's old college, Balliol, and the bride's health was proposed by the great Benjamin Jowett himself.[23]

In 1889 the Pearsall Smith family settled in England, and rented Friday's Hill House at Fernhurst in Sussex, just across the county boundary from Haslemere. Frank and Mary lived in one of the two cottages on the estate. But after Mary had borne two daughters, she became disillusioned with Frank, and resented his Catholicism. Then in 1890 a young American called Bernard Berenson came to Friday' s Hill for the weekend. He was already becoming knowledgeable about Italian art, and after experiencing his charm and his learning, Mary 'felt like a dry sponge that was put in water'. In 1891, she decided to leave Frank for Bernard, and joined him in Florence. By now, Bernard had been converted to Catholicism, so what with a Catholic husband and a Catholic lover, there could be no question of a divorce. Relations continued along the same lines until Frank conveniently died in 1899, and Mary and Bernard were then able to marry. [24]

Bernard and Mary settled in *I Tatti*, their villa outside Florence, which soon became a celebrated rendezvous for art lovers. Most people sympathised with Frank, and disapproved of Mary's behaviour. When Sidney Webb stayed with him in his cottage at Friday's Hill later in 1891, he told Beatrice that 'the *wickedness* of his wife has come home to me stronger than ever'.[25]

At this visit, Sidney Webb noted that Frank 'has gone back to work on a translation of Zeller's *Aristotle* which he has had on the stocks for ten years'. Frank undertook the formidable task of translating this work by the German philosopher Edouard Zeller jointly with James Fullerton Muirhead. It was finally published in two volumes in 1897, entitled *Aristotle and the Earlier Peripatetics, being a translation from Zener's 'Philosophy of the Greeks'*. Another of his works was a pamphlet published in 1893, containing the text of a lecture he had given to the Fabian Society, entitled *The Incidence of Taxation*. This was a thorough consideration, still relevant today, of the various possible ways of raising revenue for local authorities. He was able to draw on his experience as Chairman of the Local Government Committee of the LCC. In this capacity he had had to try to reconcile the varied taxation methods employed by the 200 different rating authorities in the London area.

Frank's Catholicism meant much to him. His religious works included *Ethics or Anarchy* (1895); *Frédérick Ozanam*, about the French literary critic who was an ardent Catholic, and worked hard to combat the atheism prevalent in early nineteenth-century France; and *The Gospel Story* (1900), a simplified version of the Gospel story, written for his daughters.

The most pressing problem caused by Mary's flight to Italy concerned the care of the two daughters she had had by Frank: Ray, born in 1887, and Karin in 1889. Frank insisted on taking charge of them until early in 1899 when he developed signs of cancer, from which he died in December of that year, aged only forty-four. Their grandmother, Hannah – whose husband, Robert Pearsall Smith, had died in 1898 – then took over, and they were brought up in her care.

Ray had a distinguished career as an author and a feminist. Her first novel, *The World at Eighteen* (1907), was probably written while she was still living at Friday's Hill with her grandmother. It was about a girl who finds herself engaged to an insufferable young man, from whom she only manages to escape on the last page, after frantic efforts. The story – based on Ray's own encounter with a presumptuous male egoist – is capably told, and her discriminating uncle, the essayist Logan Pearsall Smith, thought the book 'had decided merit'.

Ray married Oliver Strachey, the youngest member of the huge, effervescent Strachey sibship, in 1911. She lived mostly in London, where she became deeply committed to the suffragist cause. In 1919 she became secretary and adviser to Lady Astor, who had just taken her seat as the first woman MP. But Ray's heart was still at Friday's Hill, and in 1921 she bought nine acres of land nearby and built a house of *pisé* (rammed earth), which became known, appropriately, as The Mud House (it still is). Here she led a happy life, gardening, brick-laying, and entertaining her numerous friends and relations at alfresco parties round the swimming-pool. Ray had always been totally indifferent to her appearance, and at The Mud House her standard attire was described by her sister Karin as 'an amazing suit of corduroy breeches and jacket which made her look like 100 elephants. Her disregard of her appearance,' Karin continued, 'is simply stupendous, she must be very sure of her inner worth, happy soul.'

Virginia Woolf, whose brother Adrian Stephen was married to Karin, knew the family well, and when, on 24th July 1940, she heard the news of Ray's death, she remembered her in her diary as 'that very large woman, with the shock of grey hair and bruised lips ... she had a kind of representative quality, in her white coat and trousers; wall-building, disappointed, courageous, without what? Imagination? ... she cared so little for appearances; yet she was envious, I guess, of the graces ... she planned a great unconventional rough-hewn figure, and it didn't altogether come off'.[26]

The book for which Ray is best remembered is her life of *Millicent Garrett Fawcett* (1931), the suffragist leader. Ray had worked and suffered with Mrs Fawcett, and painted her character with insight and imagination. A complimentary review in the *TLS* described her writing as having 'a grave and limpid beauty'. She wrote two other suffragist books: *The Cause* (1928) – the first history of the suffrage movement – and *Careers and Openings for Women* (1937), plus two more novels: *Marching On* (1923), and *Shaken by the Wind* (1927). Perhaps her most important work was her edition of her grandmother's papers, published as *Religious Fanatics* (1928), reprinted as *Group Movements of the Past* (1934).

Karin married Adrian Stephen in 1914, and after the war they both became psycho-analysts. Karin wrote *The Misuse of Mind, A Study of Bergson's Attack on Intellectualism* (1922) and *Psycho-analysis and Medicine, A Study of the Wish to Fall Ill* (1933).

[Strachey, 1980; DNB, *Missing Persons*, 1993, pp. 639–40, for Ray Strachey.]

DAKYNS, Henry Graham (1839–1911): classical scholar; schoolmaster.

Dakyns was twenty-two when he came to Farringford as a tutor to Hallam and Lionel Tennyson; he stayed there for a year. They all liked him for his 'childlike simplicity and elfish humour', and he became a life-long friend of Hallam. He accompanied Tennyson on his nostalgic visit to Cauteretz in Spain in 1861, and acted as his 'walking-stick' as the poet revisited the valley where he had last been with Arthur Hallam. As they approached the sacred place, Dakyns had the tact to drop behind, leaving Tennyson alone as he composed his immortal lyric *All along the valley*. Dakyns's tact was rewarded when he was told of Tennyson's comment: 'Dakyns isn't a fool.' He later told his friend Miss Stawell – in 'a gruffly tender voice' – that if he hadn't already a family motto of which he was proud, he would have taken this remark as his legend.[27]

Emily Tennyson noted a visit by Dakyns to Aldworth in August 1870 – 'Mr Dakyns arrives, always welcome' – and no doubt there were others (Emily's Journal stops soon after that date). In 1892, he came to live at Highercombe on Grayswood Hill, and he was there when his step-daughter was married in April 1894 and in 1898 when he attended Conan Doyle's Christmas Ball, dressed as a Moor.[28] He visited Aldworth shortly before Tennyson's death, accompanied on that occasion by John Addington Symonds, the poet, and his gondolier; the gondolier hid in the bushes. He appears in *Kelly's Directory* at Higher Combe in 1903 but not in 1905, although a notice of the death of his wife in the *Surrey Times* for 4th January 1908 indicates that he was still there then.

Dakyns remained close to Hallam Tennyson, and contributed a chapter to his *Tennyson and his Friends* entitled 'Tennyson, Clough and the Classics'.[29] This pedantic, schoolmasterish essay is peppered with classical quotations and is remarkable for the curious practice of referring to Alfred and Emily Tennyson as 'Him' and 'Her', and to himself by an upper-case Greek delta. There is a good deal about Tennyson's views on Greek and Latin verse, but not a lot about his personality. Dakyns had written: 'The notion of collecting tiny pinhead facts, or words actually spoken but separated from their context: the idea of collecting these and calling the result biography I loathed.' Later, he regretted his restraint, as he came to realise how illuminating tiny pinhead facts can sometimes be. Poor Dakyns did not live to finish his chapter, which was completed on his behalf by his friend Miss Stawell, herself a redoubtable classical scholar and author of many translations from the Greek. Her section gives some account of Dakyns's character, his devotion to Tennyson, and also recounts the incident at Cauteretz described above.

Dakyns had been an assistant master at Clifton College for twenty years. After his retirement, he took an active part in the cultural life of Haslemere, often attending Revd Aitkens's study circle on the Rectory lawn, where on one occasion he read aloud the Manx dialect poems of T.E. Brown. His published works included *Xenophon*, an essay (1880); translations of Xenophon's *The March of the Ten Thousand* (1901), and *The Education of Cyrus* (1914) (posthumously revised by Miss Stawell).

[Martin, 1980; Tennyson, H., 1911; Sillick archives, p. 48.]

DOYLE, Sir Arthur Conan (1859–1930): author.

After qualifying as a doctor at Edinburgh in 1881, Doyle had a disappointing time sitting in his surgery at Southsea waiting for patients to turn up; so he occupied himself by writing stories. One of these, *A Study in Scarlet* (1887), introduced Sherlock Holmes to the public, to immediate acclaim. The first series of Sherlock Holmes short stories appeared seriatim in *The Strand Magazine* in 1891 and were a colossal success. The same year he married his first wife, Louisa. Not long afterwards, she contracted tuberculosis and, acting on the received wisdom of the time, Doyle reconciled himself to living abroad, either in Switzerland or Egypt. But then he ran across Grant Allen – himself a sufferer from consumption – who assured him that this was not necessary, as 'he himself had kept the disease at bay by living at Hindhead'. Doyle hurried down to Hindhead to test the air for himself, 'and was more than satisfied ... because its height, its dryness, its sandy soil, its fir-trees, and its shelter from all bitter winds present the conditions which all agree to be best'. So before departing for Egypt in the autumn of 1895, he made arrangements for the building of Undershaw (now a hotel on the A3 at Hindhead).

While in Egypt for his wife's health in the winter of 1895–96, Doyle got wind of Kitchener's expedition to deal with the troublesome Dervishes of the Sudan. For one of his martial temperament, the temptation was irresistible. So, leaving his ailing wife in a Cairo hotel, he got himself enrolled as a war correspondent, bought a huge Italian revolver and hurried to the front by train, river-boat and camel. In the event, he was disappointed, for the cautious Kitchener was not yet ready to advance, and with the hot season approaching, the Doyles had to get back to England. However, he was able to make good use of his experience in the Sudan by writing a stirring adventure-

Sir Arthur Conan Doyle

novel, *The Tragedy of the Korosko* (first published in 1897 as a serial in *The Strand Magazine*; reprinted in facsimile in *The Original Illustrated Arthur Conan Doyle* (1980)) about a captured party of tourists. It was based on an incident which Doyle had witnessed from his steamer, when a band of red-turbaned Dervishes descended on a native village. It illustrates Doyle's capacity to tell a rattling good story.

When the couple returned from Egypt in early 1896, their house was not ready, so they rented Grayswood Beeches in Haslemere. In January 1897, they moved to Moorlands, a Hindhead boarding house from which they could keep an eye on the progress of the work at Undershaw until it was finally ready for occupation in October 1897. The house, designed by an architect called Ball whom Doyle had become friendly with in his South sea days, was strategically situated. Crouching, like Wellington's guardsmen at Waterloo, just below the crest of the Hindhead ridge, it was completely sheltered from the north wind, and got its full share of sunshine.

Doyle soon made his presence felt at Hindhead. In 1898, he took over the Beacon Hotel for a sumptuous Christmas Ball. The *Surrey Advertiser* of 31st December 1898 reported that the numerous guests came in fancy dress: Grant Allen as a cardinal and his wife as a Japanese lady; Henry Dakyns as a Moor; Sir Frederick Pollock made do with his LLD robes, with Lady Pollock as a Spanish Lady; and many others. But Doyle himself outshone them all, 'his stalwart figure clad in a russet-coloured garb of a Viking', he 'towered above prince and courtier, cardinal and Arab'. He was, indeed, a large and imposing person: Frederick Whyte described him as looking 'like two stolid policemen rolled into one'.[30]

Flora Thompson, who was then manning the post office at Grayshott, records that 'scarcely a day passed without his bursting like a breeze into the post office, almost filling it with his fine presence and the deep tones of his jovial voice. As he went about the village he had a kindly greeting for all, rich and poor, known and unknown alike. He was probably the most popular man in the neighbourhood. Practically everyone had read at least one of his books, and many of his local readers fully believed him to be the greatest of living authors.'[31]

Doyle found time for a wide variety of sporting activities: cricket, football, boxing, golf and skiing – which he was said to have introduced from Norway into Switzerland – as well as being active in most local affairs. When the Boer War broke out, he immediately volunteered to serve as a physician at a field hospital. When it was over, as well as a history of *The Great Boer War* (1900), he wrote a staunchly patriotic pamphlet (1902), justifying Britain's actions to the peoples of Europe in twelve languages. It was probably for this that he received his knighthood the same year.

Stimulated by the Boer War and by the looming German menace, Doyle organised a Rifle Club – known in the area as 'The Undershaw Commando' – consisting of local lads, smartly dressed with broad-brimmed hats, and badges with the initials 'URC'. His rifle range, in the garden of Undershaw, used, in place of conventional targets, turnips scattered among the heather on the hillside to represent the enemy. This, Doyle believed, was much more realistic, as the distances were unknown to the shooters, 'and there can be no sighting shot any more than you would have a sighting shot at a skirmisher coming up the valley'. At this rifle range, 'close on a thousand rounds' might be let off in an afternoon. Doyle boasted that 'Hindhead could furnish over three hundred fighting men'.[32]

Doyle was an early and enthusiastic, though reckless, motorist. His first car was a 1902 single-cylinder 10hp Wolseley, dark green with red wheels, which he took delivery of himself at Birmingham, never having driven a car before. A crowd cheered him when he got back safely to Hindhead, but were alarmed to see the car mount a bank in the Undershaw drive; luckily he managed to right it. But on a later occasion, it overturned completely, and he was pinned underneath it for an hour until rescued. The brakes proved to be unreliable, and Doyle says he became expert at steering a car 'when it is flying backwards under no control down a winding hill'.

By the time Doyle came to Hindhead in 1897, Sherlock Holmes had, so he thought, been finally dispatched. Holmes and Moriarty had disappeared into the Reichenbach Falls locked in a death-grapple, and Doyle hoped to devote his future energies to the historical romances such as *The White Company* (1891) and *Sir Nigel* (1906) which, he thought, represented his 'high-water mark in literature'. He turned his attention first to the 'Brigadier Gerard' series of stories, most of which were written at Undershaw, as were *Rodney*

Stone (1896), *Sir Nigel* and the 'Round the Fire' series of short stories, published in the *Strand Magazine* between June 1898 and May 1899. The historical novels were carefully researched, but they lack the subtlety of the Holmes stories, and reflect Doyle's zest for adventure and bloodshed. But his devoted public insisted on the resurrection of their favourite detective, and he was obliged to comply. So the new series of stories about Sherlock Holmes – including *The Hound of the Baskervilles* – came to be written at Hindhead.

Beacon Hotel, where Doyle held his Christmas party in 1898

Sir Nigel is of interest to local readers, in that much of the action takes place in the hills round Hindhead, in the countryside as Doyle imagined it to have been in the fourteenth century. The preface shows that he had been at great pains to get the historical details right. The novel opens at Waverley Abbey, where Nigel, the young heir to Tilford Manor, leaps bareback on a great yellow horse which had proved too wild for the monks to master. The horse careers uncontrollably across country, with Nigel still precariously in place on its back, over Hankley Down, Hindhead, Shottermill, Linchmere and does not come to a halt till it reaches Henley Hill. When Nigel finally masters it, the great yellow beast becomes his faithful war-horse, and accompanies him on a series of blood-thirsty adventures in France. Although Doyle considered this novel to be 'my absolute top!', it is in fact little more than a fast-moving adventure story.

The strange dichotomy between the rumbustious physical adventures of the historical novels and the rigorous intellectual climate of the detective stories seems to reflect a genuine split in Doyle's own personality, which he himself was aware of. Writing in his autobiography about the character of Sherlock Holmes, he says: 'I am often asked whether I had myself the qualities which I depicted, or whether I was merely the Watson that I looked

... I find that in real life in order to find [Holmes] I have to inhibit all the other, and get into a mood when there is no one in the room but me. Then I get results, and have several times solved problems by Holmes' methods after the police have been baffled. Yet I must admit that in ordinary life I am by no means observant, and that I have to throw myself into an artificial frame of mind before I can weigh evidence, and anticipate the sequence of events.'[33]

The contrast between the subtle creator of the world's first fictional detective, and the writer of conventional adventure stories, is nowhere more evident than in the first of his Holmes stories, *The Study in Scarlet*. Having created Sherlock Holmes – and his counterpart, Dr Watson – with a few deft strokes, Doyle evidently feared that his readers would be too easily bored by Holmes's intellectual exercises. So he wove into the detective story a crude tale of adventure, involving a desperate attempt to escape from the clutches of the Mormons, evidently hoping that this would hold the attention of readers bored by Holmes's efforts at detection. Yet he recognised that his hero might not have approved of what he would regard as an irrelevant intrusion. As Holmes put it, it was like 'working a love-story or an elopement into the fifth proposition of Euclid'.

Doyle's obtuseness when in his 'Watson mode' is illustrated by an anecdote related by Coulson Kernahan.[34] Kernahan was then a guest at The Croft, Grant Allen's home in Hindhead. In the morning Doyle called on them. It had been snowing overnight, and on the ground there were footprints of a bird. Doyle challenged Allen to say what sort of bird it was. This was no problem for Allen, who was a very knowledgeable naturalist. He told Doyle it was a pheasant, and in his turn challenged him to use his powers of observation to deduce the sex of the bird. Doyle tried his best, but had to admit defeat. Then Allen pointed out that here and there along the trail of footsteps there were places where the bird's tail had just brushed the snow. It therefore had to be a cock pheasant, which has the longer tail, and when Allen clapped his hands, a splendid cock duly emerged from the bush towards which the tracks were heading. 'The solution of these mysteries,' Allen could not refrain from remarking, 'is as commonplace as it is simple, my dear Watson.'

Another small incident demonstrates the extent of Doyle's fame during his time at Hindhead. In 1905, a party of French naval officers was being fêted in London as part of the *entente cordiale*. When asked whom of England's great men they would most like to see, they voted unanimously for the creator of Sherlock Holmes. Doyle saw to it that they were received in appropriate style at Undershaw. As they arrived in their resplendent full-dress uniform, they were greeted by a banner inscribed *Bienvenue*, four bands, a marquee and a bevy of ladies in white costumes with leg-of-mutton sleeves and parasols.

The air of Hindhead did not, as Doyle had hoped, cure his wife's tuberculosis, and she died in 1906. In the following year he married Miss Jean Leckie, and left Hindhead to spend the rest of his life at Crowborough, in

East Sussex. Undershaw was bought in 1908 by Canon Edward Carus Selwyn on his retirement from the headmastership of Uppingham.

[DNB; Doyle, 1924; Pearson, 1943; Carr, 1949; Orel, 1991.]

ELIOT, George, pseudonym of Marian Evans, later Mrs Cross (1819–1880): novelist.

Although not legally married, the union between Marian and George Henry Lewes had become widely accepted in liberal circles by the 1860s, and they were generally known as 'Mr and Mrs Lewes'. After the success of *Adam Bede* in 1859, their financial position was much improved, and they were able to buy The Priory, their house in St John's Wood, London in 1863. By then George Eliot's fame as a novelist was firmly established, and society – or at least its more liberally-minded section – was beginning to overlook the irregularity of the Leweses' union, and to come to their soirées, which soon became a noted feature of the intellectual life of the capital. But by the beginning of 1871, the couple had decided that major alterations were needed to The Priory, and they therefore had to find accommodation for the summer while the work was being carried out.

Marian was in the middle of writing *Middlemarch*, and had reached a critical stage; it had originated as two distinct novels, which now had to be knitted together into one. It was a difficult task requiring all her great skill. So peace and quiet were essential. After some preliminary searches the Leweses settled on Brookbank, Mrs Gilchrist's cottage at Shottermill, which she had decided to sub-let for the summer while she and her children stayed with her mother in Essex. The Leweses were there from the second of May until the end of July 1871, and then at Cherrimans, across the lane from Brookbank, for the month of August. During this time Eliot completed the first part of *Middlemarch*, and Lewes arranged terms with Blackwood for its publication.

It took Marian a few weeks to get adjusted to life in a small country cottage. Writing to Anne Gilchrist on the ninth of May, she reported some problems with the commissariat: 'the butcher does not bring the meat, everybody grudges selling fresh milk, eggs are scarce, and an expedition we made yesterday in search of fowls showed us nothing more hopeful than some chickens six weeks old which the good woman observed "were sometimes eaten by the gentry with asparagus".' But after these early problems had been overcome, and the weather had improved, Marian grew very fond of the 'queer little cottage'. She wrote again to Anne on the third of July: 'During the first weeks of our stay I did not imagine that I should ever be so fond of the place as I am now. The departure of the bitter winds, some improvement in my health, and the gradual revelation of fresh beauties in the scenery ...

ELIOT

have made me love our little world here and wish not to quit it until we can settle in our London home.'[35]

Anne Gilchrist had already arranged to let Brookbank to George Smith, a water-colour artist, for the month of August, so the Leweses had to leave at the end of July. Fortunately James and Ann Simmons, who lived across the lane at Cherrimans, were going to be away that month, and agreed to let the house. Cherrimans was a more commodious house, as Marian wrote:

> We enjoy our roomy house and pretty lawn greatly. Imagine me seated near a window, opening under a verandah, with flower-beds and lawn and pretty hills in sight, my feet on a warm water-bottle, and my writing on my knees. In that attitude my mornings are passed. We dine at two; and at four, when the tea comes in, I begin to read aloud. About six or half-past we walk on the commons and see the great sky over our head. At eight we are usually in the house again, and fill our evening with physics, chemistry, or other wisdom if our heads are at par; if not, we take to folly, in the shape of Alfred de Musset's poems, or something akin to them.[36]

So, hot-water-bottle at her feet, Marian wrestled with the complexities of her great novel. *Middlemarch* had been begun in August 1869 and the first two sections of the completed work had been written before coming to Shottermill.[37] One section, called previously *Miss Brooke*, centred round Dorothea, and the other round young Doctor Lydgate. Eliot was not altogether satisfied with the initial result, and the first two months at Shottermill were spent in revision. By the end of May, the first of the eight parts in which *Middlemarch* was originally serialised, was ready to be sent to Blackwoods for publication. The second was completed by the end of June. The third section took longer, and was not quite finished by the time the Leweses left Shottermill. The work had proceeded much faster there than it did after the couple had returned to London, with all its distractions. So the peace and quiet of Shottermill may have contributed significantly to the making of what Virginia Woolf called 'one of the few English novels written for grown-up people'. *Middlemarch* was not finally completed until 1872.

Preoccupied though she was with her novel, Marian still found time to go for long walks over the surrounding hills with Lewes. Unlike many of the literary folk who came to the area, she made contacts with the local inhabitants. An American visitor, Alice Maud Fenn, who stayed at a nearby farm some ten years later, was told that Marian would often come there for a chat with the farmer's wife. Sitting on a grassy bank by the kitchen door, they would discuss 'the growth of fruit and the quality of butter in a manner so quiet and simple that the good country folks were astonished, expecting very different conversation from the great novelist'. The farmer used to drive the Leweses round the countryside in his horse and trap, sometimes visiting

Tennyson at Aldworth.[38]

After Tennyson had called on the Leweses at Shottermill, he described Marian to James Henry Mangles as 'very gentle, tho' masculine-looking, with a big nose'.[39] On another occasion, he thought her 'like the picture of Savonarola'.[40] Henry James gave a more detailed account of her appearance when he called at The Priory in 1869. He 'was immensely impressed, interested and pleased. To begin with she is magnificently ugly – deliciously hideous. She has a low forehead, a dull grey eye, a vast pendulous nose, a huge mouth, full of uneven teeth ... Now in this vast ugliness resides a most powerful beauty which, in a very few minutes steals forth and charms the mind, so that you end as I ended, falling in love with her. Yes behold me in love with this great horse-faced blue stocking ...'[41]

The Leweses' time at Shottermill had given them a feeling for the rugged heathlands of south-west Surrey, and before long they were looking for a house to buy as a country retreat. In December 1877 they settled for The Heights, at Witley, situated on a Greensand ridge similar to, though not so high as, the hills over which they had roamed during their stay at Shottermill. Here Eliot wrote her collection of essays, *Impressions of Theophrastus Such* (1879). However, late in 1878 it became obvious that Lewes was dying, and they returned to London. After she had partially recovered from the devastating blow of his death, she married J.W. Cross in 1880. The marriage had an unpropitious start when Cross became deranged during their honeymoon in Venice, and jumped from a balcony into the canal, from which he was rescued by a gondolier. But on returning to Witley he managed to recover his sanity by much felling of trees, using a special axe. George Eliot died unexpectedly in London, on 22nd December 1880.

[Cross, 1910; Haight, 1968; Bellringer, 1993; Spittles, 1993.]

GALTON, Sir Francis FRS (1822–1911): explorer, psychologist, meteorologist, geneticist, anthropologist, statistician, etc.

Galton sampled a number of houses on the uplands round Haslemere. He was at Yaffles, on Polecat Hill, Hindhead – the name was later changed to Anthony Place – August–September 1907; Quedley, Shottermill, September 1907–April 1908; The Rectory, Haslemere, October 1909–March 1910; The Court, Grayshott, August–October 1910; Grayshott House, November 1910, where he died on 18 January 1911. Like others, Galton had been attracted by the supposed virtues of the Hindhead air – when he sampled it in 1905, during a visit to the Tyndalls, he spoke of 'that wonderful air-cure Hindhead'. By 1907 he was becoming rather frail physically, though as alert as ever mentally, and hoped that the Hindhead air would revive him.

Galton was possibly the most original of all the great Victorians. Yet only two of his many projects – the study of fingerprints, and the construction of 'weather maps' – had any lasting outcome, while the proposal for which he is usually remembered, the doctrine of eugenics, though plausible enough in the circumstances in which it was conceived, is now usually dismissed as thoroughly disreputable. Galton's real contribution was probably the demonstration that mathematics can be applied to everyday life; his mistake was to exaggerate the significance of some of the results. 'Whenever you can, count,' he often remarked. So as well as physical quantities like atmospheric pressure, he counted a variety of human attributes: memory, the ability to judge the weight of cattle, the effect of prayer on life expectancy, and many other human attributes which no-one had previously thought of treating quantitatively. With a bit of ingenuity – of which he had a plentiful supply – these could all be expressed in numerical terms, he maintained. This led him to make use of, and develop, the statistical methods devised by earlier workers for the analysis of randomly-distributed attributes.

The publication, by his cousin Charles Darwin, of *The Origin of Species* in 1859, turned Galton's thoughts to the question of heredity. Many of the features he had been measuring in normal individuals were likely to be inherited, and so he devised statistical methods for studying the correlations between parents and their children. Most important of all was the likelihood that mental characteristics might be inherited. An early product was *Hereditary Genius* (1869), an attempt to show that great ability was genetically determined. The often striking effects of selective breeding in domesticated animals led Galton to speculate on the possibility of applying similar methods to man – a train of thought that was given further impetus at the end of the century, when public concern over the 'degeneracy' and perceived excessive breeding of the working-class population was stimulated by the deplorable physical condition of many of the Army recruits for the Boer War. Galton's unduly simplistic ideas on the inheritance of mental characteristics led him to propose that the state should decide which individuals were to be permitted to reproduce. He anticipated that a major improvement could be brought about in both the physical and mental state of the human stock after a few generations of selective breeding.

In his last year of life – much of it spent in the Surrey hills – Galton tried his hand at a novel. It was about an imaginary country called Kantsaywhere (which also became the title of the book), where his eugenic principles had been put into practice, and procreation was strictly controlled. The completed work was submitted to Methuen for publication, but rejected. Much of this novel was destroyed by a niece for the unusual reason that the love scenes were 'too absurdly unreal', but fragments were recovered by Karl Pearson, and reproduced in his biography of Galton. The story concerns a professor of statistics who visits Kantsaywhere, and falls in love with a Miss Allfancy. As the country is run on strict Galtonian principles, the candidate has to submit to an elaborate physical and mental examination in order to determine whether he is fit to marry. He is greatly impressed by the physique of the inhabitants; the girls have 'massive forms, short of heaviness, and seem promising mothers of a noble race'; the men are 'very courteous, but with a resolute look that suggests fighting qualities of a high order'. They are all 'gay without frivolity, friendly without gush, and intelligent without brilliancy'.

Despite the doubtless splendid qualities of the inhabitants of Kantsaywhere, Galton's vision proved unattractive to most people. Any prospects of it gaining widespread support have also long since disappeared because, although the measures for eliminating the unfit were far less drastic – they were either made to emigrate or else were kept under surveillance – Galton's ideas could be said to have anticipated, and even encouraged, Hitler's attempts to breed an Aryan race. In fairness, Galton's intentions were in fact very different, and wholly benign. His aim was to spare the human race the otherwise inevitable cruelties of natural selection, by avoiding the suffering caused by inherited disease. However, the unfortunate result has been that this highly original and many-sided genius is now chiefly remembered for his misplaced zeal for an unworkable and potentially disastrous folly. For a full discussion of the eugenic question see Kevles (1986).

As might be expected of such a practically-minded person, Galton's prose style is devoid of frills. Of his many books, the most enjoyable to read is his endlessly inventive *The Art of Travel; or Shifts and Contrivances Available in Wild Country* (1855). Should you ever wonder how you would cross an African river if you had no boat and couldn't swim, Galton has the answer. Of his various scientific ventures, the one which most strikingly illustrates his capacity for lateral thinking is perhaps his proposal for communicating with the hypothetical inhabitants of the planet Mars. In 1896, he described in the *Fortnightly Review* a code of dots, dashes and lines, intended to be used in a visual system which could be built up from these simple symbols. By this means, mathematical ideas, words, and even simple pictures could be transmitted – on the assumption that there was someone of equal intelligence to receive them.

During the period when he was residing intermittently in Haslemere or Hindhead, he wrote *Memories of my Life* (1908) and *Essays in Eugenics* (1909), as well as his usual flow of articles for scientific journals, the novel mentioned above, and numerous letters to Karl Pearson.

[Pearson, 1914–1930; Forrest, 1974.]

GARNETT, Lucy Mary Jane: authority on Greek and Turkish folklore.

Lucy Garnett was apparently living in London in 1889 when she signed Mrs Humphry Ward's 'Appeal against Female Suffrage'. But she was in

Haslemere at the time of Thomas Wright's visit of 1897, and attended there a lecture by Grant Allen, a meeting of the Primrose League, and a concert.[42] The first reference to her in *Kelly's Directory* is in 1899, when she was living at Sandy Croft, Haslemere. She was still there in 1903, but not in 1905.

Lucy Garnett was fascinated by the traditional songs and fables of the Greek and Turkish peasantry, and evidently had a complete command of both vernacular languages. She put this, and her knowledge of these countries, to good use in a series of books: *Greek Folk Songs* (1885 and 1888); *The Women of Turkey and their Folklore* (1890); *New Folklore Researches* (1896); *Mysticism and Magic in Turkey* (1912); *Greek Wonder Tales* (1913); *Greece of the Hellenes* (1914); *Balkan Home-Life* (1917).

In the first three of these books, she collaborated with John Stuart Stuart-Glennie (the hyphen was sometimes omitted). Garnett provided the translations, while Stuart-Glennie interpreted the significance of her text in the light of his own speculative theories. The title-page of one of their combined works suggests that Stuart-Glennie had a high opinion of his own contribution:

Greek Folk-Songs from the Turkish Provinces of Greece,
by Lucy M.J. Garnett,
classified, revised and edited with an Historical Introduction
by John S. Stuart Glennie MA
of the Middle Temple, Barrister-at-Law

Richard Dorson confirms this impression. He describes Stuart-Glennie as 'a dour, humourless Scot, who bored even his friends. But for his graceless personality, Stuart-Glennie's original and provocative theory would have won more adherents.' Dorson describes the joint work as 'a curious collaboration which served Stuart-Glennie as the instrument to promote his cause'. Stuart-Glennie was understandably riled when reviews of the book praised Garnett's translations but 'regarded his Introduction on pagan survivals as out of place'.[43]

The date-line to Stuart-Glennie's Preface to *New Folklore Researches* shows that he was living in Haslemere in 1896. He also attended a meeting of the Microscope and Natural History Society in that year, and Thomas Wright mentioned him as a Haslemere resident in 1897.

Another folklorist with Hilltop associations was Edward Clodd, who often stayed at Hindhead with his friend Grant Allen. He must have been well known to Stuart-Glennie as president of the Folk Lore Society in 1895. He caused a great scandal by his presidential address, in which he derived the Christian rites of baptism and Holy Communion from primitive beliefs. But I know of no contacts between Clodd and Stuart-Glennie.[44]

[Dorson, 1968.]

GILCHRIST, Anne, née Burrows (1828–1885): author.

In the autumn of 1861, Anne was living with her husband, Alexander Gilchrist, and her four children at 6 Cheyne Row (next door to the Carlyles). Alexander was well known in literary circles as the biographer of William Etty, and now he was finishing a massive *Life of William Blake*. But that autumn the two elder children contracted scarlet fever, and just as they were recovering, Alexander Gilchrist also caught it. Six days later he was dead.

Anne could not afford to keep on the Cheyne Row house. Early in 1862 she started searching for a much more modest dwelling in the country. By February she had found Brookbank, in Shottermill, in a valley among the Surrey hills.[45] On the third of April she moved in with her children. Her reasons for choosing Brookbank are not known, but she and her late husband had some knowledge of the hill country, as they had lived at one time not far away at Guildford, and she was evidently attracted to it.

Anne sent William Rossetti her first impressions of her new home in a letter dated 28th April 1862. The cottage was indeed small – 'it would fit comfortably in your drawing-room' – but she thought it 'would do well enough,' adding 'the scenery round here is of surpassing loveliness'. Anne was a great walker, and enjoyed many hikes on the heather-covered hills round Shottermill.[46] The smallness of the cottage was remedied in 1864, when she got Mr Small to enlarge it, probably by creating a bedroom in the attic, adding a dormer window.

Once settled in, Anne concentrated on finishing her late husband's life of Blake. Although he had completed a first draft of most of the text, there was still a lot of material to be gone through, checked and incorporated where appropriate. A number of visits to the British Museum were needed. Brookbank was quite conveniently situated for this purpose, as the station at Haslemere was only a mile away. Anne was fortunate also in having much help from William and Gabriel Rossetti, and Samuel Palmer; in addition much of the labour of transcription and proof-reading was done for her by William Haines, an old friend of her husband. The book was completed in the summer of 1863, and published in two handsome volumes in October of that year. It was well received, and brought about a revival of interest in Blake, who up till then had usually been dismissed as little more than a gifted lunatic. It remained the standard work until superseded by the studies of Geoffrey Keynes and others a century later.

One might have expected Anne to have been fully occupied by domestic chores, and by caring for and educating her four children, but she still found time for long walks on the surrounding hills, and for writing. She had been interested in science since she had been a schoolgirl, but had had no formal training in any scientific subject. That, however, had never inhibited Victorian literati from writing popular expositions – often highly speculative – on such topics as spiral nebulae, and botanical oddities. G.H. Lewes, a later inhabitant of Brookbank, was one of the best and most celebrated exponents of the genre, and Grant Allen was also a noted contributor. Before coming to Shottermill, Anne had written articles with titles such as 'A Glance at the Vegetable Kingdom', 'Whales and Whalemen' and 'Our Nearest Relation', an account of the newly-discovered gorilla. At Brookbank she continued the series with 'The Indestructibility of Force' and 'What is Electricity?' In all these articles she did little more than dish up the conventional wisdom of the day. Her friend Walter White thought that scientific subjects were not appropriate material for female authors, and suggested some more suitable titles such as 'On the foolishness of Women as compared with that of Men' and 'Hospitality not necessarily an expensive Virtue'.

Anne mayor may not have been influenced by his advice when she wrote an article published in *Macmillan's Magazine* for 1865, entitled 'A Neglected Art'. This was an exposition of domestic management, pervaded with a passionate sense that women ought to acquire the same professional efficiency in the running of their households as their husbands in their masculine occupations. Much of Anne's advice concerns the management of domestics. The best means of dealing with domineering cooks, she wrote, was to be prepared to roll up one's sleeves and show them how one wanted it done. But at the same time, domestics must not be treated 'like a hostile tribe' when, by setting them a good example, they could be converted into 'a faithful, loyal, serviceable race'. While at Brookbank she wrote no more books, but much later she published a workmanlike *Life of Mary Lamb* (1883).

A remarkable feature of Anne's tenure of Brookbank is the number of literary and artistic figures who came to be associated with the little cottage. The list might have been extended even further, if her former Chelsea neighbours, Jane and Thomas Carlyle, had been able to accept Anne's invitation to stay for the summer of 1863. As it was, visitors included Ford Madox Brown, Samuel Palmer, Dante Gabriel, William and Christina Rossetti and Walter White. Of these, only Christina Rossetti is likely to have written or composed anything while staying there – possibly *Maiden Song* and *Twilight Night* during her 1863 visit, and in 1864 some pastoral poems.

Perhaps Anne's most significant act during her time at Shottermill was her part in inducing Tennyson to settle in the neighbourhood. Anne had heard from Walter White that the Tennysons were looking for a site on which to build a house in the Haslemere area, but she was taken by surprise when they suddenly appeared at Brookbank one day in August 1866. They wanted to look at a possible site at The Devil's Jumps at Churt which Walter White had told them about, and with help from her neighbours the Simmonses she was able to conduct them there. That particular site was not suitable – 'very dear at the money,' thought Tennyson – but they liked the area, returning later the same year to resume the search, and again in the spring of 1867. This time Anne, in combination with James Simmons, found them the romantic site high on the escarpment of Blackdown, where they built Aldworth. Anne was a member of the party that gathered on the windswept site on 23rd April 1868 (Shakespeare's birthday) to lay the foundation-stone. She sent Emily Tennyson, who was indisposed and couldn't attend, a full account of the ceremony.

Anne saw quite a lot of Tennyson during the course of the search, and the accounts she left in letters to friends help to supplement the descriptions of the poet in diaries such as Allingham's and Mangles's. Like Allingham, Anne's two great heroes were Carlyle and Tennyson, and when the latter turned up in the flesh on her doorstep, she was not disappointed. She thought he looked 'every inch a king: features are massive, eyes very grave and penetrating, hair long, still very dark and, though getting thin, falls in such a way as to give a peculiar beauty to the mystic head'. They were soon on easy terms. 'One feels,' she wrote, 'somehow singularly happy and free from constraint in his presence – a sense of a beneficent, generous, nobly humane nature being combined with his intellectual greatness.' Anne later recorded some of her conversations with the poet. They had a common interest in scientific matters: when he accompanied her part of the way home after a lunch at Grayshott – where the Tennysons were staying in 1867 – they discussed Herbert Spencer's recent essay on the Nebular Hypothesis, which both had read. Anne was not afraid to put forward her own views, and found that they agreed about materialism. Matter, she thought, was wholly a manifestation of force and power. 'You mean,' he said, 'that we have a little bit of God in the middle of us.' She agreed.[47]

Anne had two more contributions to make to literary history. During most summers while she was renting Brookbank she was accustomed to spend several months with her mother at Earls Colne in Essex. While she and her children were away, she sub-let the cottage to friends if they wanted, or if not to strangers. The most distinguished of these visitors were George Eliot and G.H. Lewes – generally known as 'Mr and Mrs Lewes'. (Their impressions of the cottage and the neighbourhood are described under their own entries.) They had not met Anne before, and indeed never did meet her in the flesh, but there was some friendly correspondence. Some of this was about domestic details, and about Mrs Garland, their only servant, whose 'slowness and stupidity are somewhat trying to the patience of impatient people', though she was also 'kind, attentive, honest'. Lewes admired Anne's collection of books, and was soon immersed in her copy of Lacroix's *Algebra*. Eliot envied her pictures: 'If I ever steal anything in my life, I think it will be the two little Sir Joshuas over the drawing-room mantelpiece.' When the Leweses left, they invited Anne to their Sunday afternoons at The Priory. Rather strangely, she never took up the invitation. At Cheyne Row, she had been immersed in the literary society of London, but she evidently had no desire to re-enter it as a widow.

Anne's next encounter with a major literary figure was indeed bizarre. In June 1869 she wrote from Brookbank to William Rossetti, to say that Madox

Brown had lent her Rossetti's recent book of selections of Walt Whitman's poems. Whitman at that time had met with little recognition in his native America and was quite unknown in England. Anne took the book with her on her annual visit to Earls Colne, and was instantly overcome by the powerful appeal of Whitman's craggy verse, sitting reading it by the hour in a little summer-house by the banks of the River Colne. Within a few days she wrote in a letter to Rossetti: 'I can read no other book; it holds me entirely spell-bound, and I go through it again and again with deepening delight and wonder.'

Rossetti's edition had been an expurgated version of *Leaves of Grass*, from which the more steamy poems had been omitted. Now he offered, with some diffidence, to lend her the full version. She accepted his offer 'quite fearlessly', confident that Whitman's 'great and divinely beautiful nature ... could not infuse any poison into the wine he has poured out for us'.

Anne survived, and indeed thrived, on Whitman's robust verse. She wrote again at length to Rossetti, with what he described as 'resplendent enthusiasm'. Rossetti thought that it would do Whitman a good turn if something on the lines of Anne's enthusiastic letter could be published in America. Between them, they developed it into a long essay which was published in an

Walt Whitman, to whom Anne Gilchrist was attracted

American journal called *The Radical* in May 1870, under the title 'An Englishwoman's Estimate of Walt Whitman'. It did a lot to help the poet's faltering cause in his native country.

What Anne did not reveal to Rossetti was that what she felt for Walt Whitman was rather more than simple admiration for his verse, and in fact amounted to an overwhelming mental and physical infatuation. There came a time when she could no longer hold back this turbulent emotion, and it boiled over in a long letter she wrote to Whitman in November 1871. In it she described her present situation, claiming that she had never felt 'true, tender, wifely love' for her late husband, and revealing that when there 'came the voice over the Atlantic to me – O, the voice of my Mate,' she knew that 'one day I shall hear that voice say to me "My Mate. The one I so much want. Bride, Wife, indissoluble, eternal!" ... take me to your breast for ever'.[48]

It was, to say the least, a surprising letter to receive from a middle-class

Englishwoman of forty-three, whom he had never met. Understandably, Whitman treated it with some caution, and did not reply until Anne had written twice more. He then sent a tactful half-page note, expressing his gratitude for her article about his poetry. They corresponded at intervals until 1876, when Anne decided that the time had come when she could venture across the Atlantic and meet the man she loved face to face. Whitman was understandably alarmed, but could not dissuade her. In August of that year she set sail with three of her children, and on 13th September they met. Inevitably, it was somewhat of a disappointment for her, for by then the shaggy old poet had had a stroke which left him with a paralysed left foot, and he was but a pale shadow of his former rumbustious self. But Anne's calm and gracious manners concealed her disappointment, and allayed Whitman's fears of an emotional scene. It says much for the good sense of both parties that they then became, and remained, the best of friends.

Anne and her family rented a house in Philadelphia, where they could keep in touch with Whitman in nearby Camden, and they did not return to England until 1879. They visited friends in various parts of the country, and then had a spell of six or seven weeks at Shottermill. Anne had given up the lease of Brookbank when she went to America in 1876, so they stayed in a cottage on Lion Green. Tennyson called on them there, and they had lunch with him at Aldworth.

After leaving Shottermill, Anne moved to what was to be her final home at 12 Well Road, Hampstead. While there, she was visited in 1882 by John Burroughs, the American naturalist and author (see own entry). Anne had met him in America, as he was a friend of Whitman. Burroughs left Hampstead to spend a few days at Shottermill, where he hoped to hear the nightingale. It must have been Anne who recommended the farmhouse where he stayed.

Burroughs later became Whitman's biographer. Tennyson and Whitman exchanged several letters, but never met. Tennyson told his son Hallam that Whitman 'neglects form altogether, but there is a fine spirit breathing through his writings'. But when Mangles asked Emily Tennyson if she had read *Leaves of Grass*, she replied 'Of course not – it is one of the most disgusting books ever written.'[49]

Whitman had had an earlier connection with the Pearsall Smith family, whom he knew well when they were living near Philadelphia – this was before they crossed the Atlantic to settle on Friday's Hill, at Fernhurst, and became part of the hilltop community. *Leaves of Grass* had also made a powerful impression on young Logan Pearsall Smith. 'It seemed,' he wrote in his autobiography, 'to open a great shining window in my narrow house of life.'[50]

As a postscript to Anne's complex connections with other literary figures, it is perhaps worth mentioning briefly her youngest child, Grace's, encounters with three of the Hilltop Writers. When she was five she had played ball with Christina Rossetti in the garden at Brookbank, and two years later she

HAMILTON

was called upon to sit on Tennyson's lap. Later in life, at the age of twenty-six, Grace joined the Fabian Society, where she fell under the spell of George Bernard Shaw. The affair lasted some three years. For Grace it was a serious matter, which she hoped might end in marriage; for Shaw, it was only one of a series of light-hearted skirmishes with attractive girls. It was terminated by Grace's friend, the novelist Emma Brooke, who called on Shaw and lambasted him vigorously for what she saw as his callous behaviour.

[DNB; Gilchrist, 1887; Alcaro, 1991.]

HAMILTON, Bernard: novelist.

Bernard Hamilton

Hamilton lived at Hindhead Brae on the Tilford Road, overlooking the Devil's Punch Bowl. His arrival in the area is recorded in the preface to his *A Kiss for a Kingdom; or A Venture in Vanity*, a story about the adventures of the baronet hero in an imaginary European war, dated 'Hindhead, 1899'. In 1900, he addressed the Haslemere Microscope and Natural History Society on 'The Birth of an Old Nation'; and in 1902 organised the presentation to Conan Doyle, at the Hindhead Hall, of a handsome mahogany writing table and an illuminated address. This was in recognition of Doyle's work in the Boer War and his propaganda pamphlet, *The War in South Africa*.

But Hamilton had left by 1904, for his son Patrick – the successful novelist – was born in Hassocks, in Sussex, in that year *[Who Was Who]*.

Hamilton was not a great success as an author; nor did he deserve to be. The book of which he seems to have been most proud was *The Light?; A Romance* (1898), a weird mixture of fiction with a dash of history, ranging from ancient Egypt to the 1870s, and much religious propaganda in favour of the author's ideas for reforming the Church of England (see Section Two on religion). Other works were: *A Kiss far a Kingdom* (1899), referred to above, and *Coronation, a Novel* (1902).

Hamilton was the only one of the Hilltop Writers who could fairly be described as a 'brash imperialist' (Doyle was an imperialist, but of a much more dignified and restrained sort), as shown by one of the most bizarre of all his works: a hard-cover booklet of 39 pages about the South African War, published in 1900. It is a pretentious allegory, featuring characters such as' Artful Oom' (Paul Kruger, President of the Transvaal Republic), 'The Head of the Firm' (Queen Victoria), and 'Colossus Roads' (Cecil Rhodes), whom Hamilton would like to see take charge of the South African War, and indeed of the British Empire in general. His uncouth literary style is best conveyed by the title-page of his booklet:

WANTED – A MAN!
Apply John Bull & Co.
(late of Dame Europa's School)
A War Story for Big Boys

Hamilton must have been an uncongenial neighbour for gentle, peace-loving, pro-Boer Rayner Storr, who was living next door at Highcombe Edge, and was just embarking on his scholarly study of the works of saintly Thomas à Kempis.

HARRISON, Frederic (1831–1923): lawyer, historian and Positivist.

Frederic Harrison – the 'k' was omitted to distinguish him from his father – was an influential and well-known figure in intellectual circles, and author of books on law, history and literature. But he is generally remembered as the leading spirit of the Positivist movement in England – the attempt to create a religion without a deity.

In 1886, at a time when Hindhead was being actively colonised by writers, Harrison took a ten-year lease on Blackdown Cottage, at the south-east corner of Blackdown, the other great eminence round about Haslemere. There he did his writing in 'a rustic nook carved out of the hillside behind the cottage', which the family named 'Kilmainham' after the Dublin gaol in which Parnell had been imprisoned. F.W. Bockett, looking down from the heights of Blackdown, called it 'Harrison's white hut', and said it had been built by a former owner in order to 'practise the key-bugle undisturbed'. Bernard Shaw set the opening scene of *Mrs Warren's Profession* in the garden of Blackdown Cottage, and the cottage is described in detail in the stage directions. Shaw had not then been there himself, but obtained details of the setting from a friend – possibly Beatrice Webb – while Harrison was living there. (Shaw knew it later at first hand, when he leased the cottage himself in 1899.) Harrison had left the cottage in 1896, because the lease had become too expensive to renew. In 1898, he stayed for a time with the Philipson-Stowes in the new guest accommodation at nearby Blackdown House. He disapproved of Sir Frederick's background as a Kimberley diamond merchant, but was fond of Lady Philipson-Stowe. From 1902 to

1912 he lived at Hawkhurst in Kent and thereafter in Bath.

Harrison had been acquainted with the neighbourhood before he came to Blackdown. In 1871, he and his wife were living at Pinewood Cottage on Witley Heights, and from there they made their first visit to see Tennyson at Aldworth. They got lost on Blackdown, but when they finally arrived they were well received, and were shown round the grounds.[51] Soon after that, Frederic Harrison's parents leased Sutton Place, the splendid Tudor manor house near Guildford, from 1874 to 1902. Frederic often went there from Blackdown, and found that its 'strange mellow beauty … lit him up and inspired him'. In 1885, he described the house and its history in *Annals of an Old Manor House* for the Surrey Archaeological Society (published by Macmillan in 1893).

F.W. Bockett, himself a Positivist since 1883, had probably stayed with Harrison at some time between 1886 and 1892, and it was almost certainly Harrison whom he was thinking of when he wrote: 'There were other personal memories that made Blackdown very dear to me. I had climbed the hill more than once with one in whom a generous and sympathetic heart is combined with profound knowledge, and a power of expression that has rarely been equalled. We had stood side by side on the hilltop, and from revelling in the lovely scene before us had fallen into a discussion on those deep and appalling problems of our civilisation which must ever be haunting men who have hearts to feel and brains to contrive.'[52]

During the time he was at Blackdown Cottage, Harrison was serving as Professor of Jurisprudence to the Council of Legal Education. He wrote a number of important historical works and biographies, including one on *Cromwell* (1888) and another on William the Silent (1897). These, and his book of literary criticism, *Studies in Early Victorian Literature* (1895), would have been mainly written at the cottage. During the South African War he strongly supported the cause of the Boers, but later he became alarmed by the growth of German militarism, and wrote *The German Peril* (1915) as a warning. Amongst his other writings was a scholarly novel, *Theophano: the Crusade of the Tenth Century* (1904), with the empress of that name as its heroine.

But although he had a finger in many intellectual pies, it is as a leader of the Positivist movement in Britain that Harrison is chiefly remembered. At Oxford, his tutor at Wadham was Richard Congreve. Congreve was profoundly influenced by Auguste Comte's *Cours de philosophie positive*, and in 1849 visited the philosopher himself in Paris. He returned converted, resigned his Fellowship at Wadham and prepared to propagate Comte's 'Religion of Humanity' in England, under the name of 'Positivism'. In 1855, Harrison also visited Comte, and was also impressed, though it was not until 1867 that he made his position clear by becoming a founder-member of the British Positivist Society. In 1870, Congreve established a meeting-place for the new cult at Chapel Street, London. Soon afterwards, however, a schism developed between Harrison and himself, mainly over the ritual to be adopted at Positivist services (Harrison wanted to keep this to a minimum}. The majority of converts followed Harrison to new premises at Newton Hall near Fleet Street, and when he became president of the English Positivist Committee in 1880, he was recognised as the leader of the movement.

George Eliot was a close friend of Harrison, and he often tried, unsuccessfully, to convert her. On one occasion, she went so far as to write a poem, *O May I Join the Choir Invisible*, on the theme of the Positivist doctrine of 'subjective immortality' (it was later set to music as a cantata}. Some even believed that she had become converted – Tennyson told Mangles she 'was a pure Comtist'.[53] The truth was that, although Harrison did his best to persuade her to abandon her austere atheist creed, he never had any real prospect of success.

Frederic Harrison

Harrison was fortunate in retaining his mental and physical powers almost to the end. He went on playing cricket until he was 90, and even at 92 he could still read without glasses. F.S. Marvin, an old Positivist friend, saw him on the day before he died. Harrison had been reading with interest an obscure work by an Indian philosopher, published in Sweden as *Kalkaram*, and discussed the author's objections to Comte with Marvin. Austin Harrison records that his father remained 'exact and alert, hopeful and vigilant to the very morning when, as he rose from bed, he was struck down from sudden failure of the heart, even as he had always hoped might be the merciful end'.[54]

Harrison retained his faith in the Religion of Humanity till the end, though by then Positivists were becoming thin on the ground. It had sustained him through a long life; as he liked to put it, it had been 'a thought of youth fulfilled in the maturity of age'. As an outstanding leader of the movement, his passing was marked by an impressive memorial meeting, reported by J.F. Green. The ceremony opened with Mendelssohn's *Funeral March*, followed by a series of tributes and addresses, and concluded with Handel's *Dead March in Saul*. It must have been a solemn and moving event, for it not only marked the passing of their leader, but also, as many present must have sensed, the virtual end of the Positivist movement itself.

Frederic Harrison's two-volume autobiography is reticent on personal details. There are more of these in his son's rather disorderly but sympathetic

HOLL

memoir, which is not easily summarised. He divides his father's life into two phases: before and after his marriage in 1870. Beginning in his undergraduate days, Harrison became a rebel in both religion and politics, as he searched restlessly for a role in life. In the second phase his religious doubts were settled by his conversion to Positivism, and this and his tranquil marriage converted him from a rebel into a sage. The rest of his life was spent in guiding and encouraging the Positivist flock, and in writing the many books which reflect his views on events, history, biography and literature.

[DNB; Vogeler, 1984; Harrison, F., 1911; Harrison, A., 1926; tributes in *Positivist Review* (1923), Vol. 31, by F.S. Marvin, p. 30 & p. 88; J.F. Green, p. 31 & p. 75; E. May Tomkins, p. 33; M. Corra, p. 74; Edward Boyle, p. 92; S. H. Swinny, p. 94; Viscount Haldane, p. 97.]

HOLL, Henry (1811–1884): wine-merchant; novelist; playwright; actor.

Henry was the fourth son of William Holl; the other three all became engravers, like their father. William was almost certainly the 'W. Holl' featured in an extensive genealogy of the Yaldwyn family, prepared by Leslie Burton Yaldwyn (died 1981) and in the possession of his daughter, Mrs Mary Cleave, of Ipswich. W. Holl married Frances, daughter of James Cowan and his wife Caroline, the fifth child of Richard Yaldwyn, of Blackdown House. The Yaldwyn connection is substantiated by a note in the copy of Henry Holl's novel, *The King's Mail* (1863), which had been donated by his grand-niece, Mrs Constance Baker, to Haslemere Museum. This note states that Henry Holl had married 'one of the Yaldwyns of Blackdown'. The Yaldwyn link would account for the novelist's intimate knowledge of the remote and little-known country round about Blackdown House, displayed in *The King's Mail*. There is, however, nothing to indicate where he was living while writing this book. William Henry Yaldwyn had sold Blackdown House in 1844 and by the 1860s was in Australia, where he died. Blackdown Cottage remained in the possession of the Yaldwyn family; William Henry's brother, General John Whitehead Yaldwyn (1803–79) may have been living there in the 1860s, and it is possible that Henry Holl lodged with him.

Although Henry was by trade a wine-merchant, he found plenty of time not only to write plays, but to act in them. His first appearance on the stage was in a performance of *King John* at Drury Lane in 1828. He started writing plays in 1833, and in 1863 changed to writing novels, with the publication of *The King's Mail* and *The Old House in Crosby Square*. These were followed by *More Secrets than One* (1864), *The White Favour* (1866) and *The Golden Bait* (1871). His novels do not appear to have been particularly successful, for he does not secure a mention in either Sutherland (1990) or Drabble (1985), although noticed by Boase (1892).

The King's Mail provides further circumstantial evidence for the Yaldwyn tie. Not only does most of the action take place in the Yaldwyn country south of Blackdown – much of it in the area known as The Quell, whose magical woods even now seem infinitely remote – but the principal character, Martin Blakeborough, is the owner of Chase House, clearly a fictional name for Blackdown House, ancestral home of the Yaldwyn family.

The King's Mail is an adventure story, set in the late eighteenth century, in which events succeed each other at a brisk pace, so that the tale retains the reader's interest throughout its three volumes. As the name suggests, the central event concerns a coach bearing the mail, which is robbed by highwaymen. Aside from such violent happenings – of which there are plenty – the main interest centres on the character of Martin Blakeborough. He is portrayed as a fundamentally decent person, led astray by the arch-villain, Captain Nicholas Upton, who thwarts every attempt by Martin to reform. Upton is introduced in the opening chapter as he rides over Hindhead and Blackdown to Chase House in order to reclaim a five hundred pound gambling debt owed by Martin, who is already having to sell off part of his estate to meet similar obligations.

It appears that Martin fell into bad company at university, dominated by the evil Upton. As a consequence, Chase House is also infested by three other young men of bad character, all addicted to large draughts of punch and to gambling, leaving them perpetually short of cash. Martin has tried to meet his debts by recourse to a Jewish money-lender, which of course only increases his difficulties. Furthermore, he has compounded the evil nexus into which he has fallen by seducing his gamekeeper's daughter, who is now pregnant. The indignant gamekeeper later stalks Martin in the woods, intending to shoot him, but misses.

Now comes the central event of the story. Early one morning, the three young men who have been staying at Chase House ride over to Liphook, where they spend the day at the local inn, injudiciously calling attention to themselves by their sottish behaviour. After dark they ride off towards Hindhead, and lie up by the Devil's Punch Bowl, the traditional site for robbing the mail. When the mail coach eventually lumbers up the hill from Witley, the gang of three is joined by a fourth masked rider. The coach is arrested and the guard knocked on the head, though not before he had discharged his blunderbuss, wounding one of the three young men in the arm. The robbers are disappointed to find that the coach does not contain the chest of bullion they had hoped to capture, and turn their attention to the solitary passenger, who proves to be the Jewish money-lender who, armed with a document from a corrupt solicitor, is coming down to claim the whole of Martin's estate. The highwaymen remove the document, and throw the old man down the Punch Bowl.

The mysterious masked figure then vanishes from the scene, and his identity is not disclosed till near the end of the story. The other three ride off towards London, pursued by an armed posse. The man with the wounded arm is captured at Godalming and presently tried, convicted and hung from the gallows at the Punch Bowl. The other two escape, and go into hiding in London. Much of the action now shifts to the shadier parts of the capital, where the gamekeeper's daughter has also gone to hide the shame of her pregnancy.

The story returns to Chase House for its climax. By then, the iniquitous Upton is in hiding from the Bow Street runners over a five thousand pound swindle involving forgery. He comes to Chase House and persuades Martin, against his better judgement, to conceal him in a secret cellar. There he finds a cache of mail bags, proving that Martin was the fourth man at the robbing of the mail coach. The Bow Street men arrive, and the treacherous Upton denounces the man who had tried to protect him. Martin rushes from the house, pursued by the runners and by the old gamekeeper, who, unknown to Martin, had been hiding in the cellar, and emerged with Upton. Martin out-runs them all except the gamekeeper. They wrestle in the wood at The Quell, and Martin hurls the old man into a stream, where he dies. This is the beginning of a general slaughter. Martin himself commits suicide in his old home by taking a large dose of laudanum. Lucas, Martin's nefarious butler – thief, and murderer of the old Jew – does the same in more dramatic fashion by jumping overboard from the convict ship which is conveying him to the colonies. On board the same ship are the only survivor of the four highway-men, and the arch-villain, Upton, who both end their days as convicts.

There are at least two unusual characters: Lucas, the snobbish butler who constantly refers to the time he was under-footman to a duke, and who is perpetually eavesdropping on Martin in the hope of learning secrets that can be turned into cash; and Mr Dormer, the rich, benevolent owner of an estate near Chase House, who is a passionate antiquarian, obsessed with the superiority of the old ways. However, the book's main concern is with action, not characterisation. The story is well constructed, and briskly told, and wholly free of the lengthy philosophical asides which often hold up the action in so many Victorian novels. Despite the unsavoury nature of most of the main characters, the book's pace and well-planned structure make for a satisfying read. It would perhaps make a pacy film.

[Boase, 1892; Randell, 1980; Reynolds, 1912.]

HOPKINS, Manley (1818–1897): marine average adjuster; consul-general; author.

The name Manley Hopkins is more commonly thought of in connection with Gerard, the Jesuit poet, but in the context of the Hilltop Writers, it is his father that we are concerned with. Though greatly inferior as a poet, he was in some ways a more interesting character than his son; Martin rightly describes him as 'a man of startling breadth of interest'.[55]

Manley founded the London-based firm of Manley Hopkins Son & Cookes, marine average adjusters. He was an expert in this field, and wrote *A Handbook of Average* (in its fourth edition by 1884) and *A Manual of Marine Insurance* (1862). His other main interest was in the Kingdom of Hawaii, then still an independent state. Manley's younger brother Charles had been employed by the Hawaiian government, and had later settled on the island. When the heir to the throne, Prince Alexander, visited England in 1849, Manley called on him and invited him to his home. They got on well, and when the Prince succeeded to the throne in 1856 as King Kamehameha IV, he appointed Manley as the Hawaiian Consul-General and Charge d' Affaires in London, a position he held until 1896. Manley, a devout Anglo-Catholic, was concerned about the ecclesiastical affairs of the island, and corresponded with Samuel Wilberforce about the appointment of a suitable bishop to take charge of the local branch of the Anglican Church. In 1865, Manley's brother Charles accompanied Queen Emma on her trip to England, and Manley entertained her to lunch in his Hampstead home. Manley's interest in the island led him to write *Hawaii: The Past, Present and Future of its Island-Kingdom* (1866), although he had never visited the place.

Another of Manley's multifarious activities was writing reviews for *The Times*. The books reviewed included two of Tennyson's major works: *In Memoriam* and *The Princess*. Martin describes the tone of the former review as 'heavily jocular'. In it, Manley reproaches Tennyson for what he considers 'the enormous exaggeration of the grief', and 'the tone of – may we say so? – amatory tenderness … Very sweet and plaintive these verses are; but who would not give them a feminine application?'[56]

During this period Manley and his wife and growing family were living at Stratford, Essex, and after 1852 in Hampstead. By 1860 the family consisted of five sons and three daughters, the eldest being Gerard. In 1886 Manley retired, and settled at Courts Hill Lodge in Haslemere. Gerard spent a fort-night with them there in August 1887. At that time he was Professor of Greek and Latin at University College Dublin, and greatly overworked, so his visit to Haslemere gave him a chance to recuperate. This seems to have been the only time he was in Haslemere; he is not likely to have written any poetry while he was there. He died of typhoid in Dublin in 1889.

Manley Hopkins and his wife Kate moved from Courts Hill Lodge between 1891 and 1894 to a new house, The Garth, in High Lane, on the lower slopes of a ridge leading up to Hindhead. The house was designed for them by J.W. Penfold, a local architect. Manley himself died there in 1897, but his widow and some of her children stayed on until her death in 1920, at the age of 99. Apart from Gerard, the other children all lived to a ripe old age. The genius of Gerard, the eldest son (1844-89), was only recognised after his death, when his friend Robert Bridges published the first edition of his

HUNTER

poems.

Another son, Lionel, was for several years Consul-General in Tientsin, and became an expert on ancient Chinese characters; he retired to The Garth to write papers about his researches, and died there in 1952 in his ninety-eighth year. Arthur and Everard both became illustrators and commercial artists; Cyril joined his father's old business. Of the daughters, none of whom married, Kate was co-author with Kate Penfold – daughter of the architect of The Garth – of *Of Bygones in Haslemere*, by 'The Two Ks' (1903, reprinted 1919), a paperback booklet of reminiscences; Millicent became an Anglican nun; and Grace was a musician of some talent. In all, the Hopkins family lived at The Garth for more than sixty years.

At Haslemere, Manley wrote *The Cardinal Numbers* (1887) and a book of poems, *Spicilegium Poeticum, A Gathering of Verses* (1892). He described this, in his introduction, as 'the gathering out of the growth of half a century; and express *(sic)* several moods and feelings experienced during the changing hours of a long life'. The book contains a variety of short poems, some religious, some for setting to music, some epigrammatic. None of them reveals the intensity of feeling, or the technical skill, evident in the poetry of his eldest son.

The Cardinal Numbers is a very odd work. Hopkins starts his introduction by a historical review of past systems of numeration, including a section in which he shows what a long and laborious process is needed in order to multiply LXXXVII by XCIII, using Roman numerals. He goes on to relate the story of a pig alleged to be able to count numbers on playing cards, and refers to Galton's observations on the ability to visualise numbers. In the main body of this small book, each of the 'cardinal', or 'digital' numbers – the numbers one to ten – is allotted a separate chapter, with a little discourse on its principal arithmetical properties. Hopkins also discusses the merits of the decimal system at some length, and gives good reasons for thinking that a duodecimal system would have been preferable, and might have been chosen, if only Nature had endowed us with six digits. The book ends with an appendix entitled 'Arithmetic Recreations', which consist of 'magic squares', and 'a curious way of doing a sum in subtraction without seeing the figures'.

[Martin, 1991.]

HUNTER, Sir Robert (1844–1913): solicitor and co-founder of the National Trust.

Hunter and his family had earlier stayed in a friend's cottage in Church Lane; this had attracted him to Haslemere, and in 1881 he bought Meadfields in Three Gates Lane, where he lived until his death there in November 1913. Although not himself an inhabitant of the uplands, a large part of his life was devoted to the preservation of their open spaces, which he must often have explored and which he obviously loved.

Hunter became solicitor to the Commons Preservation Society in 1869, and was largely responsible for safeguarding Hampstead Heath and Epping Forest, amongst other open spaces. In informal conversations with Canon H.D. Rawnsley and Octavia Hill, he conceived the idea of The National Trust, which Parliament formally established in 1895. Among the local uplands, he secured Hindhead, Ludshott and Grayswood Commons, Waggoners Wells and Marley to the Trust, for public use and enjoyment; and he defended Blackdown against those who – like Sir Jonathan Hutchinson – wanted to put a road and a refreshment room on the summit. He also protested against

Sir Robert Hunter

the enlargement of Haslemere Church, which he maintained would destroy its character.

While at Haslemere, he published *The Preservation of Open Spaces, Footpaths and Other Rights of Way* (1896); then posthumously *Gardens in Towns* (1915) and *The Movements for the Inclosure and Preservation of Open Lands* (1915).

[DNB; Rawnsley, Cornhill Magazine, 1914.[57]]

HUTCHINSON, Sir Jonathan (1828–1913): surgeon and universal medical practitioner; eclectic lecturer; founder of museums.

Hutchinson had been living and practising in London at 14 Finsbury Circus since 1856, also the year of his marriage to Jane West. His first contact with the hills of south-west Surrey was in 1863. He had stayed at the village of Frensham near Farnham on a walking holiday with his friend Hughlings Jackson, the great neurologist. They walked south from there, over the summit of Hindhead, and returned to London by train from Haslemere. Hutchinson was greatly taken with the scenery, and from 1865 to 1874 he and his wife stayed with the Newmans at Stoatley Farm, between Haslemere and Hindhead, each summer. The only exception was in 1866, when the Hutchinsons spent the summer at Hunstanton, and Tennyson and his wife spent a month at Stoatley while looking for a site for their second house.

HUTCHINSON

In 1872, Hutchinson bought an estate of 200 acres on the low hills just north of Haslemere, known at first as Weydown, later as Inval. There was an old farmhouse, which was added to extensively. Here, Hutchinson farmed, shot, entertained, and swam. It was not long before he acquired more property in the district, much of it on Hindhead – High Stoatley, Churt Wynd, Trimmer's Wood – and in Haslemere, the Half Moon Estate. He also bought Lea Park, which later came into the hands of the financier, Whittaker Wright (who created hills and lakes to form the present Witley Park), and yet more land at Petersfield, Fernhurst and Blackwater. All these purchases were regarded as investments, for he mistrusted the Stock Exchange, and never owned any shares. On these various sites he built many houses, often constructed of wood, which he regarded as much superior to bricks and mortar. He seems to have felt a sense of mission, to enable as many people as possible to enjoy the pure air and scenery of the locality. This led him to propose, at a parish meeting, that a road and a refreshment room should be built along the ridge of Blackdown. Fortunately for future generations, his proposal was firmly opposed by Sir Robert Hunter and others, leaving Sir Jonathan in a minority of three. Hutchinson's motives were clearly benevolent, but he did not grasp that readily accessible beauty spots soon cease to be beautiful.

While Hutchinson was working in London, his wife and children lived at Inval or, if that had been let to friends, then on one of the other properties. Hutchinson came down as often as possible at weekends. Although he did not finally leave London until 1911, he had for some time before that been spending an increasing amount of time at Haslemere, where the museum which he founded had become his major interest.

Hutchinson had started his medical career in the old-fashioned way, by apprenticeship to a general practitioner, and had then gone on to the now-defunct medical school at York. He completed his training at St Bartholomew's Hospital in London, and obtained his Membership of the Royal College of Surgeons. In 1856 he began private practice, and before long began to secure several hospital appointments. He became Assistant Surgeon to the London Hospital in 1859, and full Surgeon in 1863. In 1874 his growing practice justified a move to more fashionable quarters in Cavendish Square.

Although nominally just a surgeon, Hutchinson's medical practice was in fact many-sided, and covered an astonishingly wide range of specialties. If the National Health Service, as we know it today, had had to face the task of replacing him, it would have had to appoint individual consultants in surgery, ophthalmology, dermatology, venereology, tropical medicine and pathology. In all these subjects Hutchinson acquired a considerable reputation for clinical and pathological acumen, and he made some original observations – e.g. on dilatation of the pupil in head injuries – which proved to be useful to other practitioners. (His description of 'Hutchinson's teeth' in congenital syphilis must have had some diagnostic value at a time when blood tests were not available; these teeth have preserved his name in today's textbooks, if only as a footnote.) But with such an immense spread of his resources, it is not surprising that Hutchinson made no substantial contributions to fundamental knowledge in any branch of medicine.

There was, however, one area in which Hutchinson believed that he had made a discovery of major importance. He had begun to encounter cases of leprosy in London hospitals as early as 1855, all of whom had acquired the disease abroad, as it was no longer indigenous in Britain. He studied the geo-

Sir Jonathan Hutchinson

graphical distribution of the disease, and found that it was not related to climate or race, but tended to occur on islands, on the shores of continents and along the course of rivers. This suggested to him that it was in some way bound up with the eating of fish. A visit to Norway, where leprosy was prevalent, gave him a further clue: Bergen had the largest fish-market, and the largest leper home, in the world; and also – this was the key fact – it seemed that the Norwegian peasants actually preferred to eat their fish in a state of

partial decomposition. Hutchinson concluded that some agent in rotting fish must therefore be the cause of leprosy. He believed that he had now solved the problem, and the rest of his professional life from then on was devoted to accumulating more evidence to substantiate what he called 'the fish hypothesis', and thus convince the medical world of its truth.

At the time he first thought of it, it was not an unreasonable hypothesis. But when, in 1874, Hansen working in Norway, discovered the leprosy bacillus, it became possible to put Hutchinson's theory to the test. If his theory was correct, the bacillus should be present in rotting fish. A number of observers looked for it, but their results were uniformly negative. At this point, Hutchinson should have realised that his 'fish hypothesis' was no longer tenable. Instead, it seemed to fortify his determination to prove it right. In 1890, he set out with young E.W. Swanton – recently appointed curator to Hutchinson's museum at Haslemere – to South Africa, in the hope of finding more confirmatory evidence in the eating habits of the Kaffirs. The scientific community remained unconvinced, but still Hutchinson persisted, and in 1906 he published his definitive statement in the form of a book, *On Leprosy and Fish-Eating; A Statement of Facts and Explanations*. It soon found its way to the repository of forgotten medical theses.

Hutchinson may have been unlucky in his scientific research, but there is no doubt at all about his outstanding success as a teacher. Many observers testify to his almost magical ability to hold the attention of an audience, no matter what the subject of his discourse. Sir Frederick Treves, who had been a pupil of Hutchinson's at the London Hospital, left this account of his medical teaching:

> He was not eloquent, nor did he make a practice of rhetoric, but adopted a slow, quiet, solemn and modest manner which was very impressive and effective. He made his teaching interesting by the ingenuity of his arguments, by apt illustrations and vivid meta-phors, and by an occasional quaintness of expression which impressed the memory. Above all, were a solemness and simplicity of utterance, which was almost monastic ... His teaching without question profoundly influenced the surgical thought of the time, encouraged breadth of view, and discouraged narrow-mindedness.[58]

Hutchinson had given occasional lectures at his Haslemere museum from time to time. In 1893 he started to develop these into a regular course. On Sunday afternoons, he would deliver a group of four lectures, on very varied, and apparently disparate subjects, which he yet managed to link together, thus demonstrating his belief in the essential unity of all types of human knowledge. His biographer has given some of the titles of these lectures. On 12th August, for instance, he spoke on: 'Fruits and Seeds'; 'The Chalk'; 'Hebrew History'; and 'Fenelon'. A week later, it was 'Shells'; 'Geologic Time (Since the Chalk)'; 'Historic Time (The Dark Ages)'; and 'Words-worth'.

F.W. Bockett, in the course of his cycling tour of Surrey in search of literary celebrities, called in at Haslemere Museum and chanced upon one of Hutchinson's lectures. He gave the following account of the proceedings:

> A tall, kindly-looking, elderly gentleman steps in from the garden through the open doorway; you detect the humour in the dark eyes that beam smilingly upon you through spectacles. He advances towards the expectant audience, rubbing his hands together as if looking forward with keen enjoyment to the task before him. Then comes one of the most wonderful experiences that I know of. In quiet conversational tones you have a stream of knowledge poured into you in such a way that you cannot help receiving it. Under the magic touch of the man, who has mastered the great secret of imparting knowledge to others, no science is dismal, a difficult point is fixed upon the mind for ever by a stroke of sly humour that

drives the impression home, the dry facts of science are transformed into vital realities by a tender reference to human sufferings, human love, and human fears and aspirations.

As time went on, Hutchinson tended to introduce more religious themes into his lectures. He had been brought up as a Quaker, but his religious opinions had been much modified by the implications of Darwin's theory, which he had strongly supported, without fully understanding it. His modification of orthodox Christianity has been described in the notes on religion in Section Two. The central feature was the belief that parents' qualities were passed on to their children, and in this way constituted a sort of immortality. In Hutchinson's own words, 'The change of life from parent to child is only in a sort of larger sense changing one's clothes.' One of his Sunday lectures was entitled 'The Laws of Inheritance'. It was summarised in the *Surrey Advertiser* for 11th August 1900:

Mr Hutchinson believed that not only the natural qualities of the parents, but also those that they had acquired before the birth of a child were inherited by the child. Such being the case, it was incumbent on all to improve themselves, and the world in which they lived, knowing full well that all they could acquire would be transmitted to their offspring.

It was an ingenious, and probably quite original notion – Hutchinson spoke of it as 'my great idea' – and gave much comfort to its originator. However, it did not find favour with scientists since it relied on the discredited belief that acquired characteristics can be inherited. It also involved too great a departure from orthodoxy to please religious folk. When Hutchinson gave a similar course of lectures at Selby – his Yorkshire birthplace, where he had also founded a museum – there was a considerable uproar. Local ministers thundered against him in their sermons, and the local newspapers did likewise in their editorials. Although there were similar protests in Haslemere, they were more muted, possibly due to the influence of Revd Aitken, the broad-minded rector who often attended Hutchinson's lectures, and praised him in the parish magazine.

Finally, there were Hutchinson's three museums. The first was his pathological museum in London. It started as a purely personal collection of specimens and drawings, but became institutionalised in a 'Polyclinic' in Chenies Street, in 1898. After Hutchinson's death, the contents of the museum were purchased by the Johns Hopkins Medical School, and removed to Baltimore.

The Haslemere Educational Museum started its career in 1888 in two barns at Inval. They were filled with specimens from any source that came to hand; some were collected locally, others on holidays, others again were bought in sale-rooms. They were arranged according to a formula on which Hutchinson set much store: 'Space-for-Time', an impressive-sounding title for the simple notion of arranging specimens in a graded sequence, from the oldest to the most recent. In the Inval and subsequent museums there were two such series: one in geological, the other in historical time. In 1895 the collection was moved to a purpose-built home, of wooden construction, in Museum Hill, and then in 1926 to its present home in the High Street. E.W. Swanton was appointed curator in 1897, and retired in 1948. The Museum Hill building no longer exists, but F.W. Bockett left this account of the interior, which he visited in 1900:

> At your own sweet will you enter a comfortable reading-room, the walls of which are lined with hundreds of shelves containing over 7,000 carefully selected books ... Tired of reading, you walk across the courtyard into the museum, which is happily not a museum as such dry-as-dust institutions are generally known, but a place where a man may learn something in the pleasantest and easiest manner. [59]

In 1898 Hutchinson bought the Public Rooms at Selby, and with Swanton's help converted them into a museum and lecture hall. There was never as much public support for the museum there as there was at Haslemere, but it managed to survive.

Hutchinson was clear about the purpose of his museums. They were not there to be mere repositories for locally-collected odds and ends. They were to be specifically educational, and it did not matter where the specimens came from, so long as they told a story. At the same time he recognised that a museum needs the presence of a teacher, just as the teacher needs the museum to illustrate his remarks. The combination of Sir Jonathan and his museum was an example of a happy symbiosis. The two harnessed together were an undoubted success, but he probably underestimated the contribution of his own outstanding prowess as a lecturer. Without the presence of Sir Jonathan to bring it alive, the impact of 'Space-for-Time' is noticeably muted. Swanton and his successors have, however, amply fulfilled Sir Jonathan's intention that the museum should be an enduring centre for the distribution of knowledge. Yet they found they could not altogether ignore the local context, as he apparently wished. It seems obvious that, if an institution is to retain the interest of the local population, it must put particular emphasis on building up a body of knowledge of the local environment and of local history, as well as providing access to the general body of human knowledge.

As well as his book on leprosy, Hutchinson published a large textbook on syphilis, *Illustrations of Clinical Surgery* (1877–78, 2 vols), and a large number of articles on a great variety of medical subjects. For eleven years, he edited *Archives of Surgery*, and wrote most of the articles in it himself. He delivered many addresses on even more miscellaneous non-medical themes, some of which were subsequently printed {there is a collection of these in Haslemere Museum). His ideas on the furnishing of museums were set out in *The Centuries: A chronological Synopsis of History as the 'Space-for-Time' Method*, 1897. But probably his most enduring monument is the Haslemere Educational Museum, which Bockett described in 1901 as 'without a counterpart in the wide world'.

The words on his tomb in Haslemere churchyard fittingly sum up his character:

A Man of Hope and Forward-looking Mind.

[DNB; Hutchinson, H. 1947.]

KER, David (1841–1914): novelist and war correspondent.

Ker lived at Chesham Cottage, Grayswood Road, Haslemere, from 1899 until he moved to Tileden (or Tilden) Cottage, Grove Road, Beacon Hill, Hindhead, between 1911 and 1913.

He wrote a long series of adventure stories, mainly intended for boys. The titles provide a good idea of their nature, e.g. *The Wild Horsemen of the Pampas* (1875); *Among the Dark Mountains, Or Cast Away in Sumatra* (1907); *A Knight of Honour* (1901); *Ilderim the Afghan* (1903); *Lost among the White Africans* (1909); *Blown away from the Land* (1911); *Under the Flag of France* (1912); *The Last of the Sea Kings* (1913). Some were based on his own experiences as a war correspondent.

[Sillick.]

KING, Joseph (1860–1943): MP; reviver of peasant arts.

King and his wife Maude, whom he had married in 1887, came to Lower Birtley, Grayswood, in 1894. In 1901 they moved to Sandhouse in Witley, and in 1922 to Hill Farm, Camelsdale. It was to the last of these that George Bernard Shaw came in 1930, to deliver an address commiserating with Arthur Ponsonby on his elevation to the peerage. After Maude's death, King and his second wife moved to Brownholme, Tilford. All these houses were situated in the hill country round Haslemere.

In 1894 the Kings founded the Wheel and Spindle Guild. In 1897 this became the Haslemere Weaving Industry, and moved to the Foundry Meadow. In the same year the Blounts had formed the Peasant Arts Society, in cooperation with King and his wife. Next year the Weaving House was built in the King's Road, and the peasant arts movement was firmly established in Haslemere. It flourished up until 1914, but after the First World War it never regained its early vigour, and as its founders aged and died, so the movement faltered and gradually petered out in the 1920s and 1930s. Haslemere Museum bought the collection of objects amassed by the Peasant Arts Society, and King was appointed its honorary curator.

King's main career was in politics. He entered Parliament as a Liberal, but

Joseph King

later converted to Labour. However, as far as the cultural life of Haslemere is concerned, his greatest contribution may well have been his influence in persuading Arnold Dolmetsch to settle in the Grayswood Road in 1917, and introduce the community to the delights of early music.

King was the author of *The School Manager* (1903); *The Collapse of Germany* (1923); *Peasant Arts* (1927); and a pamphlet, printed in 1913, *Filius Nullius* (Nobody's Child), in order to promote the Bill he introduced in Parliament on behalf of abandoned children. This was probably his most important political action.

[*Haslemere Herald*, 28th August 1943.]

KING, Maude Egerton, née Hine (1867–1927): author and reviver of peasant arts.

Maude was the youngest of the three daughters of Henry Hine, all of whom married men associated with the peasant arts movement. She married Joseph King in 1887, and they came to Grayswood in 1894. Maude learnt spinning and weaving from a Swedish teacher, and then instructed some of the local girls. With Miss Catherine Hird-Jones she ran the Haslemere Weaving Industry.

It seems from her brother-in-law, Greville MacDonald's, account that Maude was the real driving-force behind the peasant arts movement. She was the founder and editor of *The Vineyard*, a journal which might be looked on as the cement of the movement. She also found time to write short stories and novels.

Considered realistically, the movement seems in retrospect a belated and futile attempt, by a bunch of middle-class cranks, to roll back the Industrial

LE GALLIENNE

Revolution. But at the time, it must have inspired its adherents with a sense of doing something worthwhile, and it did bring them into contact with some of the working people of the countryside, who were largely ignored by the rest of the immigrant intelligentsia – except insofar as they ministered to their domestic comforts. Maude King's books, in particular, display a genuine sympathy with the life and labours of the country folk.

Maude King was the author of *The Country Heart and Other Stories* (1911); *Mrs Everywoman's Thoughts Today* (1943); *A Cottage Wife's Calendar* (undated).

[Macdonald, 1927.]

LE GALLIENNE, Richard (1866–1947): novelist and poet.

Le Gallienne's first acquaintance with the Surrey hills was in 1894. His brief but happy marriage to a Liverpool waitress had just ended with Mildred's tragic death from typhoid, at the cottage in Brentford where they had lived for the past year. It was a devastating blow, and Richard had come to Grant and Nellie Allen at Hindhead for consolation. He found Hindhead 'very soothing', and liked 'this heathery hill-top with thirty miles of view everywhere around us and a great infinite

Richard Le Gallienne

bracing sky'. He returned in 1895, and stayed at the Seven Thorns inn, on the Portsmouth Road, where he was joined by Julie Norregard, a young Danish journalist with whom he had now fallen madly in love. He then decided to make a permanent home at Hindhead, and after much searching found Moorcroft, almost opposite the Grant Allens – 'the sweetest little house you ever saw'. He rented this furnished, and at first was delighted with the cottage and its situation: 'It is a quite wonderful place,' he told his mother, 'so wild and bracing. We are perched right on top of a hill with nothing but hills of bracken and heather and fir-trees about us – wonderful views from every window – and nothing but a couple of cottages smoking far down the valley. Talk about "Hill-Top" novels – this is the place for them.' He set up a small wooden chalet in the garden, and began to write *The Quest of the Golden Girl*, destined to become his best-known work.

In March 1896, whilst engaged on this book, Richard had a visit from H.G. Wells, who flattered him by saying that everybody was waiting for 'a

LE GALLIENNE

new big book' by him. The *Golden Girl* was duly finished by July 1896, and published on 12th February 1897. On the same day he married Julie. The book was well received by the public of the day, and sold in its thousands. A hundred years later, however, the tide has turned against the affected prose used by writers such as Le Gallienne, and the book is now virtually impossible to read. It is a whimsical story about a young man's walking tour in search of the ideal mate. In the course of his travels, which take him through the Surrey countryside, he stops off at a 'strange old haunted forest', which Thomas Wright identified as the woods round Waggoners Wells, at Grayshott.

Moorcroft, which at first had seemed so idyllic, was rented furnished. But by the end of 1896 Le Gallienne could stand no longer the constant complaints of his two landladies about the inkstains that he was inflicting on their furniture. So he acquired Kingswood Chase, 'a medium-sized brick house in a pine-hidden hollow, at the bottom of Kingswood Lane'. The Moorcroft chalet was dismembered and re-erected in the new garden; this was where Thomas Wright interviewed him later in 1897.[60] At the same time Le Gallienne rented two rooms in Chancery Lane in London. He was not really at home on the breezy hilltops, and was better suited to city life. Kingswood Chase is in fact situated in a dank and gloomy valley – about the only place on the plateau where it is possible to escape the invigorating air. And when, bicycling round the local lanes in 1899, Le Gallienne came across The Old Manor at Chiddingfold, he found 'a feeling of peace such as I never had for a moment at Waggoners Wells'. But in the autumn of 1900, he departed for the United States, where he spent a year on his own. He rejoined Julie in London, but by 1903, she had had enough of Richard's restless wanderings, not to speak of his infidelities and his drunken bouts. So she returned his ring, and they were divorced in 1911. Richard then married Irma Hinton Perry.

While living at Hindhead, Le Gallienne wrote *The Quest of the Golden Girl* (1897); *If I were God* (1897); *The Romance of Zion Chapel* (1898); *Young Lives* (1899). He was also a contributor to the *Yellow Book*, and was active in *fin de siècle* circles. His works were often described as 'Wilde-and-water'. In 1900, he wrote *Sleeping Beauties and other prose fancies*, a book of essays chiefly notable for its devastating attack on Edmund Gosse, described – with some justice – as 'Tabby', for his combination of soft words and sharp claws.[61]

Flora Thompson encountered Le Gallienne while he was living at Kingswood Chase, and described how he 'raced about the parish at all hours on his bicycle with his halo of long, fair hair uncovered and his almost feminine slightness and grace set off by a white silk shirt, big artist's bow tie and velvet knickerbockers'.[62]

[DNB; Drabble; Sutherland; Whittington-Egan & Smerdon, 1960; Mix, 1960.]

LEWES, George Henry (1817–1878): polymath.

Lewes came to Brookbank, at Shottermill, with Marian Evans (George Eliot) – not legally his wife, but known as Mrs Lewes – on 2nd May 1871, while their London home, The Priory, was undergoing alterations. He had been down to Haslemere on 31st March to inspect the cottage, which they were renting from Mrs Gilchrist. (He had intended to go there on the previous day, but had missed the train for a characteristic reason: he had become absorbed in Hegel's *Logik* in the station waiting-room.) On 6th April he and Marian went down together to engage Mrs Garland as a servant there.

At that time, Marian was working on *Middlemarch*, while Lewes was writing what he hoped would be his magnum opus, *Problems of Life and Mind*. Both were busy, but they found time for many walks in the country-side, which they both enjoyed. Lewes's journal mentions many of these. One typical week, for instance, began on Monday 22nd May with a 'three hours' ramble over Marley Hill'; on Tuesday, they went to Haslemere, and then Marley again; on Wednesday, they walked to the Devil's Punch Bowl; Thursday's ramble was interrupted by rain; on Friday, it was Marley again; on Saturday, they 'walked towards Liphook through lanes'. Invigorated by these strenuous excursions, Lewes continued his studies of the works of philosophers: Haeckel on Monday; Whewell, Comte, and more Haeckel on Tuesday; on Wednesday, Duhamel's *Méthode générale* and Hirn's *Théorie de la chaleur*; Hirn again on Thursday, accompanied by Opzoomer's *Methode der Wissenschaft*; Stewart's *Physics*, with more Comte, Haeckel and Hirn on Friday, when he also found time to write to Blackwood, Locker and Darwin; he finished the week with Todhunter's *Calculus* on Saturday. On most days he also notes that he had been working on *Problems of Life and Mind*. The rigorous regime evidently suited him, and Marian was able to report to her friend Barbara Bodichon on 17th June 1871: 'George is glori-ously well, and studying, writing, walking, eating and sleeping with equal vigour. He is enjoying the life here immensely. Our country could hardly be surpassed in its particular kind of beauty – perpetual undulation of heath and copse, and clear views of hurrying water, with here and there a grand pine wood, steep wood-clothed promontories, and gleaming pools.'[63]

Neither of the Leweses had much inclination, or time, for social activities while they were at Shottermill, for they both had serious work to do. But at the end of July, Marian reported to John Blackwood that 'Tennyson, who is one of the "hill-folk" about here, has found us out.'[64] It happened one day, when Lewes was returning from London, where he had been to see how the work on The Priory was progressing, that he found himself sharing a compartment with Tennyson. Tennyson drove him back to Brookbank in his carriage, and came in to be introduced to Marian. A week later, he called again with his son Hallam. There must have been discussion at Aldworth about the propriety of a visit by Emily Tennyson to the Leweses, ending in a decision that the irregularity of their union could be overlooked. Tennyson told Mangles that Marian 'had been received by Lady Houghton and others. Why not? She had done nothing morally wrong'. The Leweses had asked him to read *Guinevere* to them. Tennyson had been surprised by their choice 'under the circumstances', but complied, with the result that Lewes wept copiously[65] (Emily Tennyson, in a letter to Hallam, said it was Marian who did the weeping).

After 1871, the Leweses lived exclusively in London until in 1877 they returned to the Surrey hills when they bought The Heights, at Witley. There they learnt to play tennis, and exchanged visits with Tennyson. Lewes's only writing during the time he was at Witley was an essay, still relevant today, entitled 'On the Dread and Dislike of Science' and published in *Fortnightly Review*, June 1878. But by 1878 he was a sick man, and he died at the end of that year, at the age of sixty-one.

A list of Lewes's published works gives some indication of the range of his interests. His first book was a treatise on Spanish drama (1846). This was followed by two indifferent novels, and a tragedy, *The Noble Heart*, in which Lewes himself took a part. Then in 1855 *The Life and Works of Goethe* appeared, and established Lewes's reputation, both in England and in Germany. Next he wrote *A Biographical History of Philosophy* in four volumes (1857, and later editions); it was well received. Lewes then turned his attention to science. He would like to have been accepted as a scientist, but by the second half of the nineteenth century it was becoming difficult for an amateur to be taken seriously by the scientific establishment. Lewes's science was of the Philip Gosse variety, as indicated by the title of his book: *Sea-side Studies at Ilfracombe, Tenby, the Scilly Isles and Jersey* (1858). Like Gosse's books, it was a mixture of popular exposition of the wonders of the sea-shore, and technical accounts of the morphology of the creatures encountered there. Lewes was nervous about the reception of his work by professional scientists, but was much relieved when he received a complimentary letter from T.H. Huxley, who had been severely critical of some of Lewes's earlier efforts at popular science. He gained further confidence from the reception of his next book, *The Physiology of Common Life* (1859–60). This was used as a textbook by Edinburgh medical students, and is said to have persuaded young Ivan Pavlov to give up the study of theology in favour of physiology. Huxley was again supportive.

Finally, there was *Problems of Life and Mind*, which occupied Lewes all the time he was at Shottermill. However, the first of its five volumes was not ready for publication until 1873. And then the faithful Blackwood declined to publish it; he objected on religious grounds, particularly disliking the tone of 'an anecdote about the Author of Creation'. Volumes 1 and 2, entitled *The Foundations of a Creed*, were published by Trübner in 1874 and 1875. Their subject matter was more abstract than that of most of Lewes's works, and attempted to define which subjects were admissible objects of scientific study. The main point was to show that the relationship of brain and mind, which was to be examined in the later volumes, although outside direct experience, was nevertheless a legitimate subject for the application of the methods of science. The text was diffuse and difficult, and it was not well received. Volume 3, *The Physical Basis of Mind*, came out in 1877. It was easier to read, since it dealt with a more concrete subject; but still did not please the critics. In November the following year Lewes died. The two final volumes, *The Study of Psychology* and *Mind as a Function of the Organism*, were completed by Marian from his notes, and published in 1879.

The range and quality of Lewes's published *oeuvre* can leave no-one in doubt that he was the possessor of an intellect of quite exceptional calibre, and that he had the ability to set down his thoughts in a lucid and graceful style. All contemporary observers are agreed that he was the most entertaining of companions, usually coupling their remarks with a less complimentary comment on his physical appearance. Charles Eliot Norton, the American scholar, described his arrival for one of the couple's gatherings at The Priory, in St John's Wood:

> Lewes received us at the door with characteristic animation; he looks and moves like an old-fashioned French barber or dancing-master, very ugly, very vivacious, very entertaining.

The young Henry James sat next to Lewes at a dinner; he was greatly entertained by his anecdotes, 'mostly in French', but had to agree with Mrs Kemble's assessment that 'he looked as if he had been gnawed by rats'.

But for all his own outstanding accomplishments, Lewes's greatest contribution to literature has to be his nurturing of the frail genius of George Eliot. Her timidity and lack of self-confidence were such that it is quite possible that without his encouragement she might never have published anything at all. And any critical remarks about her books were enough to discourage her from writing any further novels. Without Lewes she would have had great problems in coping with the harsh world of publishing. He negotiated all her contracts, and made sure that her work received its due reward.

[DNB; Ashton, 1991.]

MANGLES, James Henry (1832–1884): horticulturist; diarist; barrister and railway director.

Mangles features here for one book only: his diary. In this he recorded his conversations with Tennyson in 1870–72. It did not appear in print until the centenary of his death, and then only as the slimmest of volumes. But it is important, because it provides a picture of Tennyson when he was, so to speak, 'off-duty', behaving as a friendly neighbour, rather than as a great poet, and the most eminent of all Victorians.

Although Mangles tells us a lot about Tennyson, he says little or nothing about himself. His disjointed career makes him somewhat of an enigma. His father, Charles Edward Mangles, had been the captain of an East Indiaman, but later established himself at Poyle, near Tongham in Surrey, and became Chairman of the London and South-Western Railway. James Henry was the eldest of a family of ten. There was a family tradition of service in India, and James Henry was educated for the service of the East India Company at its College at Haileybury. He duly sailed for India in 1852, and in due course became a Joint Magistrate and Deputy Collector in Bengal. But in 1858 he returned home on furlough, got married and resigned from the Company's service, for reasons unknown. In 1859, he enrolled as a law student at the Inner Temple, and was called to the Bar in 1862. He had chambers in the Temple, and featured as a special pleader on the South-East Circuit from 1864 to 1882. Yet all the while his heart was set on the cultivation and hybridisation of Himalayan rhododendrons.

James Simmons, the Shottermill diarist, recorded on 11th September 1859, that Mangles had bought Valewood Park from Mrs Splatt, and had attended church with his family on the last two Sundays. The railway had come to Haslemere in January of that year – an event which Mangles would have been well aware of, owing to his father's connections. He was then still a law student at the Inner Temple, so would need easy access to London. But his special reason for choosing to live at Valewood was that he had seen that it would be an ideal place in which to exercise his passionate desire to grow and hybridise rhododendrons.

Mangles's published works consist of a posthumous collection of his numerous articles on the cultivation of rhododendrons (1917); a long essay in the *Contemporary Review* (1873-74, vol. 23) against nationalization of the railways (he had by then become a director of the London and South-Western Railway); and his diary. The diary came to light only in 1961, when Mangles's great-granddaughter, Mrs Iris Norman, and her husband discovered it in an outhouse at Valewood known as 'the old laundry house'. It had been written in an old notebook which had previously been used as a scrapbook, and was in a deplorably damp condition when the Normans found it; but they dried it with great care. Mrs Norman tried unsuccessfully to find a publisher, but was forced eventually to put it up for sale at auction. It was bought by the University of Ohio in 1971, and very ably edited by Professor Earl A. Knies for publication as *Tennyson at Aldworth: The Diary of James Henry Mangles* (Ohio University Press, 1984).

The diary opens in August 1870, when Mangles lunched at Aldworth with his wife Isabella and his sister Agnes. He found Tennyson walking on the terrace with James Knowles, the architect of the house. They discussed the garden and the view, and Tennyson made his customary complaint that 'that fellow' – Knowles – had made him have such a large house, when all he had wanted was a simple cottage. They adjourned to the study, where they had more conversation, and then joined Mangles's wife and sister for lunch, at which Tennyson's wife, sister and two sons were also present. After lunch they all set off for Tennyson's favourite walk through the woods to Foxholes, where a spring emerges from the eastern flank of Blackdown. Discussion continued on a wide variety of subjects.

This first entry shows that from the start the two men were on remarkably easy terms; Tennyson, for instance, was quite happy to discuss at some length intimate details about the itching sore on his leg. Later conversations showed that Mangles was sufficiently familiar with the current literary scene to be able to discuss most topics on not far from equal terms, and was in no way intimidated by the poet's formidable reputation. Mangles respected Tennyson as a great poet and as a man, and wanted to hear his views on the important questions of the day; but he was also quick to note his human foibles. He leaves us with a picture of a great and important, but also very human figure.

Henry Mangles

Mangles's initial visit was returned a few days later, when Tennyson walked over Blackdown to his house at Valewood. When exploring the area in the previous springtime, he had come upon Valewood and admired Mangles's rhododendrons, but beat a retreat as he feared he was trespassing. In all, Tennyson paid six visits to Valewood, mostly coming on foot over the shoulder of Blackdown; sometimes losing the way among the maze of small paths. Mangles visited Aldworth some eleven times in all, mostly walking across Blackdown to get there. The diary ends with an account of two meetings with Tennyson in London in 1872.

Mangles's main preoccupation, however, continued to be his increasing collection of rhododendrons. He was on friendly terms with both Sir William and Sir Joseph Hooker at Kew, and successfully established many of the species brought back by the latter from Sikkim. But they tended to be too delicate for the English climate, and so Mangles concentrated on growing them under protection in what he called his 'cathedral house', and then

METHUEN

hybridising them with hardier varieties. In this way he hoped to breed a race of hardy rhododendrons with the beautiful flowers of the Sikkim species. In this he was largely successful, and there are now collections of 'Mangles rhododendrons' at both the Saville Gardens and Wisley. But Mangles's death at the early age of 52 sadly prevented him from seeing many of his best hybrids in bloom.

Mangles published twenty-three articles on rhododendron culture in the horticultural press, all of which were re-published as a book by the Rhododendron Society in 1917, with an introduction by Gerald Loder. The Lindley Library of the Royal Horticultural Society also possesses a typewritten volume by Mangles, entitled *Rhododendron Notes*. In his compendious book on the genus (*Rhododendrons*, 1917), J.G. Millais described Mangles – without evident irony – as 'the High Priest of the Rhododendron Cult'.

Mangles died of abdominal cancer at his home on 24th August 1884, and is buried at Lurgashall. His wife, Isabella, and daughter, Alice, continued to live at Valewood House, and remained on friendly terms with the Tennysons and the Allinghams; when Alfred died, Hallam's wife Audrey wrote to Mrs Mangles inviting her to view his corpse. Alice later married William Daffarn, and stayed on at Valewood House. Mrs Norman recalled that both Alice and her daughter Daphne – Mrs Norman's mother – were among the select band of ladies who, like Alys Buckton and Grace Gilchrist, had sat on Tennyson's knee as small children.

[Knies,1984]

METHUEN, Sir Algernon Methuen Marshall, Baronet, né Stedman (1856–1924): author; publisher.

Algernon was the son of Dr John Buck Stedman MRCS (1820–1902), of Harts Lane, Godalming, part of a large family in the area and related to the Simmonses of Shottermill. He graduated in classics at Oxford in 1878, and wrote his first book – on Oxford – in the same year. He then took up schoolmastering, starting his own school, High Croft, in 1880 at Milford. There he wrote his own textbooks, which were printed locally under the name of Stedman. But in 1889 he abandoned teaching and set up his own publishing firm, under the name of Methuen. One of his first authors was Revd S. Baring-Gould, who later wrote *The Broom Squire* at Stedman's suggestion. The firm also took over the publication of Stedman's school textbooks. Its first big success came with the publication of Kipling's *Barrack Room Ballads* in 1892, followed by Marie Corelli's *Barabbas*. These two books established Methuens as major publishers.

Methuens' office was in London, but by 1897, Stedman was living at Shottermill and bought Honeyhanger, on the road to Hindhead. He was then still using the surname Stedman, but in August 1899 changed it to Methuen. By 1903, he was installed at New Place, built for him in Farnham Lane on the lower slopes of Hindhead, to the design of C.F.A. Voysey.

Pevsner thought it was one of the architect's best; the stones of which it was built are believed to have come from the old Christ's Hospital. The garden, too, was one of the best in Haslemere; Gertrude Jekyll is said to have had a hand in its design. Methuen was still living in Haslemere at the time of his death in 1924, and is buried there.

Methuen's habit was to spend mid-week with his publishing firm in London, with long weekends at Haslemere. He was now able to turn his attention to politics and to writing. In the former he was unsuccessful, for he failed to get into Parliament as a Liberal. As Stedman, his Latin, Greek and French readers still sold well, and as Methuen he wrote several political books: *The Tragedy of South Africa* (1905), defending the actions of the Boers; and *A Simple Plan for a New House of Lords* (1911). He compiled *An Anthology of English Verse* (1921) and *Shakespeare to Hardy* (1922); and also wrote a small book, *An Alpine ABC*, about his favourite hobby of rock-gardening.

[DNB; Duffy, 1989.]

MURRAY, George Gilbert (1866–1957): classicist.

Murray had been appointed Professor of Greek at Glasgow in 1889. He was a magnificent teacher, but it was hard work, and in 1899, as the DNB puts it, 'exhaustion was mistaken for a fatal disease, and he retired to Churt', where he lived at Barford, to the north-west of the village, which lies on the northern slopes of Hindhead. He remained there until 1905, when he became a Fellow of New College, Oxford, and three years later, Regius Professor of Greek. Between 1901 and 1909 the Oxford University Press was publishing his much-admired edition of *Euripedes*. His *Andromache* was performed by the Stage Society in London in 1901. Soon after coming to Churt in 1899, he was elected an honorary member of the Haslemere Microscope and Natural History Society, and read a paper on 'Some Conflicting National Ideals'. In 1900, he read one of his free – altogether too free, some thought – translations of Euripedes in elegant rhymed verse to the Society. Bernard Shaw was present, and moved the vote of thanks with a characteristic two-edged Shavian quip: he felt that Murray 'was reading one of his own original compositions, and being so generous as to give Euripedes the credit for it'.

Murray was Shaw's model for Adolphus Cusins in *Major Barbara* – as his mother-in-law, Lady Carlisle, was for Lady Britomart – and he was frequently consulted during the writing of the play in the early 1900s. Before moving to Barford, Murray and his wife had spent some time at the nearby village of Tilford in 1898, from where they engaged in a lengthy correspondence with Shaw about The Fox and Pelican, the Grayshott pub which Shaw and others were trying to construct as a sort of community centre, in which drinking would be permitted though not encouraged. Both Murray and his wife, Lady Mary, were strict teetotallers, and thought that no alcoholic drinks should be served there.

Gilbert Murray

Bertrand Russell was another great admirer of Murray's translations of the Greek classics, and often corresponded with him about matters of aesthetics and ethics. Murray had also known Rudyard Kipling as a boy, and renewed the acquaintance in later life. He then found him 'ridiculously like his books, and with a nice, quasi-Irish instinct for exaggeration'; this came into play when he assured Murray that 'in Hindhead, you know, *simply every day* you meet escaped kangaroos going round, frightening the farmers'. Murray tried shooting at Kipling's private rifle-range, and advised him about the Mithraic rites which feature in *Puck of Pook's Hill*.

Jane Harrison, a classical scholar from Cambridge, and an admirer, often stayed at Barford. At the end of her final visit, in 1904, she felt, she wrote to Lady Mary Murray, 'like a dove leaving a nice kind ark'. Beatrice Webb, who had met her on a visit to Friday's Hill in 1902, did not warm to her: 'a bracing personality and workmanlike scholar, not attractive either mentally or physically, a somewhat narrow mind ... she has poisoned herself with tea and tobacco'.[66] Bertrand Russell remarked that Jane was 'envied for her power of enduring excess in whisky and cigarettes'.[67] It is a remarkable tribute to the tolerance of the abstemious Murrays that they were prepared to overlook these personal habits.

In 1903, Murray accompanied Jane Harrison on an expedition to decipher some Greek tablets at Naples. On the way they stayed for a few days with Bernard and Mary Berenson at *I Tatti*, their splendidly appointed Italian villa near Florence, and this led to a small incident, recorded in the letters of three of the parties concerned, revealing the extent of the Berensons' dilettantism in the realm of literature.

The Berensons were enchanted with Murray, who was almost universally liked. For his part, Murray was impressed by Bernard's encyclopaedic knowledge of Renaissance art, but distrusted the 'over-brilliant, exotic society' of *I Tatti*. All went well until one evening they played a game known to the Berensons as 'The Urn'. In this, each person read aloud passages from their favourite authors; the company would then discuss them, and if they were not approved of, the piece of paper bearing the author's name would be thrown into an urn. Murray's disclosure that he admired Dickens's novels caused some unease, but this was nothing to the shock evoked by the revelation that he ranked Tennyson as one of the greatest of English poets. Writing to her mother – Hannah Pearsall Smith – at Friday's Hill, Mary Berenson described how 'a hush of horror fell upon us, as if someone had thrown a smoking bomb into the midst of the company ... I went to fetch a volume of [Tennyson's] poems. This I handed to Murray and asked him to read some of the "real poetry". Mother! he read *Come into the garden, Maud*! '[68]

Throughout this incident, Murray remained his usual tolerant and amiable self, but it was all too much for Jane Harrison who, unable to bear the sight of Wordsworth and Tennyson being ruthlessly discarded into the Urn, retired upstairs and 'slightly wept with indignation at the impiety and preposterousness of the whole proceeding'. According to her biographer, she paced up and down, exclaiming: 'The fops! the insolent fops!'[69] Even Murray confessed afterwards that the visit had been somewhat of a strain. But Berenson was so taken with Murray that – he told Bertrand Russell – 'even I could forgive his liking Dickens and Tennyson'.[70]

At the time of Murray's visit, Bernard Berenson was already acknowledged as an outstanding authority on Renaissance art. But in literary matters, the Berensons' arrogant dismissiveness, which so upset Jane Harrison, is evident in the little privately-circulated journal which they edited together with Logan Pearsall Smith, Mary's brother. It dealt with both art and literature; but the only poets deemed worthy of mention in its pages were Shakespeare, Milton and Keats. Called *The Golden Urn*, it announced that it was 'published by certain people of leisure and curiosity, who have thought it worth while to print for their own entertainment some impressions of art and life, some experiments in letters ... copies will be sent – not without a feeling, or at least an affectation of diffidence – to a few fastidious people'. Published in Fiesole in 1897–98, it only survived for three numbers.

[DNB; Wilson, 1987.]

NETTLESHIP, Edward FRS (1845–1913): ophthalmologist, dermatologist and geneticist.

Nettleship qualified in veterinary surgery in 1867 and in human surgery the following year. Simultaneously, he began the study of ophthalmology at Moorfields Eye Hospital. He worked part-time with Jonathan Hutchinson there, and also at the Blackfriars Skin Hospital. Early in his career he made his mark in dermatology by his original description of urticaria pigmentosa, but later he devoted himself to ophthalmology, and was appointed to the staff of St Thomas' and Moorfields Hospitals as a consultant. At the latter, he was a colleague of Jonathan Hutchinson. He gained a considerable reputation as a clinical investigator, surgeon and teacher, and also built up a large private practice.

Edward Nettleship

One of his patients was W.E. Gladstone, from whose right eye he removed a cataract in 1894. The operation was initially a success, but then came a relapse and it looked as if Nettleship might have to re-operate. However, he wisely refrained, and after some months, and with the help of four pairs of spectacles, Gladstone regained perfect sight. He was duly grateful, and spoke warmly of Nettleship as 'a man who knew what he was about'. However, when, two years later, Nettleship was called in to pronounce upon Queen Victoria's cataracts, she described him as 'cold, harsh, abrupt and unsympathetic'.[71]

In 1902 he gave all this up, and retired to Hindhead to devote the rest of his life to a scientific study of the genetics of eye diseases. But long before he retired he had spent a good deal of time in the district. In 1888, he is listed as having a house (unnamed) at Hindhead; after 1891, this is named as Nutcombe-on-Hill (now Nutcombe Hill, in Hindhead Road). In 1913, he moved to Longdown Hollow, also in Hindhead Road, where he died in the same year.

Nettleship was well integrated into local society. He was a subscriber to the Haslemere Microscope and Natural History Society from 1893 onwards, and a member of the Grayshott and District Refreshment House Association, donating some land for a garden for The Fox and Pelican. His wife Elizabeth was the sister of R.S. Whiteway, the retired Bengal civil servant and historian of the Portuguese colonial empire, who lived a little lower down the Hindhead Road.

Nettleship's study of the inheritance of eye diseases was a long and laborious task, which broke new ground in clinical genetics. It earned him the Fellowship of the Royal Society in 1912, but was only published after his death, in a memorial volume, *Anomalies and Diseases of the Eye*, in the *Treasury of Human Inheritance* (1922).

[DNB; *Lancet*, 1913.ii. p. 1354; Branford, 1994.[71]]

NEVILL, Lady Dorothy, née Walpole (1826–1913): horticulturist, society hostess and autobiographist.

Lady Dorothy was the fifth and youngest child of Horatio Walpole, 3rd Earl of Orford, and was proud to count Horace Walpole and Sir Robert Walpole among her ancestors. At the age of 20, an encounter in a summerhouse with a young gentleman with aristocratic connections but a poor reputation, led to a scandal which was only resolved by a hasty marriage to a man twenty years her senior. Reginald Nevill was a cousin of sorts, and had inherited a comfortable fortune from a Walpole uncle. For Lady Dorothy, it turned out to be a very satisfactory arrangement. Reginald allowed his wife to pursue her own interests, while he followed his; meanwhile, he provided her with whatever cash she needed.

The Nevills had of course their town house in Mayfair, and in 1851 they bought in addition an estate called Dangstein at Rogate, near Petersfield. The house and large garden stood on another branch of the same Greensand formation as that of the hills round Haslemere. Here Lady Dorothy was able to indulge her passion for horticulture by making a garden that was much written about. Its main feature was a collection of exotic plants, grown in an array of twelve hot-houses, exceeded only by that at Kew, with which plants were often exchanged. There was also – and still is – an extensive collection of fine shrubs and trees, and a magnificent view of the South Downs. But when Reginald died in 1878, Dorothy had to sell Dangstein, and move to a smaller estate at Stillyans, near Heathfield in East Sussex, which she rented until 1897.

By then her main activity was in London, where her soirées were becoming famous. But she still felt the need for an outpost in the country, and so she rented Tudor Cottage, in Haslemere High Street, from 1897 until 1905. It had been created by a local architect, W.A. Pite, by combining two old cottages. Lady Dorothy rented it from H.W. Mozley of Eton College, who had just bought it from Rayner Storr. In the advertisement of the sale in the *Surrey Times* of 30th October 1897 it was described as 'having a very picturesque elevation in the Old English Style, and containing some really attractive old rooms'. It adjoined what is now the Georgian Hotel, into which it has recently been incorporated. Until the latest alterations, the ground floor living-room was substantially unchanged since Lady Dorothy was photographed in it in the early 1900s. (The photograph is reproduced in Ralph Nevill's biography.)

Lady Dorothy gave the following account of her cottage, and of Haslemere:

After I left East Sussex I took a cottage at Haslemere, which I had known years before as a mere village, in days when the lovely surroundings were quite unappreciated by a less cultivated and less luxurious generation. My cottage there was really two old cottages, which had been most artistically united by Mr Beresford Pite, who had contrived an extremely pretty and even commodious little house, which retained every attractive feature of the old cottages, including an old chimney comer and ceilings crossed by huge beams ... The original cottage, I believe, had once been the residence of a tanner who had carried on his trade in what had been made part of a very nice little garden.[72]

The Georgian Hotel, Haslemere High Street

The architect who did the conversion was actually William Pite, not his better known elder brother, Beresford; it was his first commission. The 'very nice little, garden' is now the hotel car-park. Lady Dorothy had this to say about the town itself:

Haslemere abounds in pretty cottages, a number of which, like the one I had, are old ones transformed. But the High Street is somewhat disfigured by the architecture of a certain number of modern erections built for shops. Tradesmen in this country, alas! are too often quite devoid of taste, and seem to take an especial delight in tearing down the quaint old shop-windows composed of small panes of glass ...

But in 1887, before Lady Dorothy came to live in Haslemere – though she evidently knew the town well – Edmund Gosse recorded an offhand comment by her which was rather less complimentary about the inhabitants. It was the first time Gosse had met her, and he had been instantly fascinated by her conversation, and made a special note of what she had to say about the French novelist, Emile Zola. She particularly admired his realistic descriptions of rural life, and remarked in passing:

I wish Zola could describe Haslemere with all its shops shut, rain falling and all the inhabitants in their cups.

However, this vision of Haslemere did not prevent her from coming to live there, and enjoying the company of one of its more sober inhabitants:

Mr Elwin, whose little house was filled with a most heterogeneous collection of antiquities, including a number of quaint old chemists' jars. For years he had been gathering together all kinds of odds and ends. I used much to enjoy a chat with this original old man, and was very sorry when he died.[72,73]

Lady Dorothy wrote no fewer than three stout volumes of autobiography: *The Reminiscences of Lady Dorothy Nevill* (1907); *Leaves from the Notebooks of Lady Dorothy Nevill* (1907); *Under Five Reigns* (1910). The first of these may well have been written at Haslemere, for there were fewer distractions there than in London, where, she told Gosse, 'I am hampered by perpetual outbursts of hospitality in every shape.' Apart from these three volumes, Lady Dorothy's only other literary productions were an edited translation – with comments of her own, for she had introduced this particular species into Britain – of Guérin-Méneville's book on *The Ailanthus Silkworm* (1862); and a pedigree of her family: *Mannington and the Walpoles* (1894). She did not in truth have much literary ability; her genius was much more freely expressed in conversation and in letter-writing. In writing her reminiscences she was greatly helped by her son Ralph who, as Lady Dorothy herself put it, 'out of the tangled remnants of my brain, extracted these old anecdotes of my early years'. Their main value has been as a source of gossip about contemporaries.

Edmund Gosse considered her 'the finest female wit of the age'. He described her as:

very small and neat … Her head, slightly sunken into the shoulders, was often poised a little sideways, like a bird's that contemplates a hemp-seed.[74]

Conan Doyle, who met her late in her life, at Lord Burnham's house at

OLIPHANT

Beaconsfield, wrote of 'Lady Dorothy Nevill, with her mittened hands and her prim pussy-cat manner, retailing gossip about Disraeli's flirtations'.

[DNB, *Missing Persons*, 1993; Gosse, 1914[74]; Lady Dorothy's three auto-biographies; Nevill, R., 1919; Nevill, G., 1984.]

OLIPHANT, Mrs Margaret, née Wilson (1818–1897): novelist, biographer and literary critic.

Margaret Oliphant is perhaps the most neglected of all the major Victorian novelists, though recent reprints of a small number of her novels, and a sympathetic biography by Merryn Williams, have been a welcome sign of renewed interest. The reason for the neglect is not far to seek: she wrote far too much. Her vast output included ninety-two novels, eight collections of short stories, twenty-five non-fiction books (mostly biographies), and about two hundred and seventy articles and reviews in *Blackwood's Magazine*. Trollope is usually thought of as a prolific author, but his output seems trivial compared with Mrs Oliphant's. An *oeuvre* of such vast dimensions is bound to be uneven, and not many critics would have the stamina to read enough of her works to do them full justice.

To a large extent, this enormous output was determined by Mrs Oliphant's financial circumstances, which were always hard, and often desperate. At different times she had to support a consumptive husband, an alcoholic brother, her own three children, and three children of another brother whom she had adopted. Faced by this burden, without help from her feckless men-folk, it was indeed fortunate that, as Henry James remarked, 'her capacity for labour was infinite'.[75]

Obliged as Mrs Oliphant was to churn out a new novel every few months merely to pay off current debts, it is not surprising that the majority of her works were pot-boilers of no great literary merit. Many of her reviews and other articles in *Blackwood's* are very verbose, and it is apparent that her genius was marred by an extreme facility in writing. She recognised this her-self; it was, she wrote towards the end of her life, 'in reality easier for me to keep on with a flowing sail, to keep my household and make a number of people comfortable at the cost of incessant work, and an occasional crisis of anxiety, than to live the self-restrained life which the greater artist imposes upon himself'.[76] If she had been able to pause for a moment, and take a little more thought, she could probably have earned as much from half the output. What is perhaps surprising is that a few of her novels – notably *Miss Marjoribanks* (1866), and *Kirsteen* (1890) – were of a quality comparable to that of works by Jane Austen or George Eliot. It is interesting to speculate what might have happened, had her circumstances been easier, or if she had had someone to encourage and cosset her, in the way that G.H. Lewes watched over George Eliot. Although she clearly would have welcomed such an easement, she seems to have felt that she would not necessarily have done any better under more favourable circumstances. 'I have written because it gave me pleasure, because it came natural to me, because it was like talking or breathing, beside the big fact that it was necessary for me to work for my children.'[77] It seems that it was her nature, as much as her circumstances, which compelled her to write incessantly, without too much regard for the quality of what she was producing.

Margaret Oliphant earned the respect of some important critics for the quality of the best of her novels and her literary criticism, as well as for her personal charm. She was even admired by crusty old Thomas Carlyle, who introduced her to Tennyson as 'an old and esteemed friend ... distinguished in literature, and ... a highly amiable, rational and worthy Lady'. But when she actually met the great poet, he more or less ignored her until the time came for her to take her leave of her hostess. When she employed the conventional politeness usual on such occasions, his comment was: 'What liars you women are!'[78] Henry James was ambivalent: he thought that 'her singular gift was less recognised, less reported on, than it deserved', but when he tried to read *Kirsteen*, one of the greatest of her novels, Henry found that he was 'at once confirmed, after twenty pages, in my belief – I laboured through the book – that the poor soul had a simply *feminine* conception of literature: such slipshod, imperfect, halting, faltering, peeping, down-at-heel work'.[79] More recently, Q.D. Leavis, famously hard to please, discerned the high quality of the best of Margaret Oliphant's work, at a time when it had been almost completely forgotten. She called her a 'considerable and original novelist, intelligent literary critic and exemplary woman of letters', and placed her in the same class as Charlotte Brontë, George Sand and George Eliot.[80]

Her autobiography reveals the many trials and hardships which Margaret had to endure. None was more painful than the death of her beloved daughter Maggie. Her prose style may have seemed 'slipshod' to the fastidious Henry James, but its stream-of-consciousness quality becomes an asset in passages like the following:

> I have not been resigned. I cannot feel resigned – my heart is sore as if it was an injury – God forgive me but I feel myself calling her my ewelamb as if it was to reproach Him who has taken her from me and has not spared – Oh my darling, my Maggie – I feel as if I could go down on my knees and pray for her not to forget her poor mother and as for the other prayers my heart seems crushed and stifled – when I went to read the chapter about the many mansions even then I seemed to be stifled again – Whatsoever ...[81]

Margaret often stayed at Hindhead with her friend Mrs Christina Rogerson (see own entry) at The Log House (now The Long House). At The Log House, Mrs Rogerson had made a home for deprived children from the London slums. Margaret gave an account of this establishment in a letter to Mrs Coghill in 1888: 'I am here for a few days in Mrs R.'s very original establishment, with nearly thirty most rosy ruddy children, very unlike the slums of London, running about everywhere. They are in such good order that they are really no trouble to anybody, and interfere very little with the economy of the house.'[82] Other letters show that Margaret stayed again with Mrs Rogerson in 1890, 1891 and 1895.[83]

The action of one of Margaret's later novels, *The Cuckoo in the Nest* (1892), takes place in the Hindhead area, and is centred on the Seven Thorns inn, on the Portsmouth Road, near Grayshott.

Though not quite in the same class as *Miss Marjoribanks*, it is nevertheless a well-told and original story which moves at a fast pace and retains the reader's interest to the end. I find it surprising that Merryn Williams does not award it the accolade of an asterisk – 'indicates that a book is good, or at least interesting' – in her list of Oliphant novels, and does not mention it in her text.[84] Like *Miss Marjoribanks*, it is an ironic comment on society, this time on the world of the effete rural upper class; and, as in most of Oliphant's novels, the heroine, 'Patty of the Seven Thorns', is a determined, self-reliant girl who knows what she wants, and gets it. Although she is really no more than a self-seeking adventuress, Patty manages to retain the reader's sympathy throughout her assault on the feeble upper-class Establishment.

Patty Hewatt is the daughter of the landlord of The Seven Thorns, a once-prosperous inn which has fallen on hard times since the demise of the coaching trade. Consequently Patty has to act as barmaid and maid-of-all-work. She does this competently and cheerfully, but would much prefer the life of a lady of leisure. A possible way of attaining this ideal presents itself in the shape of Gervase Piercy, the feeble-minded son of Sir Giles Piercy, baronet, and the squire of Grayshott Manor. Gervase hangs around the bar of the Seven Thorns, and does not conceal his admiration for Patty. Seeing this, she decides to make the most of the opportunity, and soon finds that he will be only too delighted to marry her. With the help of a complaisant aunt, who lends her money, Patty contrives to get her goofy lover to London, where they marry without the knowledge of the family. Meanwhile at the Manor, Lady Piercy, who would have been Patty's formidable enemy, unexpectedly dies. On the day before the funeral, the newly-wed couple return to the Seven Thorns. On hearing the news, Patty springs into action. A dress maker is summoned to cover her costume with copious quantities of crepe, and Gervase is provided with appropriate costume and a top hat. Thus equipped, they meet the funeral cortège at the church and mingle with the mourners. Patty acts the part of the grieving daughter-in-law with conviction, and when the ceremony ends, manages by sheer audacity to insinuate herself and her husband into the coach in which Sir Giles is returning to Grayshott Manor.

Sir Giles is too bewildered to object. There follows a splendid scene, in which Patty sweeps into the Manor, routing the feeble opposition put up by the servants and the upper-class mourners, who are bemused by the pace and audacity of the onslaught. The mourners depart, the servants are quelled by Patty's air of authority, and she is left in effective possession of the house.

Patty's position is nevertheless precarious. Her first task is to ingratiate herself with Sir Giles, who is confined to a wheelchair, and clearly will not survive for long. This she accomplishes with ease, but at the price of taking her eyes off her husband. Bored by not being the centre of Patty's attention – for Sir Giles is very time-consuming – he wanders back to the Seven Thorns, where he is soon boozing heavily. Worse is to follow; by rights Sir Giles should be the first to die, so that Patty would become Lady Piercy. But one night goofy Gervase gets blind drunk, falls into a ditch, is brought to the Manor unconscious, develops pneumonia and in a few days is dead.

For Patty, this is a considerable set-back, but not a disaster. She is denied the title, which would have meant much to her, but with a bit of luck she can still get the Manor and all that goes with it. Luck is indeed with her, for without her having to exercise any pressure, Sir Giles – by now senile – gets the idea that Patty is pregnant, and will provide him with the heir he has always longed for. So a lawyer is summoned and a new will drawn up, leaving all to Patty. Sir Giles dies shortly afterwards, and Patty gets her triumph when the will is read, and the next-of-kin and all their upper-class friends are once more routed. The will is contested, but the court upholds Patty's claim. So the Manor is won; but much good it does Patty. She has by now alienated the neighbourhood; no-one calls, and her old friends shun her. Salvation turns up in the shape of an old flame, who in the meantime has become famous – and apparently well rewarded – as a professional cricketer. So, in rather a tame ending to such a spirited tale, Patty decides to abandon the Manor to the next-of-kin – making sure she gets full publicity for her noble gesture – and marries her cricketer.

In addition to her fiction, literary criticism and other biographies, Mrs Oliphant also wrote *Memoirs of the Life of Laurence Oliphant* (1891). Laurence (no relation) was an eccentric character who, after a full and adventurous career as a traveller and journalist, fell under the spell of an American evangelist, and started to propagate his doctrine of 'sympneuma' in Europe and Palestine, where he is said to have owned the Plain of Armageddon. Perhaps inevitably, Laurence encountered Mrs Hannah Pearsall Smith, the Hilltop Writer with an unrivalled knowledge of exotic religious sects. She quickly spotted that 'sympneuma' involved dubious sexual practices, and denounced the creed as 'pure unadulterated trash'.[85]

[DNB; Sutherland, 1988; Drabble, 1985; Coghill, 1974; Williams, 1986; Jay, 1990 and 1995.]

PINERO, Sir Arthur Wing (1855–1934): playwright.

By 1890 Pinero had become phenomenally successful as a writer of light domestic comedies for an undemanding public, and was just beginning to evolve into a more serious playwright, with the production of *The Profligate* at the Garrick Theatre. He had been living in London, but was now feeling the urge for a country base in which to spend the summer. So he came to Haslemere, and rented Highercombe at Grayswood from July 1890 until the beginning of 1891, 'for both work and play. We are on the top of a hill with a fine view of three counties,' he wrote to Clement Scott, the dramatic critic. He was then writing *Lady Bountiful*, which was a further step towards more serious drama, and was accepted as such by the critics. A.B. Walkley, writing in *The Times*, described it as 'a play illustrative of cross-purpose, of thwarted aims, of unblushing selfishness and noble endeavour, with an all-pervading suggestion of the divinity that shapes our ends, rough-hew them how we will'.

The next few summers were spent elsewhere, but in 1907 Pinero settled at Stillands – presumably the present-day Stillands Farm, on the road from Gospel Green to Shillinglee. Judging by the letterheads in his correspondence, Pinero must have spent the summer months there in most years until at least 1919, so a good deal of his later works were probably written there. He was buried at Northchapel.

[DNB; Dunkel, 1941.]

POLLOCK, Sir Frederick, 3rd Baronet (1845–1937): lawyer, author, mountaineer and fencer.

Pollock was one of the first settlers on Hindhead, where he arrived in 1884, one year after Tyndall and Rollo Russell. He bought twenty-seven acres of land and built Hindhead Copse, in High Pitfold Road. Originally only a weekend cottage, it was twice added to, and is now part of The Grove School.

However, by 1904, the Hindhead hilltop was no longer the place of wild beauty it had been when he first came there: 'one would have to go farther afield,' he felt, 'to find anything like what the Hindhead region was in Queen Victoria's day'. Three years earlier, in an address to the 1901 Congress of the South-eastern Union of Scientific Societies, reported in the *Surrey Advertiser* for 8th June 1901, Pollock was already deploring the loss of wildlife round Hindhead as a result of the building that had taken place during the time that he was living there. 'It would not be at all incorrect to say that at the rate the district was at present advancing there would soon be no natural history for them to study.' So in 1904, Pollock departed.

While at Hindhead, Pollock wrote several legal works of distinction (his *First Book of Jurisprudence for Students of the Common Law* (1896) was described as 'probably the most original book on the subject published in England'), as well as *Introduction to the History of the Science of Politics* (1896). He also managed to lead what Lord Wright, in his DNB article,

Sir Frederick Pollock

described as a 'vivid, many-sided, and delightful life, full of diversified interests and accomplishments'. He was well versed in philosophy, medieval history and the history of music, and he could read with ease in Latin, Greek, Hebrew, Arabic and at least five modern languages. He was active physically as well as mentally, having climbed the Riffelhorn at Zermatt with Tyndall, via a route devised by the latter. On the basis of this and other experiences in the Alps he wrote *Mountaineering* (1892), in the Badminton Library series. Another favourite activity was fencing, which he had learnt after leaving Cambridge in 1868 and which he was still doing when he wrote his reminiscences in 1933, claiming to be 'the oldest practising member of the London Fencing Club'. Fencing was, surprisingly, one of the few subjects which Pollock did not write about; but he praised *Schools and Masters of Fence*, by another Hindhead resident and keen fencer, Egerton Castle, as 'a classic not likely to be superseded'. As well as books on fencing, Pollock collected swords, starting with an eighteenth-century blade with a Persian inscription indicating that it had been made in Isfahán.

Although called to the Bar in 1871, Pollock soon abandoned the practice of law, and devoted himself to the study of legal theory. From 1883 to 1903 he was Corpus Professor of Jurisprudence at Oxford and a Fellow of Corpus Christi College. Despite so many other distractions, Pollock somehow managed to find time to take a keen interest in local affairs. He was active in the Haslemere Microscope and Natural History Society, and succeeded Grant Allen as President in 1899. In 1896 he gave a memorial address to the Society on John Tyndall, his friend for forty years, and an equally warm tribute to Grant Allen in 1900.

Pollock was also a founding member and chairman of the Grayshott and District Refreshment House Association (later taken over by the People's Refreshment House Association), which obtained permission – against opposition from local brewers – to build The Fox and Pelican at Grayshott. The Association was also supported by Rayner Storr, Bernard Shaw, Edward Nettleship, the Bishop of Winchester, and a number of prominent citizens of Grayshott.

In an obituary notice dated 23rd June 1937, the *Haslemere Herald* described Pollock as 'perhaps the last representative of the old broad culture', which fittingly sums up the wide range of his interests and activities.

[DNB; Pollock, 1931.]

PONSONBY, Arthur Augustus William Harry, first Baron Ponsonby of Shulbrede (1871–1946): diplomat, politician and author.

Despite a royal background – he was born and brought up in the Norman Tower of Windsor Castle, and became a page of honour to Queen Victoria at the age of eleven – Ponsonby evolved, by way of Eton, Oxford and the Foreign Office, into a radical politician, joining first the Liberal, and then the Labour Party. He was dedicated to the cause of international peace, and got into trouble in both World Wars for defending pacifists. He never held high office, but in 1930 he was pushed reluctantly into the House of Lords, in order to strengthen Labour's representation there.

Ponsonby had married in 1898, when he was working at the Foreign Office. His wife, a daughter of Sir Hubert Parry, was not robust, and found she could not tolerate life in London. So Ponsonby set off with his bicycle, and a packet of sandwiches, to find a country home. He chanced upon Shulbrede Priory, in a fold of the hills between Blackdown and Hindhead.

It was an old Augustinian Priory which had decayed into a farmhouse; but it still had an undercroft, and a Prior's Chamber with a frescoed wall. Ponsonby fell instantly in love with the house, leased it in 1902, and bought it in 1905. His wife Dolly lived permanently at Shulbrede, while Arthur worked in London; but he spent every moment he could there. It became for him 'the great tonic, the rock on which all else is built, the only thing that matters'. Fifteen years later, he still found it 'marvelously satisfying. The old stone walls, the gable, the chimney-stacks, the arches and vaulting, the beams and tiled floors, the aroma of wood smoke, the blazing log fires, the lattice windows, the wonderful wooded hills, the peaceful meadow all and each are sources of unending satisfaction.'[86]

At Shulbrede Ponsonby was in contact with the Pearsall Smiths at Friday's Hill, and through them with the two rival art critics, Bernard Berenson and Roger Fry. He kept in touch with the musical world through his father-in-law, Hubert Parry, who frequently stayed at Shulbrede, where he is said to have composed his setting of Blake's *Jerusalem*.

Ponsonby's delight in the place was embodied in his scholarly history,

The Priory and Manor of Lynchmere and Shulbrede (1920). He wrote some seventeen books in all, mostly at Shulbrede. The majority were on social or political themes, often oriented towards the cause of pacifism. They included: *The Camel and the Needle's Eye* (1909); *The Decline of Aristocracy* (1912); *Democracy and Diplomacy; A Plea for Popular Control of Foreign Policy* (1915); *Wars and Treaties* (1918); and biographies of Samuel Pepys (1928), John Evelyn (1933), Queen Victoria (1933) and – his best-known work – his

father Sir Henry Ponsonby (1942). Sir Henry had been Queen Victoria's Private Secretary, and when Ponsonby submitted the manuscript of his biography to the Palace, Queen Mary objected strongly to its publication. King George VI, however, was favourably impressed, and managed to talk his mother round. The book became a bestseller as soon as it appeared.

It was probably no coincidence that the subjects of Ponsonby's first three biographies were all noted diarists, for after finishing his Shulbrede book, Ponsonby had become fascinated by the study of personal journals. It began when he read Barbellion's tragic *Diary of a Disappointed Man* (1919), and

Arthur Ponsonby

continued when he studied all the diaries in the London Library and the British Museum, and any manuscript diary he could lay his hands on. The first result of his studies was *English Diaries* (1923). This was so successful that the publisher – Sir Algernon Methuen – was able, according to Ponsonby, to add another gardener to the ten he already employed at his splendid garden at New Place in Farnham Lane, Haslemere. It was followed by *More English Diaries* (1927), and *Scottish and Irish Diaries* (1927). Ponsonby's study of the subject is probably the most comprehensive made to date.

[DNB; Jones, R. A., 1989.]

ROGERSON, Mrs Christina Adelaide Ethel Athanasia, née Stewart, later Steevens (c.1839–1911): charitable worker, literary hostess, journalist, author.

Christina ('Chrissie') was a daughter of Mrs Duncan Stewart, a lady of aristocratic descent who, after the death of her husband in 1869, established a reputation as a London hostess in her little house in Sloane Street. In this she was greatly helped by Chrissie, who was similarly talented, and continued on the same lines after the death of her mother in 1884; Chrissie's husband, an elderly, alcoholic Scotsman, died in the same year. Mother and daughter between them attracted many well-known literary and artistic figures to their salons – most notably Henry James and James McNeill Whistler, who met here for the first time in March 1884. Mrs Oliphant (see own entry) was another close friend of both mother and daughter.

Soon after the death of her mother and husband, Christina became caught up in a notorious divorce case of 1885–86 in which Sir Charles Dilke, a prominent MP often thought of as a future prime minister, was cited as co-respondent by Donald Crawford, a lawyer and politician. Christina, who was a close friend both of Dilke and of Mrs Crawford, can be said to have initiated the affair, for it was she who, in July 1885, first informed Dilke that Crawford was about to file a petition for divorce. But as the case developed, it became evident that she may have been more deeply involved. The initial trial took place in February 1886; it was brief, for Mrs Crawford readily confessed to adultery with Dilke. Dilke did not give evidence himself, and the case ended with the odd verdict that although Mrs Crawford had committed adultery with Dilke (and Crawford got his divorce), the judge ruled that Dilke had not committed adultery with her. This unsatisfactory verdict left Dilke open to all sorts of insinuations by the press, and led him to invoke the Queen's Proctor to re-open the case. A much longer trial ensued, the result of which was to confirm the illogical verdict of the first trial: Dilke had not been found guilty of adultery, but the divorce still stood.

Shortly after Christina had alerted Dilke to Crawford's intention to petition for divorce, she suffered a severe mental breakdown, lasting some nine months in all and preventing her from giving evidence at the first trial. But at the second trial, she was one of the most important witnesses. This one was longer, and even more confusing than the first. The affair as a whole revealed the unbridled promiscuity prevailing among the Victorian ruling class – in comparison, the peccadilloes of present-day politicians seem like frolics in the kindergarten playground – plus the total unreliability of almost all the witnesses. Consequently it is impossible to come to any firm conclusions about what went on beneath the bedclothes in the substantial houses of the contestants, although both of Dilke's major biographers – Roy Jenkins (1965), and David Nicholls (1995) – have made valiant attempts. It has to be said that both biographers formed a poor opinion of Christina's part in the affair. Nicholls is particularly severe. He concluded that Christina had conspired with Mrs Crawford to damage Dilke because she had been his mistress but had been thwarted in her wish to marry him, and described her as 'an unpredictable, neurotic and wickedly clever woman'. I do not find it easy to reconcile this harsh verdict with what we know of Christina's subsequent conduct, and would be inclined to go along with Henry James's contemporary comment, in a letter to his brother William about the Dilke affair: 'I am sorry to say that my old friend Mrs Rogerson has been much mixed up with the whole business, though rather by her misfortune than by her fault. Enough, however, to have been both made temporarily insane (she seems better now) and virtually ruined by it.'

After the affair, Christina became deeply involved in charitable activities among the poor of the London slums. In connection with this work, she acquired an odd building in Hazel Grove, Hindhead, called The Log House (an amateur painting in Haslemere Museum appears to show that this really was built of logs). There she made a holiday home for deprived children from the capital. At the 1891 census, five boys and fourteen girls, aged three to thirteen, were living there, as well as five adult visitors and seven servants. In her autobiography Margaret Oliphant says of Christina: 'How delightful she is with these children, how loving and mother-like – and how they adore her – gutter children, with nothing but the mud of London natural to them, but now made into the healthiest children, of the fields, breathing love and care, not knowing what it is to be neglected, thought of and cared for in everything as if they were in the nursery of a duke, yet all judiciously, no absurd petting, but good honest care and love.'[87] Mrs Oliphant was clearly very fond of Christina, but she also recognised her complexity: 'She is the most varied, complex, bewildering character, yet the most simple and transparent ... always a paradox and a delightful one, always extravagant, always poor, pursuing rather oblique ways of getting that wretched money sometimes, and then flinging it away in generosity and help.'

The publisher Grant Richards gives an account of a party at The Log House. He had been staying at Hindhead with his uncle, Grant Allen, and Mrs Rogerson had invited Allen's guests to her party. Richards describes Mrs Rogerson as 'a forceful lady who lived in a remote, unusual and attractive house near Hindhead, and used it as a refuge for a dozen or so of boy waifs and strays from the streets of London ... I was told that my hostess was as clever as she was eccentric, that she was old, and that she wore her hair short like a man.' As for the party, Richards was fairly overwhelmed, and could only exclaim: 'It *was* a party!' All the important members of the staff of the *Pall Mall Gazette* were there, as well as Sir Frederick Pollock, who lived locally, and impressed Richards by the verve with which he danced the 'kitchen lancers'.

Christina also found time for journalism. She did 'the Italian reviews' for the *Pall Mall Gazette*, and it was probably in the office of that journal that she encountered George Warrington Steevens, who became her second husband in 1894. At the time of their marriage, he was 24; on the marriage certificate her age is given as 45, but in fact she was probably 55. Grant Richards wrote of her that 'in spite of her years she possessed still a fascination that made most young men her slaves'. It was perhaps fitting therefore that after her second marriage she went to live in Lady Hamilton's old house,

ROSSETTI

Merton Abbey.[88] There she entertained lavishly; amongst other guests, H.G. Wells and his wife came over from Worcester Park on their new 'tandem safety bicycle'. George Steevens had graduated at Balliol College, Oxford, and had just been appointed a Fellow of Pembroke. However, he soon forsook an academic career and became a journalist, serving on the *Pall Mall Gazette* under H.J.C. Cust, and the *National Observer* under W.E. Henley. He was a war correspondent in the Boer War, and died of typhoid at the beginning of 1900, during the siege of Ladysmith. A *Times* obituary on 22nd January described him as having 'a considerable reputation as a vivid descriptive writer'. W.E. Henley summed up his marriage as 'in the event as fortunate as in the beginning it had seemed bewildering'.[89]

After her second husband's death, Christina (under the name Mrs Christina Steevens) had a book published by Grant Richards, entitled *A Motley Crew: Reminiscences, observations and attempts at playwriting* (1901). Richards did this as an act of friendship, for he valued her lively and generous temperament, but he did not anticipate that it would pay, and it didn't.

The book opens with four slight sketches, followed by a chapter on 'Charity and Charities'. This reveals Christina's detailed knowledge of all aspects of the subject, based on her own extensive experience, and demonstrates her sensitive yet unsentimental attitude to charitable work: 'half the time of the wise,' she remarks, 'is spent undoing the mischief wrought by the good'. Then follows a light-hearted account of one of Margaret Oliphant's visits to the Log House. She is portrayed as 'The Old Lady', taking her ease on a chair on the lawn, and discoursing in a spirit of benign disapproval on the habits, morals and costume of the young. 'The Opinions of the Old Lady' was read by Margaret with amusement, and published in the *Pall Mall Gazette*. The volume concludes with two short plays, of no particular merit.

[Jay, 1990,1995; Hare, 1895; Richards, 1932,1934; *The Times*, 7th April 1911; Jenkins, 1965; Nicholls, 1995.]

ROSSETTI, Christina (1830–1894): poet.

Christina Rossetti's standing among her contemporaries was such that, despite her sex, she was recognised as a serious contender to succeed Tennyson as Poet Laureate. In the event, the Queen, who (like Christina herself) was a firm believer in the inferiority of women, did not appoint her. But neither did she appoint anyone else, until four years later. By then Christina was dead, so this was perhaps a sort of muted recognition that no other poet was more suitable for the post. Christina's technical skill in the composition of her characteristic short-line verse was, indeed, unsurpassed. She was a natural, having written her first poem at the age of five. Her range was strictly personal; not for her the mythological heroes and shepherdesses that feature in much Victorian poetry. She wrote of what she felt; and since much of what she felt was bound up with feelings of unworthiness and unrequited love, the general tone tends to be one of sadness; even, some would say, of morbidity. But she could on occasion be joyful, and even sprightly. Although a confirmed Londoner, she could on occasion sing of pastoral pleasures, and she also wrote much light-hearted verse for children. Much of her work can be taken at face value, but some, like the celebrated *Goblin Market*, invites the reader to search for deeper meanings.

Christina's visit to the hilltop country came about through her brothers' friendship with Anne Gilchrist, who was then living in the little village of Shottermill. Anne had been assisted by both William and Gabriel Rossetti in her task of completing her late husband's life of Blake, and both had probably stayed for a night or two at her cottage at Shottermill, on more than one occasion. Christina Rossetti also stayed with her at Brookbank, but there is disagreement among her biographers about the date on which this took place: Battiscombe (1981) and Jones (1992) say the visit occurred in the summer of 1863, but Marsh (1994) puts it in 1864. Both parties have seemingly valid evidence to support their case, so I conclude that both are probably correct, and that Christina paid two visits to Brookbank, in 1863 and 1864.

The first of these visits was signalled in a letter to William Rossetti, dated 'Brookbank; May 2nd, 1863', from Anne Gilchrist. She wrote 'I had a little note from Miss Rossetti yesterday, which gave me much pleasure, for it responded very kindly and cordially to my hope of her coming here with you. About the middle of May would suit me quite as well as now.' Later in 1863, in a letter to a Mrs Burnie, Anne mentioned that 'Mr William Rossetti brought down his sister, Christina, to spend a few days with me, and Mr William Haines came over to meet them. We were both altogether charmed with Miss Rossetti – there is a sweetness, an unaffected simplicity and gentleness, with all her gifts that is very winning – and I hope to see more of her.'[90] When Christina arrived at Brookbank, she was so shy that Anne had difficulty persuading her to come down to supper from her bedroom; but soon she was playing ball with Anne's younger daughter Grace, then aged five, and Anne found her 'so kind to the children and so easy to please and make comfortable that though a stranger to me, she was not at all a formidable guest'. The two women quickly became fast friends, and subsequently exchanged many letters. Christina's were usually full of enquiries after Anne's four children, and messages for them. Grace Gilchrist later remembered her as a 'fairy princess who had come from the south to play with me ... a dark-eyed slender lady ... with olive complexion and deep hazel eyes ... a voice made up of strange, sweet inflexions, which rippled into silvery modulations in sustained conversation, making ordinary English words and phrases fall upon the ear with a soft, foreign musical intonation, though she pronounced the words themselves with the purest of English accents'.[91]

In a letter to Anne dated 21st May 1864, Christina looked forward to what I believe to be her second visit: 'I have indeed often thought of my prospective visit to Brookbank. Thank you very much for remembering me and preparing for me this pleasure.' This visit probably took place in early June, for on the twenty-fifth Christina met Charles Dodgson (Lewis Carroll) at a church fête in Mitcham, and on the first of July Anne left Brookbank for her annual visit to her mother in Essex. Towards the end of 1864 Anne had evidently written inviting Christina to yet another visit to Shottermill but this time Christina declined as she was already installed at Hastings, which she found 'less *genially* cold' than Brookbank.

It seems plausible to suggest that some of Christina's more pastoral poems may have been written during, or at least have been inspired by, her visits to Shottermill. However, she was far from being a country girl; when William Sharp first encountered her in 1880 she was having a friendly argument with an unnamed lady, who I think can only have been Christina Rogerson, for she was giving a vivid account of her experiences with slum children in the country. The lady maintained 'that it is not possible to live a happy life unless he or she has at least a brief sojourn in the country every year'. At this, Miss Rossetti broke into 'a singularly clear rippling laugh' and assured Mrs Rogerson (if she it was) that there were 'hundreds and thousands of Londoners who never left the city', and that 'there are more Lambs and Wordsworths among us townfolk'. When the other lady asked 'do not you yourself find your best inspiration in the country?' she was answered with an emphatic 'Oh dear, no!'[92]

It is certainly true that not many of Christina Rossetti's poems can be described as pastoral. Some that could be so described are undated, but *Maiden Song* was composed on 6th July 1863, and may have been inspired by her walks round about Shottermill. It tells a simple tale about three country girls, Meggan, May and Margaret. Meggan and May roam the countryside, and presently sit down and pipe and sing, in the hope of attracting husbands. Margaret, being much the fairest, just sat at home and waited. The upshot was that Meggan got a herdsman and May a shepherd, but Margaret got 'the king of all that country'.

It was soon after her second visit to Brookbank that Christina wrote *A Farm Walk*, the first forty lines of which were composed on 11th July 1864. It tells a simple pastoral tale of a milk-maid encountered during a country walk:

> She wore a kerchief on her neck,
>   Her bare arm showed its dimple,
> Her apron spread without a speck,
>   Her air was frank and simple.
>
> She milked into a wooden pail,
>   And sang a country ditty,

An innocent fond lovers' tale,
    That was not wise nor witty
    Pathetically rustical,
    Too pointless for the city.

She kept in time without a beat,
    As true as church-bell ringers,
Unless she tapped time with her feet,
    Or squeezed it with her fingers;
Her clear unstudied notes were sweet
    As many a practised singer's.

I stood a minute out of sight,
    Stood silent for a minute
To eye the pail, and creamy white
    The frothing milk within it;

To eye the comely milking maid
    Herself so fresh and creamy;
    'Good day to you', at last I said;
    She turned her head to see me;
'Good day', she said with lifted head;
    Her eyes looked soft and dreamy.

And all the while she milked and milked
    The grave cow heavy laden;
I've seen grand ladies plumed and silked,
    But not a sweeter maiden;

But not a sweeter fresher maid
    Than this in homely cotton
Whose pleasant face and silky braid
    I have not yet forgotten.

A Farm Walk was followed by *Songs in a Cornfield* (26th August 1864), which may also have been inspired by Christina's stay at Shottermill. It is also a tale about a country girl, but this time a sad one, who has been deserted by her lover. Christina had herself experienced two love affairs which ended unhappily. She had had two opportunities of marriage with men she was in love with, but had felt obliged to reject them both for religious reasons: James Collinson because he was (if only intermittently) a Roman Catholic; Charles Cayley, an unworldly and lovable scholar, because his profound studies of the world's religions led him to conclude that there was not much to choose between any of them.

Bird or Beast? (15th August 1864) may also have been conceived while Christina was at Brookbank. It describes the response of the animal world to the expulsion of Adam and Eve from the Garden of Eden. The only ones that are sorry for them are the dove and the lamb:

> Did any bird come flying
>> After Adam and Eve,
> When the door was shut against them
>> And they sat down to grieve?

> I think not a lion,
>> Though his strength is such;
> But an innocent loving lamb
>> May have done as much.

> If the dove preached from her bough
>> And the lamb from his sod,
> The lamb and the dove
>> Were preachers sent from God.

A sadder poem, *Twilight Night*, was composed in two parts, the first of which, oddly enough, was written after the second. Both were composed following visits to Brookbank (25th June 1863 and 26th August 1864). It is about two lovers who have separated. The first verse of Part Two is a fine example of Christina's delicate skill:

> Where my heart is (wherever that may be)
>> Might I but follow,
> If you fly thither over heath and lea,
>> O honey-seeking bee,
>> O careless swallow,
> Bid some for whom I watch keep watch for me.

Although Christina had much correspondence with Anne Gilchrist over the years, and they remained good friends, there is no record of any further visits to Brookbank. Christina's views on the 'woman question', and on religion, are discussed in Section Two. The two friends differed on the former, for Christina had an unshakeable belief in the superiority of the male intellect, whereas Anne was a determined advocate of women's rights. But despite her respect for male wisdom, Christina was unmoved by the atheism of her two much-loved brothers, and remained throughout her life a devoted High-Church Anglican.

Like so many eminent Victorians, Christina's life was plagued by ill-health. In adolescence and early adult life, this consisted of the usual nondescript Victorian malady, variously diagnosed in Christina's case, as suspected consumption or religious mania. But later on, she was unique among her contemporaries in having two clear-cut diseases, both of which can be given a confident diagnosis. At the age of forty she was diagnosed as having exophthalmic goitre, and there is no reason to doubt the correctness of this; and an equally unquestionable breast cancer ended her life at the age of sixty-four.

The exophthalmic goitre was not finally diagnosed until a consultation with Sir William Jenner and Dr Wilson Fox on 25th November 1871. It was then regarded as a very rare disease. Sir William – the most eminent physician of the era – had seen only one or two cases in a lifetime. The condition was probably very advanced before it was finally identified. The main features are enlargement and overactivity of the thyroid gland – causing loss of weight – and, as the name implies, protrusion of the eyeballs, which caused shy Christina great distress, as strangers tended to stare at her. Not surprisingly, she did not permit any portraits or photographs while she was in this state; and she seems to have written little or nothing – though not all her poems were dated – between June 1866 and October 1872. There is, however, one notable exception: although the actual date of composition is not known, her famous Christmas carol, *In the bleak mid-winter*, was published in America in response to a request in November 1871, and was probably written while her illness was at its height.

Exophthalmic goitre is a chronic disease with a fluctuating and unpredictable course. Even with modern facilities, it is usually difficult to date its onset with any certainty. Since it is generally characterised by loss of weight, increase in weight is usually a sign of remission. Christina seems to have been in reasonable health during her stay at Brookbank in June 1864, but towards the end of that year she was sufficiently unwell to be sent to winter by the sea at Hastings. This may have been the start of the thyroid condition, although her main symptoms – headaches and cough – were not typical. They were relieved by a combination of sherry and a jelly made from seaweed; although hyperthyroidism is usually ameliorated by iodine, it is unlikely that such a jelly would contain enough to have an effect. In the summer of 1866, Christina is described as 'well and plump', and after returning from a holiday in Scotland in the summer of 1868 she is again recorded as having gained weight. So if her hyperthyroidism had indeed started in 1864, it remained in remission for several years subsequently. But in mid-1870 there was a sudden deterioration, which continued through 1871, when the diagnosis was established. In several letters during 1872, William Rossetti reported that his sister was somewhat better, though not cured; and in July 1873 she had improved 'much beyond my hopes'. But in November 1873 Christina wrote to William that her 'heart-complaint and consequent throat enlargement' had recurred. This seems to have been the final relapse of what in her case proved to be a self-limited condition; in May 1880, her brother Gabriel described her as 'quite wonderfully recovered', and Christina described herself as 'a fat poetess'.

Early in 1892, a lump appeared in Christina's left breast. It was diagnosed as cancer, and surgically removed. But by the autumn of 1894 it had recurred. She was in great pain, partly relieved by morphia, but aggravated, so her brother William believed, by the attentions of the Revd Gutch. This odious priest was determined that the dying woman should be fully cognisant of all the grisly details of the doctrine of eternal damnation.

[Rossetti, W., 1904; Battiscombe, 1981; Jones, K., 1991; Marsh, 1994.]

RUSSELL, Lady (Mary) Agatha (1853–1933), daughter of Lord John Russell, aunt of Bertrand Russell: author.

During her childhood at Pembroke Lodge, Lady Agatha had presented Garibaldi with a rose, and received in return a kiss on the forehead. As an adult, still at Pembroke Lodge, she did her best to teach her young nephew Bertie Russell to read; but without much success. She never married; she was engaged at one time to a clergyman, but it was broken off when she developed 'insane delusions'. Her first acquaintance with the Haslemere hills was probably in 1874 when she and her brother Rollo stayed at Aldworth with their parents, who had rented it for several months from the Tennysons.[93] In 1883, she accompanied her mother on a visit to Rollo, soon after he built Dunrozel at Hindhead; Lady Russell was 'simply enchanted ... the Tennysons welcomed us with the utmost cordiality'. Lady Russell liked Hindhead so much that she returned to Dunrozel for a few months each year until 1891, when she took a house of her own in the vicinity for that year and 1892.

In 1904 Lady Agatha, who was equally enchanted by the pines and heather of Hindhead, built herself a house called Rozeldene on the Headley Road, Hindhead; this was later developed into the estate of the same name (Rozel was the name of the Russells' estate in pre-Conquest Normandy). Bertie stayed with her there in 1905, and probably on other occasions, too. They talked 'of people who are dead and old – world memories – it is very soothing'.[94] She was still there in 1921, when Bertie's disagreeable Aunt Gertrude – Uncle Rollo's second wife – who was installed at the Punch Bowl Inn, started a malicious rumour about Lady Agatha's 'suspiciously friendly' relations with her chauffeur. It seems that she had bought a car and hired a chauffeur, and then sold the car but retained the chauffeur. Aunt Agatha was not above a little rumour-mongering herself, leading Bertie's elder brother Frank to characterise her as' a villainous old cat' when she alleged – for once unjustly – that Bertie was having an affair with Frank's estranged wife Elizabeth.[95] She had previously reproached Bertie, this time with more reason, for his 'misconduct with women – and married women' in a letter marked 'Private – Burn' (Bertie didn't).[96]

Captain Frank Shaw was a neighbour of Lady Agatha at Hindhead in 1922–27, and took tea with her in her 'spacious drawing-room lined with books'. He addressed her as 'Aunt Agatha', and much enjoyed her 'wit as sparkling as diamonds'. On one occasion she took down from her shelves a book by Dickens, inscribed 'To my dear little friend Agatha, from her affectionate Charles Dickens', and another by Tennyson 'To friend Agatha Russell, with devotion from Alfred Tennyson'.[97] An obituarist in *The Times*, 26th April 1933, wrote that 'Age came serenely and happily' to 'this tiny little lady', and described how 'it was one of her pleasures to have working men and women to converse in her drawing-room, to join in their talk as she dispensed hospitality to a party round her dining-table, discussing the events of the day in her cold, coherent Russell voice.'

Lady Agatha collaborated with Desmond MacCarthy in a biography of her mother, *Lady John Russell, A Memoir* (1910). She also published *Thoughts of Many Minds* (1923); and *Gleanings Grave and Gay* (1931). The latter, consisting of little snippets from a wide variety of sources, shows the eclectic nature of her reading: lofty sentiments from Rabindranath Tagore sit alongside corny jokes about Irishmen. Quotations from Lady Agatha's own writings reveal that she was an inveterate smoker – 'Who is the Master of my Fate? Tobacco!' – and looked forward to the prospect of an enjoyable afterlife, 'away from the darkness into the light'.

Lady Agatha was not the greatest of poets, but she managed a neat parody of Longfellow, in favour of autobiographies:

> Lives of small men all remind us
> We should write our lives ourselves,
> And, departing, leave behind us
> Two octavos on the shelves.

Regrettably, Lady Agatha did not take her own advice; her memoirs might well have made interesting reading.

[Russell, B., 1967 & 1968; Clark, 1975.]

RUSSELL, Bertrand Arthur William (1872–1970), 3rd Earl Russell, grandson of Lord John Russell: philosopher and pacifist.

Bertie's parents, Lord and Lady Amberley, died when he was young, and he was brought up by his grandmother – the widow of Lord John Russell – on a regime of cold baths and biblical texts in the oppressive atmosphere of the family home at Pembroke Lodge, Richmond Park. The gloom was mitigated to some extent by Uncle Rollo, a shy and amiable man who encouraged Bertie's intellectual development, and by Aunt Agatha. In 1883 Uncle Rollo moved from Pembroke Lodge to Dunrozel at Hindhead. Bertie often visited him there, and was introduced to John Tyndall, from whom he acquired an insight into the methods and power of science. Uncle Rollo also introduced him to the Pearsall Smiths, the family of rich Philadelphia Quakers who had settled at Fernhurst. Their son was Logan Pearsall Smith, the essayist, and there were two daughters. Bertie fell in love with the younger daughter, Alys, and they were married in 1894. Most of the next year was spent travelling round Europe, but in late 1895 they settled in a small cottage on her family's Friday's Hill estate. Two years later, the couple moved lower down the hill to Millhanger, a sixteenth-century workman's cottage off the Lickfold Road, in the south-east corner of Fernhurst, where they stayed until 1905. At Fernhurst, Bertie wrote his first book, *German Social Democracy* (1896), shortly followed by *An Essay on the Foundations of Geometry* (1897). It was there also that he began his onslaught on the logical basis of mathematics, the first fruits of which was *The Principles of Mathematics* (1903). He was nearing the end of this work when he began to have doubts about the validity of the underlying logic. This left him feeling dissatisfied, and led to further work with A.N. Whitehead which culminated in *Principia Mathematica* (1910–13).

Beatrice Webb visited the Russells at Millhanger, and described it as 'a workman's cottage with stuffy attic bedrooms, but with the inevitable decent size sitting-room added on to it by the Russells'. The couple, she said, 'live idyllic lives, devotedly attached to each other, living with somewhat disorderly and extravagant simplicity ... Russell working some six or seven hours at his metaphysical book.'[98]

The idyll did not last long. In the autumn of 1901 Bertie was bicycling along a Cambridgeshire road, when he suddenly realised that he was no longer in love with Alys. When he returned from his ride, he told her so. They remained together, but spent less and less time at Millhanger. After a spell at Cambridge, they took a house in London, spending the summers of 1903 and 1904 at Churt and Tilford, just north of Hindhead. Finally, they built a new home near Oxford. They were not divorced until 1921. Alys retained her affection for Bertie and in 1949, after he had got rid of his third wife, even hoped – Bertie having by then become the third Earl Russell – that he would now at last make an honest Countess of her. But it was not to be; Bertie was already in pursuit of his fourth wife.

Bertie's sister-in-law, Elizabeth – of *Elizabeth and her German Garden* – thought him 'a most charming queer creature – elf-like, Punch-like, imp-like, a Christ and a devil, angelically saintly and thoroughly malignant – the weirdest of human beings'. She also noted that he 'smelt like a bear-garden'.[99] Yet his long and distinguished subsequent career showed that, as well as possessing one of the greatest intellects of our time, he could also display integrity and passion in the pursuit of the causes in which he believed.

[Russell, B., 1967 & 1968; Clark, 1975.]

RUSSELL, Hon. (Francis Albert) Rollo (1849–1914), third son of Lord John Russell, and uncle of Bertrand Russell: meteorologist, epidemiologist and poet.

'Uncle Rollo', a shy man with a sense of humour, as well as being an important influence on the up-bringing of young Bertie, was a good example of a breed – already becoming extinct – of amateur scientists, who proliferated in Victorian times, and did much excellent work. His field of study ranged over meteorology, epi-demiology and public health, and he also took an interest in the history of science, as shown by his 1892 address to the Haslemere Microscope and Natural History Society on 'Giordano Bruno: martyr for science'.

Rollo had stayed at Aldworth in 1874 with his parents and sister, and in 1883 he established himself at Dunrozel in Farnham Lane, on the way up from Haslemere to Hindhead. He also

Rollo Russell

owned and developed land at Hindhead, as did Lady Agatha. Rollo was still at Dunrozel in 1907, but not in 1909, according to *Kelly's Directory. Who's Who* for 1910 gives Rollo's address as Steep, near Petersfield, and this seems to have been his final home.

In 1885 Rollo married Miss Alice Godfrey. The marriage was a source of great happiness to his mother, Lady John Russell, but in a little over a year, Alice died, after the birth of a son. In May 1891, Rollo married his second wife, Miss Gertrude Joachim, daughter of Henry Joachim, of Highlands, Haslemere, and a niece of Joseph Joachim, the celebrated Hungarian violin-ist. Once more, Lady Russell 'found a new joy in [Rollo's] happiness'; but in her later years, Gertrude seems to have made herself unpopular. She evidently returned to Hindhead as a widow. Bertie's elder brother Frank wrote in a letter dated 27th January 1921: 'Did you know that our disagree-able Aunt Gertrude was running the Punch Bowl Inn on Hindhead? I feel tempted to go and stay there for a week end but perhaps she would not take me in. The Aunt Agatha was very bitter about it when I last saw her and said the horrible woman was running all over Hindhead poisoning people's minds against her by saying the most shocking things – we can guess what about.'[100]

Rollo's scientific interests were primarily concerned with the weather and its effects. He made a serious study of the strange sunsets which followed the Krakatoa eruption of 1883, summed up in a lecture to the Haslemere Microscope and Natural History Society in 1891. He took a general interest in possible effects of atmospheric changes on the spread of plant, animal and human diseases. His weighty monograph, *The Atmosphere in relation to Human Life and Health* (1896), published in *Smithsonian Miscellaneous Collections* (Vol. XXXIX, 1899), is a lengthy and far-ranging review of all that was then known about the atmosphere: its chemical composition, its content of particulate matter – including bacteria – and its relationship to human and plant diseases. One of his particular interests was in the effect of topography on rainfall; he cited the difference between the rainfall at Midhurst and that at Fernhurst as evidence of the influence of quite minor hills, in this case the South Downs. He then went on to speculate about the further effect that an artificial barrier, 300–400 feet high, along the top of the Downs might have on local rainfall. He gave several lectures to the Haslemere Microscope and Natural History Society on meteorological subjects. In 1894, his title was 'Rain Drops, Hailstones and Snowflakes'. He was an early member of the Society, and its President from 1903 to 1907.

Rollo's interest in human disease was not confined to the effects of the weather. He wrote two quasi-medical works: *Epidemics, Plagues and Fevers; Their Causes and Prevention* (1892); and *Preventable Cancer: A Statistical Research* (1912). In the first of these, he showed that he had a sound grasp of contemporary advances in bacteriology, and was well aware of the potential benefits to human health, if only politicians would make better use of that knowledge. He was a strong advocate of a national public health service, condemning the ignorance of voters who were prepared to elect 'a Town Councillor who builds pestiferous dens where fever always lodges, and who cares nothing for the powers we possess for the security of the people.' In the 1890s he took a practical interest in the sanitary arrangements in Haslemere, after they had been the subject of an uncomplimentary review in the *Lancet*.

Rollo's ideas on the influence of overcrowding on the spread of respiratory infections were substantially correct, but he was inevitably wrong – as the vectors had not yet been discovered – about insect-borne diseases such as malaria and yellow fever, which he thought were disseminated by microbes oozing up from the soil. Equally inevitably, since its causation is still so poorly understood, he is much less impressive when he comes to deal with cancer. He takes his opinions from contemporary medical authorities, who, before specific carcinogens began to be identified in the 1930s, were content to ascribe the cause of cancers to the vague and virtually meaningless concept of 'chronic irritation'.

Rollo's views on the 'degeneracy' which had been so strikingly revealed in the medical examination of Army recruits during the Boer War have already been referred to (see Section Two). Rollo saw the underlying cause of most of the current ills of society as the great migration from the countryside to the towns, where health was undermined by foul air and overcrowding. Despite being a scion of an aristocratic family, he argued persuasively for the nationalisation of land, in a booklet entitled. He had studied the question in Germany and France, and was impressed by the contented, healthy and prosperous peasantry, each owning his own small farm, and by the absence of crime and drunkenness. He contrasted this happy state with that in Britain, which suffered under what he called 'oligarchic despotism', with the country split into a small number of huge estates, ruled by uncaring landlords. As a result, 'hundreds of villages have been sacrificed to the prehistoric pleasures of the pursuit of small animals'. Rollo thought that the best remedy for this sorry state of affairs would be wholesale nationalisation, but recognised that it would not be possible to get such a measure through a Parliament dominated by the landed interest. So he favoured simplification of the purchase of land, combined with heavy taxes on landlords.

In 1889, while living at Hindhead, Rollo published two small works, both anonymously: a book of poems, *Break of Day, and Other Poems* (1893), and *Psalms of the West* (1889). The latter had a format resembling that of the Psalms of David, although Rollo maintained there was no connection; his intention was to show the superiority of Western thought, as opposed to the fatalism of the East. The little book was evidently very popular, running to three editions and eight impressions. The last of these was published post-humously in 1922, when the author's name was revealed in an introduction by his widow.

Rollo's poems and psalms reveal an equal devotion to science and religion. In a poem entitled *Ad Scientium*, he explains his attitude to both:

> Come with triumph songs about thee,
>   Noble, fair one high descended,
> Teacher of divine discoursings,
>   Angel of eternal truth,
> Sister to religion holy.

He felt that Christianity should accept and assimilate the truths of science, and discard what he saw as obsolete superstitions which obfuscated true religion.

In 1913, Rollo edited Early Correspondence of Lord John Russell 1805–40 (1913).

[Russell, B., 1967; Clark, 1975.]

SALVIN

SALVIN, Osbert (1835–1898), FRS: naturalist.

Osbert was the son of Anthony Salvin, a well-known Victorian architect who had been active locally, doing restoration work on Petworth House and Blackdown House, as well as on Fernhurst church. When his father died in 1882, Osbert inherited Hawksfold, built by his father, on the western out-skirts of Fernhurst, and lived there until his own death in 1898.

Osbert Salvin collected all manner of animals, but particularly birds, during several expeditions to Central America. He became the Strickland Curator of Ornithology at Cambridge from 1874 until he retired and moved to Fernhurst in 1882.

Salvin was joint author – with Frederick Du Cane Godman – of the gigantic *Biologia Centrali-Americana* (1879–98) which described, in its sixty-three volumes, a total of 50,263 species of animals and plants native to Central America. *The Times* called it 'the greatest work of its kind ever planned and carried out by individuals'. He was also the sole author of: *Catalogue of the Picariae in the British Museum*, 1892; *Catalogue of the Turbinares in the British Museum*, 1896.

[DNB.]

SHAW, George Bernard (1856–1950): playwright.

In June 1898, Shaw married Charlotte Payne-Townshend, an event he described with typical gusto: he had arrived at the registry office in his oldest jacket; the registrar naturally assumed that he was 'the inevitable beggar who completes all wedding processions', and was on the point of marrying Charlotte to the best man when the latter, 'thinking the formula rather strong for a mere witness, hesitated at the last moment, and left the prize to me'.[101]
For the honeymoon, the Shaws rented Pitfold House, on Woolmer Hill – between Shottermill and Hindhead – from Henry and Annette Beveridge.

Shaw arrived there on crutches; in the previous April, before his marriage, his left foot had become painful, and swelled up 'to the size of a church bell'. An abscess developed, and had to be opened, revealing that the source of the trouble was an infected bone. Charlotte had returned from Italy to find him in a deplorable state, and had installed herself as his nurse; it was largely in order to regularise this situation that Shaw consented to be married. She intended the move to Hindhead to be as much a convalescence as a honey-moon. Shaw had other ideas, and determinedly kept on working, as was his habit – much to Charlotte's annoyance – wherever he happened to be, and in whatever physical state. The choice of Hindhead was probably made by Charlotte, who had heard about the health-giving properties of its air, and

176

hoped that it would be curative. The air, in fact, did little to heal Shaw's infected foot; but rather stimulated him to work even harder than usual. Almost immediately, he was dictating *The Perfect Wagnerite* (published in late 1898), completing *Caesar and Cleopatra*, and starting to write *Captain Brassbound's Conversion*.

George Bernard Shaw

One week after arriving at Pitfold House, Shaw fell down the stairs. He described the event in a letter to Beatrice Webb. He had hobbled upstairs on his crutches to fetch something from his bedroom; on the way down, 'the crutches got planted behind my centre of gravity and shot me into the air. I snatched at a bannister on the landing above, and caught it in my right hand; but it snapped like an Argoed[102] tree; and I was precipitated fifty fathom or thereabout into the hall, with my left arm doubled up in ruin under me.' The capable Charlotte applied two butter-pats as splints, and while they waited for the doctor, Shaw lay in the hall 'with all the strain gone, perfectly relieved and happy'.

Then the infected foot got worse, and a bone specialist was summoned from London. He removed a piece of bone, and was supposed to deal with the arm at the same time but forgot, enabling Shaw to have a good chuckle at the expense of the medical profession. Charlotte then took him off to the Isle of Wight, and he returned to Pitfold so much improved that he threw away the crutches, and took to his bicycle. Shaw was always accident-prone where bicycles were concerned, and it was not long before he fell off and sprained his ankle. But over the next six months the infected foot very gradually improved, even though in April 1899 he had another bad landing from his bicycle, making the bad foot 'collapse like a leg of mutton which had been stabbed with an area railing'. Nevertheless, an X-ray showed that the bone was now healed; Shaw of course attributed the happy result to his vegetarian diet.[103]

The Shaws found Pitfold House too small – it was not until the next year that the Beveridges had it enlarged to its present size – and in November 1898 they moved to Blen-Cathra, now St Edmunds School, in Hindhead. Shaw by then was becoming thoroughly involved in local activities. He became a temporary music critic for the *Farnham & Haslemere Herald*, joined Grant Allen in a play-reading society, and in a Disarmament debate in

Hindhead Hall. In February 1899, he gave an address to the Haslemere Microscope and Natural History Society on 'Why I am a Socialist'. At another meeting in 1900 he proposed a vote of thanks in his own inimitable style to Gilbert Murray for reading his translation of Euripedes (see Murray entry).

On another occasion, Shaw went with Richard Le Gallienne, who was living nearby at Kingswood Firs, to address the pupils at the local school. He caused consternation by telling the children: 'The first duty of a child is to disobey its parents, and grown-ups generally.' The poor mistress in charge of the school told him 'it would take weeks to bring them back to law and order again'.[104]

Shaw also took a leading part, with Frederick Pollock, Edward Nettleship and Rayner Storr, in the campaign to forestall the attempt of a local brewer to open a pub in Grayshott, by founding The Grayshott and District Refreshment Association, which built and ran The Fox and Pelican inn (see Section One). The project was regarded with disapproval by totally committed tee-totallers like the Gilbert Murrays, then living at Tilford. Lady Mary Murray wrote a letter of protest to Charlotte, to which Shaw replied at length. He maintained that if he could not get his regular drink, the average workman 'sulks, mopes, beats his wife and children'. He himself disapproved of alcohol – it grieved him to see his wife drinking whisky at dinner – but he thought that moral attitudes were 'more potent than alcohol as generators of madness, ruin and despair'.

In August 1899, the Shaws left Blen-Cathra, going first to Cornwall, and then on a Mediterranean cruise. In the early part of 1900, Shaw spent occasional nights at the Beacon Hotel at Hindhead, and in May took a lease of Blackdown Cottage, where he stayed until the end of October. The cottage, nestling beneath the south-east corner of Blackdown, was a great deal more secluded than either of the Hindhead houses. Although he had not set eyes on it before, Shaw was in a sense familiar with the cottage, as he had used someone else's account of its garden to depict the setting for the first scene of *Mrs Warren's Profession*. The stage directions call it 'a cottage garden on the eastern slope of a hill a little south of Haslemere'. The house has 'a thatched roof and porch, and a large latticed window to the left of the porch'; behind the house 'the common rises uphill to the sky line'. Whilst living at Blackdown Cottage, Shaw was probably writing *Three Plays for Puritans*, published in January 1901.

One result of Shaw's residence at Hindhead was that the action of his play, *Misalliance*, although not written until 1909, was sited there, in the luxurious villa of the founder of 'Tarleton's Underwear'. It was a pure conversation piece, only momentarily interrupted when an aeroplane crashes into the greenhouse. The pilot and his passenger – she turns out to be a Polish acrobat – step out unscathed, and immediately join in the crossfire of paradox and sophistry; and then again when a decidedly incompetent revolutionary emerges from a portable Turkish bath and threatens to shoot both Tarleton and himself – 'Begin with yourself, if you don't mind', is Tarleton's sensible response. Shaw said of the play: 'I have carefully cherished, repeated and exaggerated every feature that the critics denounced ... no division into acts, no change of scene, no silly plot, not a scrap of what the critics call action.' Although he does not say so specifically, the fact that the play was sited in a property owned not by a literary person – as it might have been ten or twenty, years previously – but by a manufacturer of underwear, may reflect Shaw's awareness of the change that was taking place in the area, as the men of commerce took over from the men of letters, and the area was rapidly ceasing to be a thriving centre of literary activity.

[Laurence, 1972; Holroyd, 1988 & 1989.]

SILLICK, William Austen (c.1877–1955); journalist.

In 1897, a 'callow youth' of 20 was sent to Haslemere for a fortnight by his editor, to relieve the regular reporter there – and when that reporter left the paper's employment the following year, Sillick succeeded him as the representative of the *Herald* in Haslemere and the surrounding area.

He was 'unfledged, untrained and inexperienced' – but was determined to make a success of his post. However, he had not much to build on, for although *The Herald* had started in Farnham as early as July 1892 as an advertising sheet,

William Austen Sillick

and although it had made some progress in that neighbourhood, it cannot be said that after six years it was very prosperous or influential.

One of Sillick's first jobs on coming to Haslemere was to carry on his shoulders the entire Haslemere edition from the station to the *Herald* office in East Street, to be dealt with there by himself and a lad named Snelling.

He travelled his district seeking out the news, first on bicycle and then in a small car. He was Mr Sillick to some, 'Old Bill' to others, and he made himself welcome, often coming away with a piquant story which, we are told, he loved to retell with far louder laughs from the teller than from the hearers.

An entertaining example of his style of reporting may be seen in his report in the *Herald* dated 25th February 1899:

SILLICK

The Novelist and the Dog – Anyone coming down from Hindhead on Tuesday afternoon might have seen one of the most distinguished residents actively engaged in parting two of the canine tribe who were settling old differences. Dr Conan Doyle is quite an adept at describing warfare of any kind, and in his next novel we shall expect to find a glowing account of "A dog fight, and how it terminated," derived from actual experience.

He also records an early example of what was to become a dominant problem in Hindhead a century later:

Saturday 8th April 1899: The Bank Holiday – There was not so much business on the Hindhead on Good Friday as has been the case on previous occasions, but on Bank Holiday the traffic was overwhelming. During the day there must have been thousands who passed the cross-roads – bicycles, traps and brakes continually coming and going. The weather was fine, and in a large measure added to the pleasure of the holiday-makers.

Flora Thompson recalls him in *Heatherley*. On a visit to Grayshott in the 1920s, she says she 'saw coming towards her the reporter of the local newspaper and thought "Ah, it's Tuesday!" for she remembered that Tuesday had been his day in the past for coming to the village to collect such scraps of news as the place afforded. He was evidently then engaged in the same pursuit for he was walking, notebook in hand, in close converse with the village policeman.'

She tells us that this reporter had been one of her friends during her period of employment at Grayshott (1898–1901), and that 'there had been a time when he would even have risked losing an item of news' for the sake of a talk with her. She says that they shared some happy experiences together, such as a primrosing expedition on Good Friday, and an August Bank Holiday tramp over the moors with stewed whortleberries and cream for tea at a wayside inn.

She describes him as having 'a sturdy figure, bright inquisitive eyes and head bent a little forward as though perpetually in search of news for his paper'.

Sillick was an enthusiastic compiler of notes on the eminent people who came to the area, as shown by his papers and scrapbooks in Haslemere Museum which were the inspiration for this book. How ironic, then, that they include no mention of the girl with whom he had walked on the heaths, and sat for hours by Waggoners Wells. But he could not have known then that, one day, she also would have been worthy of a place in his collection.

An article published in the *Haslemere Herald* in September 1948 summed up Sillick's fifty years in the town by saying that he had 'not only been recording mere news all these years, but writing local history... All the important changes in local administrative affairs have been reported by his pen and nothing of note has occurred unless he has been there.'

[*Haslemere Herald*, reports on Sillick: September 1945 and 17th September 1948; Flora Thompson: *Heatherley*]

SMITH, Hannah, née Whitall (1832–1911); mother of Logan Pearsall Smith and mother-in-law of Bertrand Russell: author of religious works.

Hannah and her husband, Robert Pearsall Smith, whom she had married in 1851, were born into the Quaker community of Philadelphia. After several trips to Europe, the family finally moved across the Atlantic in 1888, and settled in England. In 1889 they found a permanent home at Friday's Hill House, on the southern slopes of the hill just north of Fernhurst. The house was big and ugly, with a fine view of the South Downs, and the estate of ten acres included two cottages. When Beatrice Webb stayed there in 1901, she described it as 'a pleasant, comfortable house – with no special distinction, surrounded by tall spreading trees, a terraced lawn, with meadows sloping in curved lines towards the Fernhurst valley'.[105] They remained there until about 1906, when Hannah and her son Logan moved to Court Place, near Oxford. They also had a flat in London.

Hannah was a most unusual person. Although her life was dominated by an intense desire for 'the deep things of God' and a strong urge to impart such knowledge to others, this evangelistic impulse was balanced by an equally strong endowment with common sense. Her search for a knowledge of God led her to explore a variety of religious sects, of which there was an abundant supply in nineteenth-century America.

Her sturdy common sense successively revealed their weaknesses, but did not shake her faith. She ended her life as profoundly religious as ever but uncommitted to any sect, believing, as Christ did, that true religion could be summed up in two commandments: 'God is', and 'Be good'.

A valuable by-product of her unusual combination of mysticism and commonsense was a written account of her experiences with one fanatical sect after another. As a result, she became a connoisseur of bizarre offshoots of the Evangelical movement. She left this account of her researches with her grand-daughter, Ray Strachey (see under Costelloe), to be published only after her death. Ray carried out these instructions faithfully with *Religious Fanaticism: Extracts from the Papers of Hannah Whitall Smith* (1928), reprinted as *Group Movements of the Past* (1934). In her own lifetime, Hannah had published a number of works expressing her attitude to religion. Most of these were written while she was still in America, the most popular being *The Christian's Secret of a Happy Life* (1875). During her time at

Friday's Hill she wrote *Educate our Mothers* (1896); *The Unselfishness of God* (1903); and *The God of All Comfort* (1906).

In her exploration of what various sects had to offer, Hannah was accompanied by her husband Robert, who shared her enthusiasm, but lacked her common sense. Starting as Quakers, they tried successively Methodists, Plymouth Brethren and Baptists, and some even more exclusive sects. During the course of this odyssey, they became entangled with a succession of evangelists, many of whom tended to mingle their religion with dubious sexual practices. Robert was readily beguiled by these seductive notions. In 1872 he suffered a nervous breakdown, and retired to a hydropathic sanatorium run by a Dr Foster, whose main form of treatment was prayer. Foster was a believer in the doctrine of Christ as the Bridegroom and his people as the Bride, and this required him to act from time to time as a proxy Bridegroom. Robert was converted, but his ailment was only partially cured. In the hope that a change would be beneficial, the Smiths set sail for England. There, Robert proved to be an effective preacher, and drew large audiences. As well as disseminating Dr Foster's doctrines, he seems also to have put them into practice. This became public knowledge in 1875 when Robert, feeling a call to act as a proxy Bridegroom, had departed for Paris with a complaisant Bride. The scandal was considerable, and the Smiths were forced to retreat hurriedly to America. Hannah was remarkably tolerant of her erring husband, and maintained in public that he was wholly innocent.

In view of these experiences, Hannah not surprisingly developed a deep mistrust of the male sex. Apart from the peccadilloes of evangelistic ministers, she had observed with distaste the way most husbands treated their wives, 'by which the man is considered, and considers himself, *master*'. As has been noted in Section Two, Hannah's disgust with the male sex had led her to propose to the Annual Council of the British Women's Temperance Association the ultimate remedy: 'Resolved that it is the sense of this Council that all men should be castrated.'

Hannah devoted her life to religion, feminism, the temperance movement and her children. Her niece, Carey Thomas, wrote: 'Aunt Hannah is the most completely honest woman, grand and noble in many ways … only deluded in two things, her slavish devotion and real selfishness for her children, and her Christianity.' Her children were devoted to her, but her son-in-law, Bertrand Russell, in what must be seen as a gross misjudgement, considered her 'one of the wickedest people I had ever known'. He believed that she was the cause of her son Logan's homosexuality. Virginia Woolf, however, enjoyed Hannah's conversation, particularly relishing her anecdotes about the Quakers. Hannah told her 'how the Friends prophesy at dinner, out of malice, so as to cheat someone of a hot dish'.

[Strachey, B. 1980; Strachey, R., 1914.

SMITH, (Lloyd) Logan Pearsall (1865–1946): man of letters.

Logan Pearsall Smith was born in New Jersey, USA, the son of Robert and Hannah (Whitall) Pearsall Smith. The Smiths were descended from a Quaker family which had migrated to America in the seventeenth century, and 'settled on the banks of the Delaware among the wigwams and papooses of the Indians, thinking their mild Quaker thoughts in their meeting-houses'. His desire to study English literature, and later to contribute to it, dated from an encounter with Walt Whitman in 1882. His enterprising elder sister Mary – later Mrs Costelloe, and then Mrs Berenson – had been carried away by Whitman's verse, and determined to meet him, despite his disreputable reputation among the Quaker community. She prevailed upon her distrustful but weak father to convey Logan and herself to his cabin at Camden, not far from their Germanstown home. All three fell for the amiable old ruffian, and carried him off to their house for the first of many visits.

Both Logan and Mary were educated at Harvard, where Mary met her future husband, Frank Costelloe, an English lawyer. They were to be married at Oxford, and it was arranged that Logan should attend, and then spend a year in Germany. This initiated his life-long affection for European culture, and distrust of the American way of life. In 1888 Robert and the whole family crossed the Atlantic, and settled the next year at Friday's Hill House, Fernhurst. Logan continued his education at Balliol College, Oxford, where he was befriended by the Master, the great Dr Jowett. He read *Literae Humaniores* ('Greats'), and was impressed by the rigour and depth with which he was expected to study the classics, compared with the relative superficiality he had experienced at Harvard. But after graduating in 1891, he came to perceive as petty the prevailing Oxford mores, where the ultimate objective was the gaining of First Class Honours in the Final Examination, for the greater glory of the College. Logan then had a spell in Paris; after that, he spent the summers at Friday's Hill House and the winters in Italy. In 1897, he rented High Building, in the western outskirts of Fernhurst, and lived there on his own.

He was there for ten years, and then accompanied his mother when she moved to Court Place, near Oxford.

In later life, Logan evidently returned to the Surrey Hills, for when writing about his old friend Gertrude Jekyll in his 1936 book of essays, he remarked that 'when, after a large lapse of time, I found myself living again in the old neighbourhood', he had re-visited her at Munstead Wood.[106] This does not necessarily imply that he had his own establishment; he may have been staying with his niece, Ray Strachey, at The Mud House, Fernhurst. Miss Jekyll was then, he says, 'almost on the threshold of her ninetieth year'. (She would have been 90 in 1933, had she not died at the end of 1932.) Logan shared with the great designer and maker of gardens a common interest in the derivation and meaning of words. When expecting a visit from him, she would prepare in advance a list of words to be discussed.

After Oxford and Paris, Logan gradually lapsed into the life of what he would probably have thought of as a 'man of letters' – reading widely, becoming acquainted with leading figures in the world of literature, and from time to time writing small pieces of carefully fabricated prose. His first published work was a collection of short stories, *The Youth of Parnassus* (1895), mainly written in Paris. It was not a success; he sent a copy to Henry James, who promptly mislaid it on the Underground. He also wrote a play about sin – 'in its British sense' – but it too disappeared without trace.

When in Italy, Logan often stayed with his sister Mary after her marriage to Bernard Berenson, the great authority on Renaissance art. The three of them jointly edited what Logan rightly described as 'a pretentious little review' called *The Golden Urn*. In this ephemeral journal Logan published little literary snippets which were the forerunners of his best known work, *Trivia*. This was first published in 1902, in a small private edition, of which about thirty copies were sold. It was later republished, in an enlarged public edition, in 1918. Logan's model was Baudelaire's *Petits Poèmes en prose*; he intended his book to be a collection of disconnected fragments of elegant prose, each piece having 'a life of its own, and some of them life enough to amuse the reader'. *Trivia* could be described as a graceful miscellany of random jottings, on topics which were not in themselves important, but which reflected Logan's view of the world as largely absurd, futile and transitory.

Logan's mother Hannah, herself an author, found *Trivia* 'quaint and interesting', but concluded that 'it begins nowhere and ends nowhere and leads to nothing'. It was, however, praised by such discerning critics as Desmond MacCarthy, George Santayana and Robert Bridges. Virginia Woolf, reviewing the 1918 edition, described the book as 'a handful of chosen flowers, a dinner of exquisite little courses, a bunch of variously coloured air balloons'. She concluded that 'there is little to be got from this book except pleasure'.[107]

Trivia contains a beautifully told little anecdote, which also happens to be of local interest, for it concerned a deranged vicar of Linch, the remote little hamlet deep in the Sussex countryside between Fernhurst and Milland. His derangement took an unusual form, whose significance would have passed unnoticed, had it not been for Logan. Before this happened, Logan, bicycling through the local lanes, had come upon the vicar in his church, and had engaged him in conversation. It emerged that until recently the vicar had spent most of his life at Oxford, where he had become a scholar of distinction, and an authority on Vegetation Deities in Greek religion. It so happened that Logan was acquainted with the book which the vicar had written on that subject, and so they had a happy conversation. A year or two after this encounter, Logan was dismayed to hear that the vicar had become odd in his behaviour, and then frankly mad; and to add to the scandal, his madness had taken a blasphemous turn. Logan alone was able to unravel the significance of these events. His interpretation was that the sudden transition, late in life, from the cloisters of Oxford to the remote depths of rural Sussex, with its luxuriant vegetation, had so unhinged the unfortunate vicar's reason, that he tended to confuse the Deity who presided over the Church of England with Demeter, the Corn Goddess of the ancient Greeks. The end came when the sight of the abundant fruits of the earth at the Harvest Festival finally convinced the poor man that his true allegiance was to the ancient fertility goddess, and he astonished the congregation by appearing for the service clad, as was appropriate for a hierophant of Demeter, in a fawn skin, with a crown of poplar leaves on his head. The startled communicants were offered a strange wheaten posset, and the service culminated when the vicar reverently placed upon the altar the figure of a woman, representing the holy Wheatsheaf. Shortly after these strange events, the vicar disappeared; whether to his death or to a lunatic asylum, was never determined.[108]

Logan had many literary friends; among them was 'Michael Field' a pseudonym for two spinster ladies: Miss Katherine Bradley (1846–1914), known as 'Michael', and her niece, Miss Edith Cooper (1862–1914), 'Field'. Together, they churned out a large volume of verse, mostly in the form of poetic dramas, all of which was almost totally ignored by the world at large. Logan's sister Mary (then Mrs Costelloe) and her lover (and later husband) Bernard Berenson had met the two ladies at Dresden in August 1891 while on a tour of German art galleries. Both 'Michael' and 'Field' were in hospital with scarlet fever, and were much touched by their visitors' gift of a bowl of roses.[109] When Logan got to know them they were living at Reigate, and later at Richmond. On one occasion, his sister lent them a cottage at Friday's Hill.

The ladies' susceptibilities had to be handled with the greatest care. When, in 1907, their dog Chow died, they were in great distress, so Logan and his sister Mary went to great lengths to write an appropriate letter of commiseration. However, it was judged to show inadequate appreciation of the depth of the tragedy, and for some years they were ostracised by the Michael Fields. During their lifetime, Logan carefully refrained from reading their works, lest he should be expected to express an opinion on its merits. After their deaths, he found, rather to his surprise, that much of it had 'a beautiful distinction'. T. Moore and D.C. Sturges published extracts of their copious and incoherent correspondence and diaries, which reveal their contacts with many prominent Victorian literary figures: Browning, Meredith, Wilde and Ruskin, amongst others. In an Introduction, Sir William Rothenstein, who had known them well, described the spinster ladies as 'two indomitable spirits'; but the most perceptive portrayal is to be found in Logan's sympathetic essay.[110]

Another literary personality whom Logan also met through the Berensons was none other than Gertrude Stein, the American author of many works in

STORR

her own idiosyncratic style of prose and poetry. She and her brother Leo visited the Pearsall Smith home at Friday's Hill in the summer of 1902, accompanied, it seems by other relatives, for Logan describes how 'a large black contingent of Steins ... led by the great Gertrude herself ... settled like a flock of birds on our terrace'.[111] In the autumn of that year Gertrude and Leo rented a cottage nearby, evidently in one of the more pastoral parts of the hilltop country, for Leo admired 'the springy English turf on which some nice red cows, lamby sheep, white ducks, lordly roosters and clucky hens wander in pastoral freedom'.[112] But the onset of winter blunted the charm of the rural scene, and brother and sister retired to London, and, so far as is known, did not return.

Logan was passionately concerned with the preservation of the English language and, with Robert Bridges and others, founded the Society for Pure English. The old-fashioned term 'man of letters' seems best to describe his somewhat dilettantish activities on the fringes of literature. He himself seems to have felt dissatisfied, and perhaps a little puzzled, that he had not been able to achieve something more substantial. A description by Beatrice Webb, when she was staying at Friday's Hill in 1901, gives a convincing portrayal of this likeable but ultimately ineffectual figure:

A refined and gentle-natured bachelor, with a pretty talent for turning out sentences, and a taste in collecting bric-à-brac ... tall, delicately featured, always smiling. But behind the smile there is a deep-seated melancholy, due to a long record of self-conscious failure to become an artist in words. The world has proved too complex for him to grasp; he is perpetually breaking off before he has mastered even a small portion of it.[113]

[DNB; Smith, L. P., 1936 and 1938; Drabble; Strachey, 1980; Russell, J., 1960.]

STORR, Rayner (1835–1917): auctioneer, medieval scholar and Positivist.

The catalogue of the British Library lists two works by Rayner Storr: his *Record of Lectures and Addresses of the Haslemere Microscope and Natural History Society* (1893–98), and his *Concordance to the Latin original of De Imitatione Christi* (1910). The first displays him as the competent and conscientious Secretary of the Society, careful to check his detailed account of each lecture with the author, and shows his respect for every sort of objective knowledge, and its practical application; the second reveals him revelling in the rich poetic imagination and idealism of Thomas à Kempis's great work. With this wide range of interests he was soon at home among the eclectic hilltop community.

But Rayner started his career in a much narrower groove. He and his brother John were partners in the family firm of Debenham, Storr & Sons, Auctioneers, of King Street, Covent Garden, which had prospered under the care of their father, William Bromfitt Storr. In 1871, when only 36, Rayner retired; he had discovered that auctioneering was not his *métier*; and he was evidently not under any necessity to earn his living. He continued for a time to live in Upper Norwood, but then, in 1875, he heard of Haslemere as a suitable country retreat, and decided to investigate. But so remote was the little village at that time – even though it had had its station on the Portsmouth line for sixteen years – that when Rayner asked at Clapham Junction for a ticket to Haslemere, the clerk denied that such a place existed.

Having eventually arrived, Storr acquired The White House, in the High Street, together with Tudor Cottage next door (they are now united as the Georgian Hotel). Both were put up for sale in 1897. The White House was then a large mansion, with twelve bedrooms – though no mention of a bathroom – gallery, music room, studio, dining-room, drawing-room, school room and an ornamental garden-house according to an advertisement in the *Surrey Times*, 30th October 1897. Tudor Cottage was sold separately to H.W. Mozley of Eton College for £4,500, and was then leased to Lady Dorothy Nevill.

Rayner Storr

In 1897 Storr moved to Highcombe Edge, Tilford Road, Hindhead. It was a newly-built house, designed for him by a local architect, W.A. Pite – brother of the better-known architect Beresford Pite – whose first commission had been the renovation of Tudor Cottage. Highcombe Edge was a large, solid, brick building, with nine bedrooms and four bathrooms, plus a central tower with four lunettes. It was situated on the western edge of the Devil's Punch Bowl, with magnificent views but full exposure to east and north winds. Storr had only recently settled in there when Thomas Wright called upon him in his 'handsome residence … a few steps' from Grant Allen's house.[114]

During his time at Haslemere, Storr was an active member of the parochial council, and showed the practical side of his nature in his concern with the local drains – or rather, the lack of them, since as late as 1890 the sewage generated by the inhabitants had been collected in cesspits. His concern may have been initiated by the death of his first wife from typhoid in 1877, and reinforced by the diphtheria epidemic which hit the town in 1886. A proposal for a drainage system, supported by Storr, had been rejected as too expensive. Matters came to ahead when two articles appeared in the *Lancet* deploring the existing system as 'both offensive to the senses and fraught with grave danger to health', particularly as 'some of the most eminent in arts, science and literature possess houses there to which they resort for the renewal of health of body and mind'.[115] This attack caused much indignation among the citizens of Haslemere, and a search was started for the culprit who had 'leaked' to the *Lancet*. Storr was the prime suspect, but he stoutly rejected the charge in letters to the two local newspapers.

After his move to Hindhead, Storr continued to be active in many aspects of local life, becoming Vice-President of Grayshott cricket club and Undershaw football club, and President of the Grayshott and District Refreshment Association, which ran The Fox and Pelican (see Section One). In 1908 he left Hindhead and settled in Hampstead, where he remained until his death in 1917.

Storr was one of the little band of enthusiasts who started the Haslemere Microscope and Natural History Society. He was a committee member in 1889, honorary treasurer in 1890, and honorary secretary from 1891 to 1900, and did much to broaden its scope to include the study of Man as well as of Nature. He impressed Thomas Wright by quoting from memory 'choice passages from the latest lectures of Mr Grant Allen and Dr Hutchinson'. He compiled and published full accounts of the lectures and addresses to the Society during 1893–98, submitting his version to the speaker for verification – the only Secretary to do this.

Storr was brought up a Methodist, but after his retirement he became an adherent of Positivism – the 'Religion of Humanity'. He first heard of the movement through his sister-in-law. She knew Susan Bridges, whose husband, Dr John Henry Bridges, was a friend of the leading English positivists, Richard Congreve and Frederic Harrison. In 1871, at the time of his retirement, Storr got to know the French Positivist, Gustave Pradeau, and became a lifelong friend. Although he did not formally join the movement till later, Storr was sufficiently impressed by Pradeau to educate his two sons on the lines recommended by the movement's founder, Auguste Comte, in his *Synthèse*. During the Boer War – to which he was vigorously opposed – Storr got to know another leading Positivist, S.H. Swinny. Swinny stayed at Highcombe Edge in 1907, and from then on Storr contributed regularly to Positivist funds, becoming a formal member of the Society in 1909. He also contributed two articles to the *Positivist Review*: 'The Consecration of Suffering' (October 1913), and 'Love and Service of Country' (November 1915). Wilfred Storr, Rayner's surviving son from his first marriage, became Treasurer of the Positivist Funds.[116]

The broad scope of Positivism, which respected equally the objectivity of science and the idealism of religion, appealed to Storr's eclectic *Weltanschauung*. Although rejecting, on rational grounds, the existence of a personal deity, he nevertheless cherished the piety and devotion of the older religions, and believed that they came to their full fruition in Positivism. He was deeply sensitive to the beauty of poetry, and particularly admired the works of Dante. But his greatest love of all was for *De Imitatione Christi*, the famous devotional work supposedly written by Thomas à Kempis (c.1380–1471). Storr taught himself to read the medieval Latin, greatly aided by his friend Gustave Pradeau, and with some help also from Gilbert Murray and Lord Morley. His objective was to compile a Latin concordance which would then 'forward the habit of reading *The Imitation* in the tongue in which it was conceived by its Author, the language then common to the learned throughout the West, and the beauty of which as used by him no translation can reproduce'. He was not alone among the Positivists in his love and admiration for *The Imitation*, for Comte himself had a great regard for what Storr called 'this incomparable poem'. Nor was it only the poetry that appealed to Positivists; so powerful did they find its advocacy of selflessness and spiritual striving, that they were able to overlook irrelevancies like 'God, his Christ, his Eucharist, his Bible, and Hell, and Cross and Heaven'.

Storr therefore devoted much time and labour to the production of his weighty *Concordance to the Latin original of the four books known as De Imitatione Christi, given to the world AD 1441 by Thomas à Kempis, compiled with full contextual quotations* (1910). This impressive work was not only commended by Positivists, but also in conventional ecclesiastical circles, and a second edition was soon called for. Storr even received a letter from the Vatican, saying that the Pope (Pius X) considered that his book 'cannot fail to be of real service'. This must surely be the only occasion on which the work of a Positivist has been praised by the Holy See.

Storr's religious outlook is best summarised in the preamble to his will:

> First of all, I wish to declare my firm hope and earnest belief in the final ascendancy of the Religion of Humanity, by the light of which I have endeavoured to conduct my life for many years past; which solves for me the problem of my existence and which through Love reconciles me to its conditions and keeps me in touch with all who aspire after a better and more spiritual life, however widely their Faith may seem to differ from my own. To my dear wife and children and to all who have learnt to love me in spite of my many faults and shortcomings I commit the memory of my character, which I regard as the immortal element of my life ...[117]

Storr's memory was in safe hands, for he was well loved. The publisher, Sir Stanley Unwin, who had married, Storr's daughter Mary, described him as 'a perfect dear', and used to tease his wife by saying that he 'fell in love with her father before he fell in love with her'[118] Stanley Unwin's nephew, Philip, wrote of his 'highly individual outlook' which 'kept him and his

189

family somewhat apart from the normal stream of social life'.[119] F.W. Bockett, a fellow Positivist, visiting Haslemere on his cycling tour, referred to 'great-hearted Rayner Storr', and praised the work he was doing for the Haslemere Microscope and Natural History Society.

Storr married twice: his first wife was Winifred Maria (1834–77), daughter of William and Ann Milton of Worcester, by whom he had two sons, Milton (1860–99) and Wilfred (1865–1933). His second wife, whom he married in 1881, was Alice Severn, a niece of Joseph Severn (painter, and the friend of John Keats who was with him at his death in Rome). Their children were Alice Mary (b.1884), who married Stanley Unwin, and Winifred (b.1885), who married Gerald Brooke (of Brooke Bond tea).

[S.H. Swinny: *Positivist Review* (1917), pp. 161–4, 'In Memoriam Rayner Storr'; *Haslemere and Hindhead Herald*, 2nd June 1917; *Hampstead and Highgate Mail*, 15th July 1933.]

SWANTON, Ernest William (1870–1958): museum curator, naturalist and local historian.

In 1888, Jonathan Hutchinson appointed the youthful Swanton to assist him in the museum he was just starting at his house at Inval. Swanton later recalled that the first exhibit was a fox, kept in a pig-sty. When the collection acquired a more permanent home on Museum Hill in 1895, as the Haslemere Educational Museum, Swanton became its first curator, living nearby at Brockton, in College Hill from 1905. When the museum moved to its present home in the High Street, Swanton occupied the living quarters attached to it, until his retirement in 1948.

Swanton's interests were in natural history, and in the past development of the town of Haslemere and the surrounding district. Another resident, the architect J.W. Penfold, was also keenly interested in local history and had collected a vast amount of miscellaneous information about the past of Haslemere, which he would probably have put together in a book, had he not died in 1909. As it was, Swanton inherited Penfold's notes, and collaborated with another friend and correspondent of Penfold's, Percy Woods, in writing *Bygone Haslemere* (1914).

Woods, who was a medieval scholar of great erudition, contributed the chapters on Haslemere in the Middle Ages. Swanton wrote the rest, including the section on archaeology. It was in many ways a pioneering work, and demonstrated that local history could indeed be a subject for serious study. It had merit in showing what could be made of somewhat unpromising material, for it has to be said that for the greater part of its history, nothing much happened in Haslemere. The two authors, and Penfold before them, had amassed a great deal of laboriously gathered information about who owned which plots of land at different periods of the town's history, making for a scholarly if hardly enthralling work. Apart from this, there was little to record, except for some brawls during elections in the eighteenth century, and the peccadilloes of Revd James Fielding, a curate of Haslemere who is believed to have supplemented his income by highway robbery. Swanton did not attempt to bring his history up to date – apart from biographies of a few local worthies – and he has little to say about the coming of the intelligentsia in the late Victorian period.

Swanton's abiding interest was in all aspects of natural history. He was a Fellow of the Linnean Society, and had been President of the British Mycological Society. It was during his tenure of the latter office that an unfortunate lapse led him to mistake an aberrant specimen of *Psalliota xanthoderma* for a field mushroom, resulting in what he described as 'a smart stroke of affliction'. It was probably this event which was mentioned by Flora Thompson in one of her *Peverel Papers* as a reason why she gave up collecting fungi for her table.[120] She was a member of the Haslemere Natural History Society during her time in Liphook, and had no doubt heard it from Swanton herself.

Ernest William Swanton

Swanton was the author of a number of books about natural history: *Pocket Guide to the British Non-Marine Mollusca* (1906); *Fungi, and How to Know Them* (1909); *Monograph of the Mollusca of Somerset* (1912); *British Plant Galls* (1912); *A Country Museum* (1912), and *The Rise and Development of the Haslemere Natural History Society* (1939). His many contributions to the local press were collected and published as *Country Notes* (1951).

[Obituary notices in *Haslemere Herald*, 24th October 1958; *Nature*, 22nd November 1958; *Proceedings of the Linnean Society*, April 1959.]

TENNYSON, Alfred, 1st Baron Tennyson (1809–1892): poet.

There are many possible ways of approaching Tennyson, and they are all well worn. Here, I have tried to see him as he was at home at Aldworth, mainly through the eyes of his neighbour, James Henry Mangles, who got to know him well as they strode over Blackdown together, or smoked post-prandial pipes in each other's houses. The notes which Mangles jotted down in his diary of their conversation, though necessarily much abbreviated (they were written up from memory each evening, in a sort of 'telegraphese'), give a sense of what it was like to have a friendly conversation with the great poet. They supplement, and extend, the similar account in William Allingham's diary.[121] Another local witness was Anne Gilchrist, who entertained Tennyson at Brookbank, her cottage in Shottermill, and helped Tennyson to choose a site for Aldworth. The original suggestion seems to have come from Walter White, who wrote in his journal on 20th November 1864: 'Talked about the encroachment of buildings around Farringford … I suggested his [Tennyson] buying an estate of heathland, ninety acres including a hill, one of the Devil's Jumps, at Chart [Churt] near Haslemere, which was on the market for £1,500. He seemed to like the notion, but started objections.' Mrs Gilchrist records that White had heard of the estate through her neighbour, James Simmons. But it was not until August 1866 that the Tennysons were able to come to Haslemere to inspect the site, as described in Anne Gilchrist's entry.

In the event, the site at Churt was rejected as 'very dear at the money'. Later in 1866, the Tennysons stayed for a month at Stoatley Farm, on the lower slopes of Hindhead, to resume their search. They were back again in the following summer, when they took rooms for themselves and three servants in Grayshott Farm (re-named Grayshott Hall by a subsequent owner, and later rebuilt). Whilst they were there, they discovered, with the help of Anne Gilchrist and James Simmons, the site on which Aldworth was later built. It was a windy platform, with an enormous view, on the eastern face of Blackdown. James Simmons arranged the purchase from the Cowdray estate of Lord Egmont. The foundation-stone was laid on 23rd April 1868, and the Tennysons moved in at the end of July 1869.[122]

Tennyson had intended that Aldworth should be a simple cottage, but James Knowles, whom he had engaged as an architect after a chance meeting on Haslemere station, gradually persuaded him that he needed something more imposing. Opinions of its architectural merits have varied a good deal, but have not, on the whole, been particularly complimentary. Walter White's was probably a just assessment when he called it 'a palatial-looking house on a small scale', though he did not commit himself on its aesthetic merits. Nairn and Pevsner, in the *Buildings of England* series, likened it to 'a small fussy hotel half-way between the French and English C16 style'; Peter Levi called it 'a grander, private version of the Grosvenor Hotel' (designed by

Knowles and his father). A later architect, Thomas Mawson, who arranged the sale of the house to the Gaekwar of Baroda in 1920, thought it 'a passable Gothic structure ... too small in scale for a site possessing such a spacious character; but the stone terrace, with its Gothic balustrade, does far to atone for this defect'. F.W. Bockett, peering at the house down the drive marked 'Private', reported that 'there is nothing about it to impress one. A common-place millionaire might have a dozen such houses built at short notice.' He added, 'The site, however, is one that even millionaires cannot command every day.' Alfred's grandson, Sir Charles Tennyson, who often stayed at Aldworth in his youth, gave a detailed account of the interior. Of the exterior, he said that, 'Like Farringford, it was essentially a Georgian house in a Gothic dress, but built in stone instead of brick, and more formal in design. Moreover, where Farringford had grown rather haphazardly over half-a-century, the design of Aldworth was remarkably logical, seeming to express the clarity and luminosity of the later Tennyson'. In her biography of James Knowles, Priscilla Metcalf described the thinking behind the design. The house was, she said, 'a fantasy on the idea of an Anglo-French manor-house' of four hundred years ago, when Malory's *Morte d'Arthur* was first printed. Like Tennyson, Knowles was fascinated by the Arthurian legends, so Aldworth was to be a sort of Victorian Camelot. The embodiment of this fantasy was 'an English late-fifteenth-century stone manor-house of a gener-alized sort, with the steep-roofed French skyline English architects liked in the 1860s, modern conveniences, and poetic resonance too'.[123]

The problem with Aldworth is that it never quite matches up to the grandeur of the site, with its stupendous view. Any building of lesser dimen-sions than Blenheim Palace would probably appear fussy and insignificant in such a majestic situation.

Whatever the merits or demerits of the house, the situation fulfilled Tennyson's desire for solitude and for protection against what he called the 'Cockneys' who, he told Mangles, at Farringford would even 'come up to the windows when he was at dinner'. However, if the following letter, dated 21st October 1877, is not some sort of curious spoof, there appears to have been one occasion when his defences were penetrated:

Mr Alfred Tennyson presents his compliments to the Governor of Witley Hospital for Convalescent Lunatics and requests him to be so kind as to take precautions, that his patients should not pay visits to Aldworth, as two did yesterday (one describing himself as assis-tant librarian of the British Museum). Mr Tennyson is very glad if they in any way enjoyed themselves here, and hopes that they did not suffer from their long walk.[124]

At Aldworth, Tennyson felt free to roam the Blackdown plateau at will, taking with him, as an additional precaution, a whistle with which to warn off other walkers, lest they should approach too closely while he was in the throes of composition (the whistle can be seen in a photograph taken in about 1888).[125] As Lord Houghton remarked, 'he has built himself a very handsome and commodious home in a most inaccessible site, with every comfort he can require, and every discomfort to all who approach him. What can be more poetical?'

Alfred Tennyson, with his whistle

Inaccessible it might be, but there was also the convenience afforded by the newly-opened railway; once the carriage had negotiated the rutted lane to Haslemere station, one could be in London in another hour and a half. Tennyson was keen to escape the vulgar sightseers, but he also liked the company of his friends, and very soon after he had moved into Aldworth the house was full of them.

They were probably all curious to inspect Tennyson's new quarters. The news that he had settled in Haslemere must have caused quite a stir in literary circles; for most, it was probably the first time they had heard the name of this obscure little Surrey town. The fact that the Laureate evidently thought that it was a desirable place for a literary person to live and work must indirectly have influenced some of the writers who subsequently settled here. It is impossible to know how many were actually influenced in this way, but Tennyson's reputation at this time was such that it cannot have failed to have an effect. For he was much more than just a poet; for many, he was – after the Queen – the leading figure of the age; the pre-eminent Victorian. There was solid evidence of his standing in the mundane fact that no poet, before or since, had ever earned enough from his poetry to enable him to own two large houses; and was soon to be endorsed when he became the one and only poetical peer.

As was evident, Tennyson's choice of the site of his house was primarily based on its being a place where one could find solitude, yet be within reach of one's London friends and publisher. But he was also enthralled by the altitude, and the stupendous view it afforded over the Sussex Weald. From the upper windows of the house, or strolling on the terrace, where crimson flowers 'burn like lamps against the purple distance', the wooded plain, bounded by hills to right and left, stretched far away to distant Kent. 'It wants nothing,' said Tennyson, 'but a great river looping along through the midst of it'.[126] It was beautiful, and it was also symbolic of Tennyson's place on this Victorian Olympus. From here he could survey his realm, brood over its lack of moral tone, utter warnings when necessary, and keep a wary eye on those untrustworthy French.

But although Tennyson must have been aware of the tremendous respect and affection in which he was held by the educated public, he was even more conscious of some critical voices that were beginning to make themselves heard. They were, in fact, few indeed, and it was only very recently – with the appearance of possible rivals, such as Swinburne – that any cracks had appeared in the almost universal adulation which followed the publication of *In Memoriam* in 1850. Tennyson's conversations with Mangles reveal his extreme sensitivity to these few critical voices. One day in March 1871, Mangles was drinking a glass of post-prandial claret with the poet in his study. Tennyson was in a black mood; the Aldworth drains had been giving trouble, and now, he complained, 'the admirers of Swinburne gave him no peace'. One of the worst of these was James Hain Friswell, whose *Modern Men of Letters Honestly Criticized* had just been published. It contained, so he told Mangles, 'the most abusive passages', alleging that Tennyson, 'spent his whole time lying on the sofa, smoking tobacco'.[127] Friswell, who considered Tennyson 'a half-hearted and polished rhymster', was one of several critics who felt that Tennyson had had an altogether too-easy life, apparently believing that adversity and despair were essential for the production of great poetry. Others were even more offensive, sending him 'the most libellous letters, addressed "Miss Alfred", "The Poet Laureatess", and worse things than that'. Tennyson was hypersensitive to adverse criticism, and was grossly exaggerating when he complained to Mangles that 'all the press was teeming with insults and abuse'.

Tennyson hit back at the odious Friswell with a hendecasyllabic counterblast:

> Friswell, Pisswell – a liar and a twaddler –
> Pisswell, Friswell – a clown beyond redemption,
> Brutal, personal, infinitely blackguard.[128]

Other criticisms were more discriminating, and were not so much directed against the poetry itself, still less against the poet, as against the implication that it was the vehicle of a profound philosophy. Everyone recognised Tennyson's great virtuosity as a creator of beautiful verse; what they were less sure about was the significance of the content. Thus Matthew Arnold said 'the real truth is that Tennyson, with all his temperament and artistic skill, is deficient in intellectual power'.[129] Frederic Harrison, who had been an early visitor to Aldworth and who later lived for a time near by at Blackdown Cottage, knew Tennyson and his works well. He thought that 'it would have been well had he felt clearly that it was his destiny to be the poet – not the philosopher –

much less the moralist, the reformer, the evangelist.' Such views are not dissimilar to the general assessment of Tennyson a hundred years after his death; few would deny that he was one of the great English poets, or claim that he was one of the great English thinkers.

Another characteristic of Tennyson, which emerges clearly in Mangles's account, is his constant anxiety about what happens after death. Frederic Harrison said of him that 'the problem of life beyond the grave haunted his mind till it became a kind of cerebral nightmare'.[130] This worry had been with him most of his life; when his father died in 1831, young Alfred spent the night with the corpse, hoping that his ghost would appear and confirm the existence of life after death. It didn't.[131] As a consequence, he was greatly intrigued – as were many late Victorians – by spiritualism. The first séance he attended was held at Aldworth, when, under the influence of the medium, a Mrs Acworth, the table in Tennyson's study 'heaved like the sea'. The subject of spiritualism cropped up several times during his conversations with Mangles, who seems to have been somewhat of a sceptic, declining Tennyson's offer to lend him a book on the subject.

But although Tennyson was apt to brood at times about his critics, and to worry about his prospects in the after-life, he was also ready enough for a cheerful gossip about some of the less creditable goings-on in literary circles. He was intrigued, for instance, by Byron's supposed incestuous relations with Augusta Leigh, and told Mangles how he had 'tried to pump' Thomas Campbell about the scandal when he was 'full of brandy' after a publisher's dinner. Another brief report by Mangles of a comment on Swinburne: 'told of how he had bitten Menken', shows that Tennyson was familiar with the story of Dante Gabriel Rossetti's offer of £10 to the actress Adah Menken to seduce Swinburne, and how all she had managed to achieve was a bite. Tennyson was also familiar with the tale of how the grief-stricken Rossetti had buried the manuscript of his poems in his wife's grave in 1862, only to retrieve it in 1870 so that the poems could be published.[132]

Much of Tennyson's conversation with Mangles was concerned with plants, for he was aware of the latter's horticultural and botanical expertise and often sought his advice about his own garden. When he first visited Mangles's house, he told him 'I have come to see some flowers. I have seen none all the year', the newly-created garden at Aldworth being as yet largely bare. The sight and smell of flowers were important to him, and they often feature in his poems, and – meticulous wordsmith that he was – he had to be sure he had got his facts right. Not only flowers; when Mangles walked over to Aldworth on 21st September 1872, Tennyson was still brooding over the composition of *Gareth and Lynette*, and told Mangles that it was by his advice that he had used the phrase 'as one/ That smells a foul-fleshed agaric in the holt', in his account of how the snobbish Lynette turned up her nose at Sir Gareth when he was pretending to be a scullion, saying that he smelt of the kitchen.[133] Thomas Wright also detected a reference in the poem to the

Punch Bowl at Hindhead – 'saw / bowl-shaped, thro' tops of many thousand pines/ a gloomy-gladed hollow slowly sink/ to westward'. Emily Tennyson wrote at Aldworth on 7th October 1869 that Alfred had read to her the beginning of *Gareth and Lynette*, and Mangles's diary shows that he was still composing it there nearly two years later. Much of the poem therefore originated at Aldworth.

The acquisition of Aldworth had coincided with the end of a period of stagnation in Tennyson's creative life, and may indeed have been the stimulus which reactivated his genius. He resumed work on *Idylls of the King*, and in 1870 published four of the idylls as *The Holy Grail and other Poems*. Also included in this volume was the much-loved *Flower in the crannied wall*, written in 1869–70, and based on a plant which Tennyson is said to have plucked from a wall at Waggoners Wells – a place he would have known from the time he stayed at Grayshott Farm in 1867, while looking for a site for Aldworth.[134] *Gareth and Lynette* was sent to press and published in 1872, and completed the *Idylls*, with the exception of *Balin and Balan*, which was not in print until 1885.[135] Hallam Tennyson said that the poem was 'written mostly at Aldworth', between 1872 and 1874. Sir Charles Tennyson believed that the down on which Arthur beheld 'Balin and Balan sitting statuelike,/ Brethren, to right and left the spring, that down,/ From underneath a plume of lady-fern,/ Sang, and the sand danced at the bottom of it', referred to Foxholes on Blackdown, the terminus of the poet's favourite walk from his house.

There are other indications of Tennyson's response to the scenery of Blackdown. His description, to General Hamley, of the view from Aldworth is well-known: 'You came, and look'd and loved the view,/ Long-known and loved by me,/ Green Sussex fading into blue/ With one gray glimpse of sea'.[136] Less often quoted is the delicate *June Bracken and Heather*, which formed the dedication of *The Death of Oenone and other poems* (1892), and is addressed to his wife Emily in celebration either of her seventy-seventh birthday (8th July) or the fortieth anniversary of their wedding (13th June):

There on the top of the down,
The wild heather round me and over me June's high blue,
When I looked at the bracken so bright and the heather so brown,
I thought to myself I would offer this book to you,
This, and my love together,
To you that are seventy-seven,
With a faith as clear as the heights of the June-blue heaven,
And a fancy as summer-new
As the green of the bracken amid the gloom of the heather.[137]

Martin, Page and Pinion suppose that this poem was composed in June 1891, during Tennyson's visit to Exmoor, and assume that it was descriptive of the scenery there.[138] This cannot be the case, for before this visit, in April 1891, Tennyson had read 'the little dedication to Oenone' to Herbert Warren (President of Magdalen) and others.[139] It must therefore have been composed during the previous year, just before Emily Tennyson's birthday on 8th July 1890. The Tennysons were at Aldworth for most of June 1890, so it can be said with confidence that *June Bracken and Heather* is, as Sir Charles Tennyson believed, descriptive of the landscape on the broad summit of Blackdown.[140] In Tennyson's time, the whole of the summit was covered with heather and bracken, for grazing by cattle and sheep prevented the growth of the Scots firs, which now dominate the area. Mangles does not have a lot to say about Tennyson's personal appearance, though at their first meeting he noted that the poet was dressed in 'a shabby coat and a wideawake', referring to the broad-brimmed hat which, with the cloak that he habitually wore out of doors, he had adopted as being an appropriate uniform. Thomas Carlyle had described Tennyson in his early thirties as 'A fine large-featured, dim-eyed, bronze-coloured, shaggy-headed man'; and again as 'One of the finest-looking men in the world. A great shock of rough dusty-dark hair; bright-laughing hazel eyes; massive aquiline face, most massive yet most delicate, of sallow brown complexion, almost Indian-looking; clothes cynically loose, free and easy – smokes infinite tobacco.'[141] From others, Tennyson's often, and – some thought – deliberately, dishevelled appearance produced a different response. Thus T.W. Higginson, an American Unitarian minister, visited Tennyson at Farringford, and thought that 'his brilliant eyes and tangled hair and beard gave him rather the air of a partially reformed Corsican bandit, or else an imperfectly secularised Carmelite monk'.[142]

It was at Aldworth that Tennyson died, and he did so in a style appropriate to the passing of a great poet. At a little after midnight, on 6th October 1892 the full moon streamed through the oriel window on the majestic figure, as he drew his last breath. In one hand he held a volume of Shakespeare, his finger near a favourite passage from *Cymbeline*:

> Hang there, like fruit, my soul,
> Till the tree die.

In the evening of 11th October the coffin was set upon the Aldworth wagonette, draped with moss and scarlet lobelia, and was led by the coachman down the sunken track now known as Tennyson's Lane, to Haslemere station, and thence to Westminster Abbey. H.D. Rawnsley, a cousin of Emily Tennyson's and an old friend of the family, was among the cortège that followed it down, and recorded the event in appropriate verse:

> The moon rose black against the dying day,
> And purple grew the dewy woodland dell,
> But from those lamps that lit the funeral wain

Shone such a glory through the hollow lane,
We felt, 'with him that leads us all is well',
And bravely followed down the darkened way.[143]

[Hoge (1981); Knies (1984); Lang & Shannon (1990); Page (1992); Levi, (1993); Martin (1980); Ricks (1969); Tennyson, C. (1977); Tennyson, H. (1897); Tennyson, H. (1911).]

TENNYSON, Lady Emily, née Sellwood (1813–1896): wife of Alfred.

Emily Tennyson published nothing under her own name during her lifetime, but she was in effect a co-author with her son of Hallam Tennyson's *Memoir* (1897). Not only was she constantly at Hallam's elbow, as a source of memory, advice and encouragement; while he was preparing the work, he also relied heavily on the *Journal* which she had tirelessly compiled from 1850 to 1874, and was only prevented from

The Tennysons with sons Lionel and Hallam, circa 1862

completing by her own illness. The diary, much truncated by Hallam, was eventually published in 1981; it had been preceded by the publication of Emily's *Letters* in 1974. Both of these works have been of inestimable value to Tennyson scholars.

After a long engagement, Alfred and Emily were eventually married in 1850. From then on, she was not only an affectionate wife, efficient house-keeper, mother and hostess, she also conducted most of Alfred's correspon-dence, took care of his finances, protected him from importunate strangers and adverse critics, and made helpful comments on his poetry. She was, Alfred said, 'my life-long and truest critic' – and encouraged him in his times of depression. Edward Lear calculated 'that 15 angels, several hundreds of ordinary women, many philosophers, a heap of truly wise and kind mothers, 3 or 4 minor prophets, and a lot of doctors and schoolmistresses, might all be boiled down, and yet their combined essence … fall short of what Emily Tennyson really is'.[144] Without her support, Tennyson's output of poetry would certainly have been less, and might have been much less.

Although the perception of history, and likewise of Emily herself, was that her prime mission in life was to be the guardian of her husband's genius, hints of a more robust personality can be glimpsed here and there. At her first

199

meeting with the redoubtable Thomas Carlyle, she told him, after one of his more outrageous remarks, 'Mr Carlyle, you know that is not sane'.[145] With equal audacity, she wrote in 1869 to Gladstone, who had recently become prime minister after a long spell as Chancellor of the Exchequer, proposing a novel system of taxation of her own devising. In a tactful note, Gladstone said he would like to discuss the proposal with her; but no more is heard of it. These are not the acts of a woman content always to remain in her husband's shadow, though that was where she wished to be seen to be.

All this was done by someone whose physical frailty was remarked on by every commentator. Much of her immense labour on behalf of her husband was carried out from a couch or an invalid chair. The cause of her frailty is obscure. It seems to date from her youth, when she was said to have a 'weak back'. Then, in 1858, frailty drifted into more definite illness, with extreme weakness and often much pain. It may be that some previous bone condition – possibly spinal caries – had been aggravated by menopausal osteoporosis (she was forty-five in 1858); but this is the merest speculation. Despite these disabilities Emily managed to carry on with her multifarious tasks until her final breakdown in 1874. Although supposedly just the result of overwork – which may well have been a contributory factor – this seems to have been some sort of severe physical illness. But, like so many of the maladies recorded in Victorian biographies, it was not immediately fatal, for Emily lived another twelve years, and died at the respectable age of 83. As with most other Victorian illnesses, its nature remains completely obscure.

[Hoge, 1974; Hoge, 1981; Martin, 1980.]

TENNYSON, Hallam, 2nd Baron Tennyson (1852–1928): biographer.

After his father's death, Hallam Tennyson lived intermittently at Aldworth before it was sold to the Gaekwar of Baroda in 1920. He was there in 1904 – having just returned from Australia – when Helen Allingham and her brother, Arthur Paterson, paid a visit. Amongst other things, he showed them his father's study, which he used for his own writing.

Hallam devoted most of his life – apart from some distractions, such as acting as Governor-General of South Australia, and then Australia, from 1902 to 1904 – to the propagation of what he conceived to be an appropriate image of his father's life and work. His instruments were successive carefully edited editions of the *Poems*, and, above all, his *Alfred Lord Tennyson, A Memoir*, which was published in two volumes in 1897. This was supplemented in 1911 by a volume of tributes, edited by Hallam, entitled *Tennyson and his Friends*. He intended the *Memoir* to be a comprehensive representation of 'the grandness, the unity, the nobility' of his father's life. It was a task for which he had been preparing well before Alfred died; indeed, he may be said to have been coached for it by his father, who was terrified of having his personality picked to pieces by strangers – as he put it to Henry Graham Dakyns, 'In life the owls – at death the ghouls.' In the Preface to his *Memoir*, Hallam made it clear that his father 'wished ... that my notes should be final and full enough to preclude the chance of further and unauthentic biographies'.

Hallam's cosmetic restructuring of his father's personality necessarily required suppression of some of its earthier aspects, with a consequent loss of many of the little quirks which give verisimilitude to the portrayal of the dead. There is no hint in the *Memoir*, for instance, that the poet's language in ordinary conversation could on occasion be decidedly coarse. There is an example of this in Mangles's record of his conversations with Tennyson, as they walked across Blackdown. The poet spoke of the pleasures of scratching an itchy place on his leg, saying 'No luxury like scratching – beats fornication all to pieces.'[146] Hallam had evidently heard his father make a similar remark, but thought it more seemly to translate it as 'I scratched till I could have shrieked with glory.'[147] Then again, one would never suppose, from Hallam's *Memoir*, that his father would stoop to retailing scandal, yet Mangles faithfully recorded several instances in which Tennyson refers to odd goings-on by some of his well-known contemporaries.

In portraying his father not just as a great poet, but also as the embodiment of all that was finest in the Victorian Age, Hallam was certainly echoing popular sentiment of the time. What he sought to do by his *Memoir* was to stamp this image indelibly on the minds of future generations. For quite a long time he was largely successful. Adverse criticism was almost wholly muted until after the 1914–18 War, when Lytton Strachey began his attack on Victorian hagiography, and Harold Nicolson published his unsympathetic *Tennyson* of 1923. Since then, a more favourable view of Tennyson has prevailed; but it is no longer Hallam's version of unalloyed veneration. Tennyson was undoubtedly one of the greatest of English poets, but, as recent biographers have emphasised, he was also a quirky, and therefore interesting, human being.

[Tennyson, H., 1897 and 1911; see Millgate, 1992, pp. 38–72, for a full discussion of the effect of Hallam Tennyson's editing on his father's texts and image.]

THOMPSON, Flora Jane, née Timms (1876–1947): historian of rural life.

Flora Thompson is best known as the author of *Lark Rise to Candleford* (1945), an evocative account – using assumed names – of her childhood in Oxfordshire. At the age of fourteen she became an unofficial post office counter clerk at Fringford ('Candleford Green'), and at twenty-one a post office assistant at the Hampshire village of Grayshott, adjacent to Hindhead. She remained there for three years, and soon after she left met John Thompson, another post office clerk, whom she married in 1903. They lived for thirteen years in Bournemouth, then returned to the hilltop country when John Thompson became sub-postmaster at the neighbouring Hampshire village of Liphook, from 1916 until 1928. While she was there, Flora was a member of the Haslemere Natural History Society.

Flora's career as a writer started only after her marriage and the birth of two children. Then in 1911, while she and her husband were living in Bournemouth, she won a competition in *The Ladies Companion* with an essay on Jane Austen. This encouraged her to write occasional articles for magazines, despite opposition from her unsympathetic husband. At Liphook, she wrote the 'Peverel Papers' articles which were published monthly in the *Catholic Fireside* magazine – some of these

Flora Jane Thompson – from the bust erected in Liphook

were collected together after her death and published in *A Country Calendar* (1979). But it was not until the late 1930s, after she and her husband had moved to Dartmouth, that she discovered how best to express her great gift for observation and recall. She had the ability to observe both people and nature with quite unusual intensity, coupled with an unusually retentive memory. She taught herself to express her recollections of long ago in a simple prose which created a vivid image of a long-vanished rural society. The first part of her major work was published as *Lark Rise* in 1939, and followed by *Over to Candleford* in 1940, and then by *Candleford Green*. The three were eventually combined and published as *Lark Rise to Candleford*. After this, Flora wrote *Heatherley*, intended as a sequel to the trilogy, which described the three years she spent at Grayshott. But she was dissatisfied with it, and did not attempt to have it published. It only appeared in print after her death, in a combined volume edited by Margaret Lane, entitled *A Country Calendar and other writings* (1979) – this went out of print, but *Heatherley* has since been republished locally (1998) to mark the centenary of her arrival in the Hindhead area.

Flora was immediately captivated by the beauty of the heathlands around Grayshott, which she explored in many long solitary walks, and soon got to know the flora and fauna, both of the open heath on the uplands and the pools and swamps of the valleys. It was a completely different landscape from the cultivated countryside in which she had been brought up, and which she also loved. Not only was the countryside different; the village of Grayshott, unlike the old-established villages and hamlets of Oxfordshire, was a new, raw settlement which had grown up to service the large houses which were springing up at nearby Hindhead. Thomas Wright stayed at Grayshott at the same time as Flora, and commented on the 'temporary look' of its newly-built houses.[148] Grayshott consisted, Flora wrote, 'of a couple of roads with shops, a new model inn with an artistic signboard' – The Fox and Pelican, with its sign by Walter Crane – 'and a few modern cottages and villas, many of them with an "Apartments to Let" card in the window. Since a famous scientist had discovered the virtues of the moorland air ... the place had come into being to serve the convenience of those living in the large houses and staying at the hotels which had sprung up at every favourable viewpoint for miles around.'

Flora was effectively in charge of Grayshott post office and its telegraph machine, for the nominal postmaster, Walter Chapman ('Mr Hertford'), spent most of his time and effort at his cabinet-making business. At first, Flora lodged with Chapman and his wife Emily above the shop which housed the post office. Although relations between Flora and her boss were superficially cordial, it emerged before long that Walter Chapman had marked psychotic tendencies. These became apparent at night-time, when he took to prowling round the house, and peering in through Flora's bedroom door. He did not molest her, but the effect was unnerving. He had a phobia about burglars, and alarmed Flora one night by firing at an imaginary intruder with a revolver. This decided her to leave and seek lodgings elsewhere, which she eventually found, after some difficulty. Although it was only a barely furnished room in a workman's cottage, Flora – somewhat of a loner – was much happier there.

It was as well that she left the post office lodgings when she did, for shortly after Flora left Grayshott, Walter Chapman's tendencies became more extreme. Becoming convinced that his wife Emily was unfaithful, he threatened to shoot her. She was then pregnant with her fifth child, and fled to Walter's brother Ernest. Unhappily, Walter Chapman managed to persuade her to return. Very soon, his delusions about her infidelity returned, and he also developed paranoid fantasies, sending a telegram to the postmaster of Petersfield which read: 'Diabolical plot to ruin me.' In this grim atmosphere Emily's baby was born. Six weeks later, Emily was discovered lying covered with blood from twelve stab wounds, with a cabinet-maker's carving tool embedded four inches in her back. She died shortly afterwards. At his trial, Walter Chapman was found guilty but insane, and committed to Broadmoor.

While Flora was working at Grayshott post office, Chapman behaved rationally enough, and as he was mostly engaged at his workshop, she conducted the post office business herself. This had an important bearing on her future as a writer, for since at that time Hindhead did not have a telegraph office, the Hilltop Writers who lived there had to come to Grayshott to do their business. Often several of them were there chatting together, and Laura listened enthralled to their witty conversations, though she could not of course join in. The effect was to give her an intimate insight into the literary world and its ways, which she could never have got from reading books alone, avid reader though she was. This instilled into her mind the first glimmering of an idea that she might herself one day become a writer.

Flora does not name these writers who came to her post office, but some are readily recognisable from her descriptions. On her first Sunday at Grayshott, she had seen 'a tall man on a crutch, with a forked red beard and quick, searching eyes, surrounded by a group of younger men who appeared to be drinking in every syllable' – unmistakably Bernard Shaw. Her favourite, and also that of the villagers, seems to have been Conan Doyle – 'the most popular man in the neighbourhood', who 'had made a great impression on the villagers; not so much by his literature as by the big fancy-dress ball he had given at the new hotel on the hill to celebrate it'. Another frequent visitor to the post office was Grant Allen, but although Flora refers to the shock and excitement caused by his novel, *The Woman Who Did*, she does not describe his appearance. Richard Le Gallienne she describes as 'a new young poet whose work was then held in high esteem in literary circles', but who was 'little regarded locally'.

Many other, mostly minor characters are also described, whom it is not possible to identify, largely because of Flora's habit of giving them fictitious names. But 'Madam Lilywhite', 'a small, elderly, daintily dressed lady', who advertised herself as *Milliner and Costumier, Baby Linen and Real Lace, Lending Library (frequent books from Mudie's)*, must be Mrs Fanny Warr, the 'draper and bookseller' at whose house Thomas Wright stayed when he came to write his book about Hindhead. She seems to have been a somewhat hoity-toity lady, who insisted upon being addressed as 'Madam', which caused some resentment among the other tradespeople. Flora could not afford her expensive clothes, but made much use of the lending library.

Flora's view of the village as a temporary settlement which had sprung up to serve the big houses at Hindhead was confirmed when she revisited Grayshott twenty years later. The place was shabbier, but otherwise little changed. Hindhead was by now a large, thriving suburb, fully capable of supplying its own needs from its own shops and post office. Grayshott, the small satellite which had nourished it in the early days, was no longer needed, and was looking decidedly faded.

[DNB: *Missing Persons*; Margaret Lane, *Introduction* to Thompson, 1979; Lindsay, 1990; J.O. Smith, 1997; Bloxham, 1998.]

TYNDALL, John FRS (1820–1893): natural philosopher.

The old-fashioned term 'natural philosopher' seems appropriate to describe the range of Tyndall's scientific work, which included studies on the properties of crystals, radiant heat, diffusion of light in the atmosphere, the motion of glaciers, spontaneous generation of bacteria and the germ theory of disease. He was a strong supporter of Darwin's theories, and, like Galton, he made a serious study of the efficacy of prayer. Perhaps because of the great diversity of his interests, Tyndall made no outstanding discoveries. His scientific work, though important, is not of the same calibre as that of great nineteenth-century physicists like Faraday, Maxwell and Kelvin; yet to the public, Tyndall was possibly the most famous of all the Victorian scientists.

In his celebrated – or infamous – address to the British Association at Belfast in 1874 he strongly defended scientific materialism, which led to him being attacked as a 'materialist'. However, in the printed version he admitted the existence of 'awe, reverence, wonder, woven into the texture of man'.[149] Tyndall's old friend Sir Frederick Pollock defended him against the charge of materialism in an address to the Haslemere Microscope and Natural History Society on 30th December 1896, in which he said that Tyndall 'did not want, as the theologians assert, to drag down spirit into the world of matter, but to lift up matter into the world of spirit'.

John Tyndall FRS

Tyndall was a forthright and outspoken character, always ready to make his views known on social and political affairs. Although a vigorous advocate of scientific progress, in some social matters he took a conservative line. Like Tennyson, he defended Governor Eyre when he was arraigned in 1866 for his over-vigorous suppression of the Jamaican rebellion; and – again like Tennyson – he strongly opposed Gladstone's Home Rule Bill, having been brought up in Ireland as a staunch Orangeman.

In 1856, Tyndall and his friend T.H. Huxley went to Switzerland to study the nature and formation of glaciers. This not only led to Tyndall's continued work on this topic, but also to his becoming an enthusiastic mountaineer, and engendered a life-long love of high places. He had the physique for mountaineering; even at the age of sixty-two he said 'I think no more of a march of twenty miles in cool weather than a walk across the room'. Like his friend and rival Edward Whymper, he made several assaults on the Matterhorn. Unlike Whymper's, they were not successful; but in 1861 Tyndall did

205

make the first ascent of the Weisshorn, and he was also noted for his solitary climb of Monte Rosa. He was so enamoured of the Alps that he built himself a house high up in the mountains near Bel Alp; Sir Frederick Pollock, another mountaineer living at Hindhead, visited him there on two occasions.[150] A feature of this house was that the ground-level bathroom had a hole in the stone floor into which a stream could be diverted by moving a boulder higher up the mountain. This ensured that Tyndall could have his customary bath of ice-cold water whenever he felt like it.

Tyndall had been appointed Superintendent of the Royal Institution in London in 1867, and occupied a flat at the top of the building from then until his resignation in 1887. In 1883, he and his wife Louisa – who was twenty-six years younger – felt the need for somewhere they could go to escape the murky atmosphere of London. In a letter to his sister, he described how they had built themselves a little hut 'on a wild and lovely moorland, about two hours distant from London ... We have but one room; but we have a capital little kitchen range where we make our own tea, cook our own chops, and boil our own potatoes. A tidy woman comes to us now and then to wash up and arrange matters.' The hut was situated in what was to become the garden of Hindhead House, which they planned to build in 1885; the architect was J.W. Penfold of Haslemere. Tyndall had already sunk a well 220 feet into the Greensand, from which he anticipated drawing water 'soft as the dew and clear as crystal'. Meanwhile, he enjoyed 'the simplicity and peacefulness of life in the small hut' adding that 'nowhere else do I get such food as my wife gives me here'.

On 22nd December 1885, Tyndall and his wife spent their first night in the new house. But by the next year he was already becoming alarmed by the number of people who were beginning to follow his example and building houses on Hindhead. So he bought up as much land as he could to preserve his privacy, eventually amounting to fifty-two acres in all, of which thirty-six were later given by his widow to the National Trust as Tyndall's Wood. Despite these frustrations, he wrote in 1886, 'I think our house is a perfect heaven upon earth.' In March 1887, Tyndall resigned from the Royal Institution, and from then on lived wholly in Hindhead.

However, Tyndall's purchases of land were not enough to prevent his neighbour from putting up stables within 200 yards of his study window. Soon he could hear the neighing of horses, the noise of voices and stable buckets, and the ringing of a bell summoning the coachman to the house.[151] He consulted his friend Sir Joseph Hooker at Kew, and was advised to plant a row of trees. Tyndall felt that this would take too long to become effective, so he built his famous screen of larch poles and heather in order to shut off the offending sights and sounds. Later, another screen had to be erected to exclude the view of a rather dilapidated cottage. Tyndall was proud of these hideous erections, calling them 'not only a thing of beauty but a noble thing'; but most other people disapproved. He went so far as to write an article in defence of his screens, which he sent to James Knowles, editor of the *Nineteenth Century*. Knowles declined to publish it, on the grounds that it 'contained too many personal allusions'; Tyndall was always ready for a quarrel, and when engaged in one he did not pull his punches. The screens survived until they were blown down in a gale in early 1901. Later that year, F.W. Bockett was toiling up the Hindhead road on his bicycle – slightly miffed by having been overtaken on the steepest section by a lady cyclist – and when passing 'the familiar dull-looking gabled house', he exclaimed 'But … where was the famous gargantuan screen that once shut off all signs of humanity? A few forlorn-looking poles swayed ludicrously in the wind, fragments of fir branches fluttering about their base.'[152]

One of Tyndall's screens, viewed from Hindhead Road

Tyndall wrote to James Simmons about his problems with the neighbours. He hoped that Simmons, who was active locally in the buying and selling of land – and very likely arranged the original purchase of his estate – might be able to prevent 'this lovely piece of moorland' from falling into the hands of 'these *damned* building speculators'. He was also concerned about the public footpath which he had diverted to a route further from his house. To indicate the change, Tyndall had planted a row of small Scotch Firs along the old path. Now, he told Simmons, his manservant had caught Mr Mason – presumably the occupant of one of the offending buildings – rooting up these trees. When detected, 'he slunk away'. Tyndall was something of a victim of his own fame: as soon as it became known that he regarded the air of Hindhead to be comparable to that of Switzerland, people flocked to take advantage of it.[153]

Along with his friends Frederick Pollock and Rollo Russell, Tyndall was a strong supporter of the Haslemere Microscope and Natural History Society in its early days, donating a microscope and a lantern. It was Rollo Russell who introduced his young nephew Bertrand to him. Tyndall was impressed by Bertie's attempts to find the centre of gravity of two walkingsticks balanced on his finger, and did much to stimulate his interest in science. Tyndall was also a friend of Alfred and Emily Tennyson, and often visited them at their houses Farringford and Aldworth.

Like so many of the great Victorians, Tyndall was frequently troubled by illness. His two long-standing complaints were indigestion and insomnia. He constantly suffered from the food provided by the Royal Institution – 'Had a boiled rabbit for dinner. These bad dinners do more moral damage than many are aware of' – and much preferred his wife's cooking, when they were having their alfresco meals in the hut which preceded Hindhead House. Insomnia was even more troublesome. To combat this, he had three musical boxes, given him by his friend T.A. Hirst, which helped to pass the night watches. The one he liked best played *Bonnie Dundee*; this enabled him to imagine himself marching up the Pass of Killiecrankie with the Highlanders. When this failed, he had to resort to chloral hydrate.

It was, however, neither of these afflictions, but a misadventure with the remedies he used against them, that led to the great tragedy of Tyndall's death on 4th December 1893. Every morning his wife Louisa was accustomed to give him his regular dose of magnesia (for indigestion) and every evening his dose of chloral hydrate (for insomnia). On the fateful morning she somehow mistook the bottles and gave him chloral hydrate, in a dose appropriate for magnesia. This was many times greater than his usual dose, and Tyndall instantly recognised by the taste that something was amiss. When Louisa told him what she had done, he exclaimed: 'My poor darling, you have killed your John!' And so it proved. Despite heroic efforts with emetics and stomach-tubes, he lapsed into coma, and by the evening was dead.[154] He was buried in Haslemere churchyard under a heather-covered mound, reminiscent in shape of a neolithic long-barrow. Louisa lived on at Hindhead House with her memories for another forty-seven years.

Tyndall published a large number of papers and several books on his scientific studies. He also wrote, for the general public, *Fragments of Science for Unscientific People* (1871); and, while at Hindhead, *New Fragments* (1892).

[DNB; Eve & Creasy, 1945; Brock et al., 1991; 'Hindhead House', *Haslemere Herald*, 17th July 1953.]

WALES, Hubert, pseudonym of William Piggott (1870–1943): solicitor and novelist.
According to Sillick, Wales lived at Hindhead for forty years, implying that he came there in about 1903. However, his first entry in *Kelly's Directory* is not until 1913, when he was living at The Long House – the site where Christina Rogerson had housed her slum children – Hazel Grove, Hindhead. Between 1919 and 1922 he moved to Homeward Heath, also at Hindhead, where he remained until his death. But his novel, *The Yoke*, shows that he was familiar with the hills round Haslemere much earlier than that; most likely, like the hero of that novel, he had stayed with friends in the district in about 1900.

Wales was best known for *The Yoke*, which evoked a scandal when it was published in 1907, causing the National Vigilance Association to denounce it as 'immoral garbage' (even in 1993, the London Library was still keeping its copy under lock and key). This reaction is not altogether surprising. The main theme is the affair between young Maurice Heelas, who is studying to be a barrister, and his friend Angelica Jenour, who is twenty years older. One day Maurice, overcome by sexual urgency, is about to sally forth to look for a prostitute. Realising the danger he is in, Angelica nobly offers herself as a substitute, and is accepted. A happy relationship ensues, which lasts some years, until Maurice falls in love with Cecil Grahame, the sister of his friend Christopher. Angelica then gallantly releases him to the younger woman. The novel ends conventionally with the marriage of Maurice and Cecil; but Angelica, less conventionally, feels no regret for what she has done.

The local interest starts when Maurice, who is not as yet interested in Cecil, is invited by Christopher to visit their mother's home in Haslemere. The house is described as situated in the High Street, but backed by pine trees and approached by a new road; the detailed account suggests that it may well have been a house visited by the author. Haslemere people are described as 'the sort who go in for high art and the simple life, and affect slovenly dressing'.

One Sunday afternoon, Maurice is persuaded to go on a bicycling tour of the neighbourhood with Cecil, and they set out up the Hindhead Road. She points out the houses of various notables on the way: that of a well-known publisher [Algernon Methuen, at Honeyhanger since 1897]; then 'the famous stockade erected by an eminent scientist to keep his neighbours at arm's length' [an obvious reference to Tyndall's screen; this suggests that Wales's visit to Haslemere took place before 1901, when the famous screen was blown down in a gale]. Near the summit they pass 'the house of the novelist who had given the world *Micah Clarke*, and with that enthralling story revived the historical romance' [Conan Doyle]. They then cross the 'hill-top' which had inspired 'the novels which bore that title, though the hand which had penned them would write no more' [Grant Allen, author of the Hilltop Novels, died in 1899]. These observations, taken together, suggest that Wales visited Haslemere in about 1900.

The couple freewheel down the long descent to the Pride of the Valley, and return to Haslemere by way of Frensham Ponds and Churt. Later in the story, Maurice again visits Haslemere. By then, the fate from which Angelica had saved Maurice has overtaken his friend Christopher Grahame: he has caught syphilis from a prostitute, and committed suicide. Maurice has to bring the bad news to Mrs Grahame and her daughter Cecil. On this visit, he walks to Blackdown with Cecil, and they 'filled their lungs with the pure air and their eyes with the scene amidst which a great poet had chosen to live and to die'. This is the last reference to the Surrey hills; the story reaches its conclusion in Devon, where Angelica finally hands Maurice over to Cecil.

Hubert Wales wrote a number of other novels, including: *Mr and Mrs*

WARD

Villiers (1906); *The Wife of Colonel Hughes* (1910); *The Spinster* (1912); *The Thirty Days* (1915); *The Rationalist* (1917). He also wrote *The Purpose – Reflections and Digressions* (1913), in which he sets out his philosophical position on some weighty issues. He is revealed as a mystically-inclined deist. All religions of the world are right,' he thinks. Yet on the other hand, 'Evolution is a great synthesis, it is working to lift the quality of all existence to one supreme calibre.' The central truth is:

> There must always have been Something – an unbeginning to eternal Something – and that Something is your Self.

No doubt this meant Something to him. In a later section, Wales set out his views on the qualification of parliamentary voters. At that time there was still a property qualification; he rightly pointed out that the amount of property someone owns is a poor guide to his ability to assess political issues. Instead, he proposed that all first-time voters should have to take an examination, of an hour's duration, in which they had to write a simple essay on a theme such as divorce, arbitration, trial by jury, capital punishment, etc.

Wales was also a member of the Society for Psychical Research, and published a paper in its *Proceedings* on 'A Series of Cases of Apparent Thought Transference' in 1920.

[Who Was Who.]

WARD, Mrs Mary Augusta, née Arnold [generally known as 'Mrs Humphry Ward'] (1851–1920): novelist.

Mary Augusta was a granddaughter of Thomas Arnold of Rugby and a niece of Matthew Arnold. Her father held for a time a teaching post at Oxford, and her husband, Humphry Ward, whom she married in 1872, was then a Fellow of Brasenose. Mary, although barred by her sex from formal studies at the university, was nevertheless soaked in the academic atmosphere, and educated herself to a high standard by reading at the Bodleian Library. In 1881, she and her husband and three children moved to London, where Humphry had a job on *The Times*, and Mary started writing fiction.

Her second novel, *Robert Elsmere* (1888), had a quite phenomenal success in Britain, and even more in America. Not only was it extraordinarily popular with subscribers to Mudie's lending library; it also found favour among the intelligentsia. An immense review by Gladstone admitted the author's brilliance, but vehemently attacked the book's main theme. This concerns the doubts, and finally rejection, of Anglicanism by the hero, an Oxford-trained clergyman. Despite his disapproval of Mrs Ward's religious views, Gladstone's review gave a further large boost to the sales.

The Wards had been living in a rather unsatisfactory London house in Russell Square – there was trouble with the drains – and liked to escape to the country in the summer. From 1883 to 1889 they had been accustomed to rent half a dozen front rooms at Borough Farm, situated among the heathlands just west of Milford (and later used for a time by Sidney and Beatrice Webb as their summer retreat). Here Mary was able to recuperate from the ardours of London in a *chaise-longue* in the garden, and it was there that she wrote the greater part of *Robert Elsmere*. (Mrs Ward told Thomas Wright that 'the commons between Borough Farm and Thursley are described in the beginning of the second book of *Robert Elsmere*.') William Allingham visited the Wards at Borough Farm in August 1887, and thought it 'a beautiful wild place – much vext by the rifle range close by'. He encountered Henry James there; he had come down from London for the day. Mary had first met James in 1882; even then he was becoming something of a literary guru, and Mary looked on him as a sort of father figure, whose approval was very important to her.

As well as writing *Robert Elsmere*, it was at Borough Farm that, during an evening walk, Mary had the first inspiration for its successor, *The History of David Grieve*, and dashed off the first few pages. Most of the rest of this novel was written at Haslemere.

As a result of the huge success of *Robert Elsmere*, the Wards were now in a position to replace Borough Farm by something more permanent. In August 1888, Humphry was despatched to Haslemere to buy land on which to build a house. He found and bought a suitable plot on Grayswood Hill, just north of Haslemere. There were delays in building the house, so in the early months of 1890 the Wards rented Grayswood Beeches – the same house that Conan Doyle was to rent briefly in 1896, while waiting for Undershaw to be built – and did not move into Lower Grayswood until July 1890. The house was re-named Grayswood Place by a later owner.

However, it was not long before Mary began to realise that this was not really the sort of establishment she wanted. She had been unsettled by a brief stay in 1889 in John Hampden's old house at Great Missenden; its antiquity and spaciousness appealed to both her romantic nature and her snobbery. For she had social aspirations; her aim was to become integrated into the landed gentry. Haslemere society was altogether too bourgeois for such ambitions, and, besides, she could not possibly invite her upper-crust friends to share her 'old gowns and milk puddings' at what now seemed to her just a suburban little house. Even the view of Blackdown, where Tennyson lived, was being obliterated by more and more plebeian villas. So when, in January 1892, the Wards discovered Stocks, next door to Ashridge in Hertfordshire, and with the Rothschilds almost within hailing distance at Tring Park, Mary decided that the time had come to leave what she called 'the villadom of Surrey'. Stocks, a mellow old house, with three hundred acres of parkland and 'an avenue of limes like a cathedral aisle', belonged to Sir Edward Grey, from whom the Wards first rented, and later bought it. Haslemere could not compete with such attractions, and so the Wards left for their new and imposing home in July 1892.[155]

David Grieve, mainly written at Haslemere, was very well received by reviewers, and was generally considered to be superior to *Robert Elsmere*. Mary Ward went on to write many other successful novels, and to engage in many additional activities in the social field. There is no record of her having returned to the hills of Haslemere, though it is quite likely that she visited E.C. Selwyn – the ex-headmaster of Uppingham who bought Undershaw from Conan Doyle – with whom she was doubly connected: her sister Lucy (1858–94) was Selwyn's first wife; his second was Maud Dunn, Mary's favourite cousin on her mother's side.

During the period when the Wards were spending the summer months at Borough Farm, Humphry was editing his two-volume history of *The Reign of Queen Victoria* (1887), to which Lord Wolseley contributed a chapter on 'The Army'.

[DNB; Sutherland, 1991; Trevelyan, 1923.]

WEBB, Sidney James, 1st Baron Passfield (1859–1947); **WEBB**, (Martha) Beatrice, née Potter (1858–1943): social reformers.

After their marriage in 1892, the Webbs were so inseparable in their life and work that it is convenient to treat them as a single unit (as the DNB does). But although theirs was an ideally successful partnership, as individuals they could scarcely have been more different.

Beatrice Potter, beautiful, elegant and rich, swept through the upper echelons of society with all the assurance of a born aristocrat. But she was also intelligent and perceptive, and conscious of the obligations of persons with her advantages towards those less fortunate. When, in 1883, she encountered Joseph Chamberlain, he was immediately attracted. For her part, Beatrice became totally infatuated with the handsome and eloquent Radical politician, thought by many to be a future prime minister. It must have seemed an ideal match, and Beatrice felt that she had in it her power to provoke a proposal of marriage whenever she wished. But then she became aware that Chamberlain would expect his wife to drop all her own interests in order to promote his political career, and moreover, to accept all his opinions without question. This was altogether too much for such an independently-minded young woman, and so, despite the strongest physical yearnings, she refrained from inviting a proposal. But the inner conflict continued for many years, and was liable to be reawakened at any chance encounter with Chamberlain. It was partly to assuage the pain that Beatrice threw herself into social work in the London slums.

It was in this context that she came across Sidney Webb. Beatrice had been struggling with the historical section of a book she was writing on *The Co-operative Movement in Great Britain* (1891), and when she turned to a friend for advice she was told: 'Sidney Webb is your man. He knows everything; when you go for a walk with him he literally pours out information.' It was an accurate description; at their first encounter, Sidney immediately wrote out for her a list of all the references she needed.

Sidney came from a lower middle-class family, whose meagre income was mainly derived from his mother's small hairdressing business in London. He did well at school and passed with distinction into the Civil Service, where he remained until 1892. But his real interest was in social reform, and he and George Bernard Shaw – who thought him 'the ablest man in England' – together formed the effective nucleus of the new Fabian Society. But he was handicapped by his physical appearance, which Beatrice appraised with cool objectivity in her diary after their first encounter:

Sidney and Beatrice Webb

A remarkable little man, with a huge head on a very tiny body … a Jewish nose, prominent eyes and mouth, black hair, somewhat unkempt, spectacles and a most bourgeois black coat shiny with wear; regarded as a whole, somewhat between a London card and a German professor … his pronunciation is Cockney, his H's are shaky, his attitude by no means eloquent, with his thumbs fixed pugnaciously in a far from immaculate waistcoat, with his bulky head thrown back and his little body forward he struts even when he stands, delivering himself with extraordinary rapidity of thought and utterance and with an expression of inexhaustible self-complacency.[156]

'But,' she added, 'I like the man.'

Not surprisingly, Sidney's love-life had not been a great success. He had been attracted to a succession of girls, all of whom had rejected him. So when someone as attractive as Beatrice made it clear that she welcomed his companionship (he was the first person to whom she confessed that she had been converted to socialism), it was inevitable that he would fall head-over-heels in love. Soon he was pestering her to marry him. Beatrice was still very much under the spell of the handsome Chamberlain, and, greatly though she admired his intellect, she found poor Sidney personally repulsive; and did not hesitate to tell him so. But his sheer perseverance eventually won the day, and Beatrice reluctantly agreed to marry him, much to the disapproval of her eight sisters and the consternation of many of her friends. Sidney and Beatrice were married in a registry office in 1892, and thus began a historic partnership. Despite Beatrice's lingering physical aversion, they became, in Bertrand Russell's words 'the most completely married couple I knew'.[157]

After their marriage, the Webbs had a house in Grosvenor Road in London, but they usually spent the summer months in the country, either at The Argoed, in the Wye Valley – Beatrice's parents' holiday home, which she had inherited – with friends or in rented accommodation. Although these were nominally holidays, it was not in their nature to stop working, and so they continued to write wherever they happened to be. They often stayed at The Argoed, where they were sometimes joined by Bernard Shaw. Others of these working holidays were spent, either separately or together, with friends among the hills round Haslemere. Even before their marriage they were walking the hilltops together. In July 1890, Sidney was staying with the Pearsall Smiths at Friday's Hill, while Beatrice was with the Frederic Harrisons at Blackdown Cottage.[158] In September 1891, Sidney wrote to Beatrice from Frank Costelloe's cottage at Friday's Hill, where he had gone to commiserate with Frank, whose wife Mary (née Pearsall Smith) had deserted him for Bernard Berenson. Sidney had liked the scenery – 'We will go up Blackdown together one day' – but not the barbecue at Friday's Hill: 'We all sat shivering in rugs and shawls round a fire of faggots … We toasted "marsh mallows", an American sweetmeat, and sang evening hymns.[159]

The Webbs (now married) spent August and September 1894, at Borough Farm, among the heathlands at Milford. In June 1896, they 'rode from Guild-ford through the Milford country to Millhanger, the little cottage in which [the Bertrand Russells] have settled themselves'. On returning from their world tour at the end of 1899, Sidney became anxious about Bernard Shaw's state of health, and visited him and Charlotte at Blen-Cathra, Hindhead, on three occasions. In July 1901, the Webbs were with the Pearsall Smiths, for an extended stay at Friday's Hill, Fernhurst. They were at Fernhurst again for nine weeks in May and June 1902, this time staying with the Bertrand Russells at Millhanger. During this period, the Webbs were embarking on their enormous treatise on *English Local Government*, published in nine massive volumes between 1906 and 1929; this is probably what was engaging their attention during their two sojourns at Fernhurst.

It was during their 1894 stay at Borough Farm that the Webbs heard that a wealthy solicitor had left £9,000 to the Fabian Society. Keeping the news quiet from their fellow Fabians, they hatched a plot to use the money to found what became the London School of Economics. They needed to make sure that the new institution should be solidly based on the methods of empirical investigation of the structure of society, which they were exploiting so successfully in their own work. It was to prove their most lasting memorial.[160]

The Webbs evidently had a liking for the heathland country, for eventually they bought their own house at Passfield Corner, near Liphook, in 1923; although only a few miles from Haslemere, the country there is less hilly, but the extensive heathlands are similar. When Sidney was reluctantly ennobled in 1929, in order that he could become Colonial Secretary in the Labour Government, he took the title of Baron Passfield, though Beatrice steadfastly refused to be known as Lady Passfield.

When Beatrice died in 1943, Sidney kept her ashes in a jar on the mantelpiece, which he used to show to visitors, remarking 'That's Beatrice, you know.' After he died in 1947, their combined ashes were transferred to Westminster Abbey. It was a fitting tribute to a remarkable partnership; no other married couple has been so honoured.

[DNB; MacKensie, 1978; MacKensie, 1982; Webb, 1979; Seymour-Jones, 1992.]

WELLS, Herbert George (1866–1946): novelist.

H.G. Wells had a number of connections with the hills of south-west Surrey. While he was living at Woking, and then Worcester Park, he explored the Surrey heathlands on his bicycle, and made at least two excursions to Hindhead. His novel *Tono Bungay* (1909) was based on Lea Park (later Witley Park). Finally, there was his sojourn at Cochet Farm, on the flanks of Blackdown, in 1911.

In his *Experiment in Autobiography* Wells describes a visit he made to Grant Allen at Hindhead in 1895. He had written a strongly critical review of Allen's *The Woman Who Did*, to which Allen had responded with his usual courtesy by inviting Wells to lunch. So, Wells:

> ... ran down by train one Sunday, walked up from Haslemere station and lunched with him in Hindhead. In those days Hindhead was a lonely place in a great black, purple and golden wilderness of heath; there was an old inn called The Huts and a score of partly hidden houses. Tyndall had built a house there, Conan Doyle was

close by, Richard Le Gallienne occupied a cottage as tenant, motor-cars and suburbanism were still a dozen years away. Le Gallienne came in after lunch. We sat about in deck chairs through a long sunny summer afternoon under the pines in the garden on the edge of the Devil's Punch Bowl.[161]

In March 1896, Wells was again at Hindhead, this time visiting Richard Le Gallienne in his cottage Moorcroft. They had an agreeable conversation, and Richard found him 'very comforting'.[162]

There is no record of any further visits to the hill country until he stayed at Cochet Farm, beneath the western flank of Blackdown. The precise date of Wells's visit is uncertain, but it must have been shortly after the appearance of the first instalments of his *New Machiavelli* in the autumn of 1910, probably in the spring of 1911. In his posthumously published autobiographical fragment, Wells wrote of this visit: 'I happened to go alone to lodge at a certain Cochet Farm near Haslemere to complete some work.' The work on which he was then engaged was probably his novel *Marriage*, the successor to *The New Machiavelli*.

But it seems that he also had another motive in going to Cochet. Towards the end of 1910, he had met Elizabeth von Arnim, well-known as the author of *Elizabeth and her German Garden*, and other novels. Her autocratic Prussian husband, Count von Arnim, had died in August 1910, and she had thankfully escaped to England. *The New Machiavelli* was just then appearing in serial form, and Elizabeth read it avidly, and with approval. She called on Wells at his house in Church Row, Hampstead, and found him alone. They got on famously together, and went for a walk on Hampstead Heath.

Not long after this encounter, Wells arranged his visit to Cochet Farm, situated at the top of the Valewood Valley. Although by this time much of the countryside round Haslemere had disappeared under bricks and mortar, the surroundings of the farm remained – and still do – as virginal as when James Mangles and Alfred Tennyson settled nearby in the 1860s. It so happened that Elizabeth had just then gone to stay with her sister, Mrs Charlotte Waterlow, at Ropes, on the eastern outskirts of Fernhurst, and less than a mile from Cochet Farm. Wells says, perhaps somewhat disingenuously, 'I forget now how far this proximity was arranged.' Arranged or not, before long Elizabeth and he were tramping together over the 'heathery hillside' which separated them, and they 'soon came to an easy understanding'. This understanding lasted for another couple of years, during which they were frequently together, either discreetly in London or, with less need for concealment, on the Continent. Elizabeth found Wells's lively frolics a great improvement on the ponderous Teutonic embraces of her late husband, and they also relished each other's intellectual company. On one occasion, finding themselves in an alpine meadow with a copy of the previous day's *Times*, they took great delight in making love on top of a letter from Mrs Humphry

Ward in that issue, in which she denounced the moral tone of the younger generation.[163]

Despite these distractions, some at least of *Marriage* probably got written at Cochet Farm, for Wells – ardent lover though he was – did not usually allow his love-life to interfere with his work. Considered as literature, it is one of his worst novels; but unlike some of its predecessors, its morals were impeccable, for it concerns a failing marriage saved only when the troubled pair resort to the rather desperate expedient of spending the winter together in a hut in the interior of Labrador.

In 1912, the young Rebecca West wrote a brilliantly destructive review of *Marriage* in *The Freewoman*. This attracted Wells's attention. He invited her to lunch, found she was attractive as well as intelligent, and in due course she succeeded Elizabeth von Arnim as his mistress.

[DNB; Wells, H.G., 1934; Wells, G.P., 1984; Dickson, 1969]

WESTON, Dame Agnes Elizabeth (1840–1918): sailors' benefactor.

Miss Weston's life-work began when she started a coffee-bar in Bath for the men of the 2nd Somerset Militia. She continued to correspond with them after they had been posted abroad, and through one of them heard of a ship's steward who had expressed a wish for a pen-friend who would 'help him in the Christian life'. This led her to send out regular monthly newsletters for distribution to ships' companies. In 1873, she went to Devonport, where some of her correspondents were being paid off, and there met Miss Sophia Winz, who became her life-long friend and partner. They joined in the work of the Royal Naval Temperance Society, but soon realised that something more was needed as a distraction from the sort of things that sailors on shore-leave are apt to get up to. So Miss Weston and Miss Winz founded 'Sailors' Rests' at Devonport and Portsmouth. Here, sailors were offered religious services, and were encouraged to sign a pledge of abstention from alcohol. Even if these offers were spurned, though, they could still get a meal and a bed for the night. The next forty years of Miss Weston's life were devoted to the management of these establishments, which eventually provided accom-modation for 1,600 men at the two naval bases. These good works earned her a DBE in 1918.

In 1901, Miss Weston and Miss Winz set up house at Ensleigh in Cross-ways Road, Grayshott. Miss Weston described it in her memoirs as 'a little chalet, among the pines and heather, with some picturesque woodland attached'. The two ladies had settled there partly because the rail service enabled them to reach their Portsmouth base within an hour, but they were also greatly taken by the local scenery: 'a lovely tract of country called Hind-head, rising to some 800 feet above the sea. It looks a bit of the Highlands let

WHITE

down promiscuously near London. The pines, the birch and the mountain-ash, the, heather and the fern, and also, in quiet corners, the lovely sylvan scenery makes the place unique ... the air is magnificent.'

Not surprisingly, Miss Weston had not been long at Grayshott before she became President of the Grayshott and Hindhead Temperance Guild, founded in 1903. Her work for the sailors was nearing its end, and in 1909 she summed it all up in *My Life Among the Bluejackets*. Despite its saucy-sounding title, her book provides a straightforward account of a long life of service to sailors, and concludes with an appropriately nautical reflection, in emphatic capitals:

'GOD'S HAND HAS BEEN UPON THE TILLER.'

[DNB; Weston, 1909; Chappell, 1949.]

WHITE, Montagu (d. 1916): South African civil servant; Consul-General and propagandist for the Boer Republics.

White was born in Cape Colony, South Africa and served in the Cape Colonial Service from 1874 to 1878. After taking part in the Gaika War, he moved to the independent Boer Republic of Transvaal, where he was the Mining Commissioner of Boksburg until 1892. In 1892, he was appointed Consul-General for the Boer Republics in Great Britain, and took up residence in London. During the tense summer of 1899, White sent repeated reports to Pretoria on the state of public opinion in Britain, and advised the Boer government to agree to a joint commission to sort out the disputes between the two countries. His advice was not taken, and war was declared in October of that year. That was the end of White's career as Consul-General. He then left London, and settled in Haslemere. His reason for choosing Haslemere can only be guessed at; it is not likely to have been simply a desire to escape from the fog of London to the pure air and open spaces of the Surrey uplands, though that may have been a factor. A more cogent consideration would have been a desire to get away from the rabid imperialism prevalent in the capital, to somewhere where there was likely to be a more tolerant attitude to supporters of the Boers. It seems possible that his friend Lady Dorothy Nevill told him that Haslemere was such a place.

Once arrived, White settled at a house called Goodwyns in the High Street. He remained there until 1910, when he married the daughter of Revd James Legrew Hesse, (last Rector of the combined parishes of Chiddingfold and Haslemere) who lived at The Lodge – also in Haslemere High Street – from 1848 until his death. Miss Hesse stayed on there after her father died, initially with her brother George, but on her own since 1883. After the marriage, White moved into The Lodge. When he himself died in 1916, his widow remained there until a few years before her own death in 1925. The Lodge was sold by her executors in 1926, and became the new home of the Haslemere Museum.

Montagu White, although technically an 'enemy alien', seems to have been for the most part treated tolerantly by the inhabitants of Haslemere throughout the South African War. But on 5th November 1899, at a time when the war was going badly for the British, a mob of thirty or forty youths 'hooted and howled' outside White's house in the High Street. A report in the *Surrey Times* of 11th November 1899 states that stones were thrown and windows broken. However, this seems to have been more in the nature of a drunken Guy Fawkes night revel, rather than a politically motivated demonstration. There do not appear to have been any other anti-Boer agitations at Haslemere.

Lady Dorothy Nevill, who occupied Tudor Cottage in the High Street from 1897 to 1903, had this to say about White and his wife:

> A great friend of mine at Haslemere was Mr Montagu White – before the Boer War representative of the Transvaal Republic in England. Not long ago he married another Haslemere friend of mine – a lady who owns a considerable property there, and also a charming house filled with interesting things, which I often went to admire.[164]

This passage was written after Lady Dorothy had left Haslemere, though she was evidently keeping in touch with her friends there. Although herself a staunch Conservative, she was not, in her own words,, overenthusiastic about the war', and many of her friends – notably Frederic Harrison – were strongly opposed to it.

Montagu White contributed the opening chapter, entitled 'The Policy of Mediation', to *The Story of the Boers* (1900). This was a propaganda book, published in London and New York, which was intended to sway American opinion in favour of the Boers. White advocated mediation to end the war, and thought that the United States would be the most suitable mediator.

White went back to South Africa at the end of 1914. In 1916, he had been about to return to England, but unexpectedly died – together with his sister, Mrs Hann – from mushroom poisoning.

[Who's Who; obituary in The Times, 22nd April 1916.]

WHITEWAY, Richard Stephen (d. 1926), JP: civil servant and historian.

Whiteway spent twenty-three years in the Bengal Civil Service, before retiring to Brownscombe, on the Hindhead Road at Shottermill, in 1892. He soon

WHYMPER

became active in local affairs; he was a subscriber to the Haslemere Microscope and Natural History Society from 1895, a JP, and a member of Farnham and District Council for 25 years. In World War One he also acted as
Honorary Secretary of the Haslemere Platoon of the 6th Battalion of the
Surrey Volunteer Regiment. He remained at Brownscombe until about 1920.

Whiteway's sister, Elizabeth, married Edward Nettleship, the ophthal-
mological geneticist who lived a little higher up the Hindhead Road at
Nutcombe-on-Hill. Whiteway's daughter Logie, then aged 14, was staying at
Nutcombe at the time of the 1891 census. Another daughter, Helena Isabel,
married Revd Leake, a curate at Shottermill, who later became the first vicar
of Grayswood. For the last six years of Whiteway's life he lived with his
daughter at Grayswood Vicarage.

At Shottermill, Whiteway taught himself Portuguese by studying the
Bible in that language. This enabled him to study Portuguese colonial history
in depth, and then to write: *The Rise of the Portuguese Power in India 1497–
1550* (1899), and *The Portuguese Expedition to Abyssinia 1541–43* (1902).

Whiteway's wife was associated with Mrs Beveridge in forming a
Shottermill branch of the League Against Women's Suffrage. She died in
1911.

[Sillick; obituary notice of Mrs Leake in *Haslemere Herald*, 10th June 1949.]

WHYMPER, Edward (1840–1911): wood-engraver, mountaineer and
author.

Edward was born in Ealing, where his father, Josiah Wood Whymper (1813–
1903), had his wood-engraving business. In June 1859 the family moved to
Town House, in Haslemere High Street. The move had been made because of
Mrs Whymper's ill-health – even at that early date, the area was thought to be
health-giving – but only a few months later she died suddenly after the birth
of her youngest daughter, Annette. James Simmons (the Shottermill diarist)
recorded her death in December 1859, adding that her husband had gone to
London that day, 'and before he returned she was a corpse'.

Edward is said to have disapproved of the move to Haslemere. His biographer thinks this may have been because of his poor opinion of the railway
service, which had only started in January 1859, and may well have been
functioning rather erratically. Edward often recalled – with perhaps a slight
touch of exaggeration – that there were occasions when he and the other
passengers had to get out and help to push the train up the gradient from
Witley to Haslemere. He himself sometimes preferred to walk the forty-five
miles from London to Haslemere.

Edward entered his father's business at an early age, and soon became a
skilled wood-engraver. It was in this capacity that he first encountered the

Alps, having been commissioned in 1860 to provide illustrations for a book on the mountains of the Dauphine. Thereafter he was hooked, and spent an increasing amount of time attempting to scale more and more formidable peaks. Finally, there was the Matterhorn, then thought to be unconquerable. Eight times he tried to climb it from the south side, and failed each time. (Amongst others, John Tyndall had also made two unsuccessful attempts.) But in 1865, he attacked the mountain from the north, and succeeded. This was the dramatic climb so vividly described and illustrated in Edward's *Scrambles among the Alps*, in which four members of the party tragically fell to their death on the descent.

Edward combined his mountaineering with writing. The book that made his reputation, *Scrambles among the Alps* (1871), was, according to his biographer, written at Town House. Edward was a chronic insomniac, and did all his writing between 10 pm and 3 am, or even later. A plain but ample supper would be laid out for him, and the rest of the household would then retire to sleep. In his book both the text and the engravings provide a graphic, not to say dramatic, account of his adventures, and it was deservedly a great success. Successive editions were called for in 1879, 1893 and 1906. For the following generations, it is a vivid reminder of the era when the tweed-jacketed and knickerbockered young men of the Alpine Club opened up the high mountains of Europe as a playground for the adventurous.

Edward subsequently explored mountains in other parts of the world, notably in the Andes, where he made a number of major climbs. He became interested in the problems posed by altitude sickness, concluding (wrongly) that oxygen would be no use in combating it. These experiences led to another successful book, *Travels among the Great Andes of the Equator* (1892). Most of this was also written at Town House. In 1906 Edward, then aged 66, married Edith May Lewin, and shortly afterwards they moved to Teddington. He died while on holiday in Chamonix on 16th September 1911.

Two other members of the Whymper family wrote books: Edward's stepmother, Emily Whymper, a talented water-colour painter, wrote and illustrated *Beauty in Common Things* (1874), in praise of native flowers.

Edward' s sister Annette (1859–1944) was also an author and artist. Annette, known as 'Miss Nettie', was the youngest child of Josiah Wood Whymper by his first wife, Elizabeth, and the only one of his children to be born in Haslemere. For many years, she kept house for her father, but after he died in 1903, she lived with her sister Elizabeth in Beech Road, Haslemere. Like most of the Whymper children, 'Miss Nettie' was a gifted artist, but she is mostly remembered for her lively stories, all with a moral or religious lesson. Best known are: *Kesiah Crabbe, Spinster* (1901), and *Celia's Fortunes* (1901), both published by the Religious Tract Society.

[DNB; Smythe, 1940; Sillick.]

WOLSELEY

WOLSELEY, Garnet Joseph, first Viscount Wolseley (1833–1913): Field Marshal and historian.

Lord and Lady Wolseley were living at Manor House, Three Gates Lane, Haslemere, when William and Helen Allingham called on them on 5th June 1887. Wolseley was then in semi-retirement after his Sudan campaign, but was continuing his efforts to modernise the British Army. For this, he needed to live part-time in London; but retirement also gave him an opportunity to write his historical works, which he probably did largely at Haslemere. When the Allinghams called on him, he had just completed a chapter on the army for Humphry Ward's *The Reign of Queen Victoria* (1887), and was already at work on his *Life of Marlborough*, the first two volumes of which were published in 1894. It was never completed, as he was then appointed Commander-in-Chief, and had too many other things to do. In 1890 he was named to command the army in Ireland. Some time later, he had a country home at Glynde in Sussex.

Garnet Joseph Wolseley

Like a number of other distinguished soldiers, Wolseley came of an Irish Protestant family, and although Allingham – also an Irish Protestant – could detect no trace of Irish accent, he noted some Irish idioms in his speech. The Allinghams were received at The Manor House by 'the General, in grey jacket, corduroy breeches (with flap), black riding-boots and spurs; a light figure, about five feet seven in stature; bright, almost boyish face of roundish shape, with small ashen-coloured moustache, the forehead full and smooth, the hair close-cut, of a steel gray'. Later, they walked in the garden with Lord Wolseley, now wearing 'a large, soft but high-crowned grey hat, thrown loosely on to one side, handkerchief hanging half out of his breast pocket, corduroy breeches, bright eyes and merry face, seeming as if he only wanted a shillelagh to enable him to present, if so inclined, a genteel version of the typical Paddy'.

Despite his jolly appearance, Wolseley had some forthright things to say about the 'degenerates' who so perturbed the middle class at the turn of the century. He told Allingham, 'in his usual easy cheerful way' that 'we have nowadays an absurd and superstitious respect for human life ... I would have supplies of chloroform for gaols and hospitals, for cripples and so forth, and the world would be *débarrassé* of much trouble and expense.' Allingham was uncertain how seriously to take this remark.

Lady Dorothy Nevill, who knew Wolseley well, does not record any such bloodthirsty sentiments. She regarded him as 'a man of culture as well as a soldier, his conversation and letters are best described by saying that they seem to bubble over with vitality. Keen and alert by nature, no one more than he is endowed with the faculty for observing and enjoying everything which is going on around him.'[165] Henry James described him as a 'very handsome, well-mannered and fascinating little man – with rosy dimples and an eye of steel: an excellent specimen of the *cultivated* British soldier'.[166]

Lord and Lady Wolseley's letters show that they rented Manor House from February to September 1887, or perhaps a little longer (the *Surrey Advertiser* reports that they were both at Miss Agatha Stewart Hodgson's wedding in October 1887). Lady Wolseley seems to have been at Manor House for most of that period, with Lord Wolseley dividing his time between Haslemere and his house at Hill Street, London. On 11th September, Wolseley and his daughter Frances walked up from the Manor House to Aldworth. Allingham happened to be there also, and records that Tennyson called for 'a chair for the great Soldier'. Wolseley then related some of his experiences in Egypt. He had watched the mummy of a Pharaoh being unrolled, but didn't know which one. He had 'rather wished for a scarabaeus or two; the Khedive said to me, "Go down to the Museum and take as many as you like!"'

On another occasion, Wolseley told Allingham that Tennyson was a 'queer old chap!' He admired his poetry, but thought it 'effeminate'.

[DNB; Arthur, 1922; Allingham, 1985; pp. 354–361 & 364–65.]

WRIGHT, Thomas (1859–1936): schoolmaster, historian, biographer and novelist.

Wright was born and lived most of his life in a house at Olney, Bucks, next door to where William Cowper (1731–1800), the 'mad poet', had lived. (In time he would write Cowper's biography.) To distinguish him from other Thomas Wrights, he is usually designated 'of Olney'.

Wright wrote many other biographies, including those of Blake, Walter Pater and Defoe. An obituary notice in *The Times* noted that 'his skill and industry in the collection of facts were superior to his literary style'. His exaggeratedly flowery manner of writing is amply displayed in his Hindhead book.

WRIGHT

Wright paid two visits to the Hindhead area in 1897, and described what he had seen in the following year in *Hindhead; or the English Switzerland, and its Literary and Historical Associations*. A short introduction by Edward F. Beesley gives an account of Thomas Wright and his works.[167] Despite its stylistic deficiencies, this small book is a valuable source of information about the writers who were living there, and their homes, at a time when the district's fame, both as a place of great beauty and as a centre of literary activity was at its peak.

Wright and his wife had set out for Hindhead with high expectations. Yet when they approached the Hindhead hills in July of 1897, on 'a quick train from Waterloo', they were almost overwhelmed by the beauty of the rugged scenery. As the train toiled up the incline from Witley to Haslemere, 'we began to look out for our mountain, and it soon loomed gloriously before us. Presently we were close under it. High above towered the huge mass with its precipitous pine-clad sides, and its foxgloves and fern stretching down, or so it seemed, under the very wheels of the railway carriage. We had been prepared for beauty, but this was more than beauty – it was enchantment.'

Having reached Haslemere station in this ecstatic frame of mind, they made their way to Grayshott, where they were to stay – via Shottermill, pausing to look at Brookbank, and comment on George Eliot's visit there. Eventually they arrived by devious tracks at Hindhead, where the only sign of human life was 'a bright red pillar box knee-deep in bramble and fern'. When at last they came upon the Portsmouth Road, they became lyrical with delight at the 'measureless expanses of glorious purple heather. Every bank was prodigal with the rich tufts. It was purple, upon purple, upon purple. An exclamation of astonishment – and then we drank in the beauty in silence.'

A by-road brought them to Grayshott, where they stayed with a Mrs Fannie Warr, 'where the five roads meet' – the crossroads where St Luke's church now stands. *Kelly's Directory* for 1898 lists Mrs Warr as a 'draper and bookseller', from which we can deduce that she was the snobbish 'Madam Lillywhite' described by Flora Thompson in *Heatherley*.[168]

In his *Autobiography*, Wright mentions that Mrs Warr 'was also interested in pottery, and at her request I sent her a couplet for an earthenware candlestick which she was placing on the market'. Wright's little poem displays his ingenuity as a rhymster:

> Sleep is beauty's best elixir,
> Light my wick, ma'am, light my wick, sir.

Writing in the 1930s, Wright says that 'these candlesticks may still be picked up in Surrey shops'.[169]

This first visit, which extended into August 1897, was mostly spent exploring Hindhead and the Punch Bowl. It started with a pre-breakfast walk to nearby Waggoners Wells. Wright thought that the pines there smelt like 'blackberry jam at boiling-point'. On their way to the Punch Bowl after breakfast, the Wrights passed Conan Doyle's new house Undershaw, still not quite finished but with a wonderful view. The Devil's Punch Bowl, Wright thought, was so beautiful it should be re-named 'God's Chalice'. But he noted that it was 'now much less wild than formerly', when black cocks were commonly encountered on the surrounding moors.

Wright's second visit to Hindhead, this time without his wife, was at the end of September 1897. His first expedition was to The Devil's Jumps at Churt. On the way, he passed Grant Allen's house, The Croft. At Hindhead, he discovered, Grant Allen was spoken of 'not merely with respect, but almost with affection'. Although unable to accept 'the teaching of *The Woman who Did*, Wright speaks of its author's 'kindly and sympathetic spirit, his love for pine and heather and dew drop', his desire 'to elevate woman', and his universal knowledge.

Wright's next encounter was with Rayner Storr at his new 'handsome residence' next door (Highcombe Edge). He too, 'was all kindness and cheerfulness', and showed Wright a copy of Morley's 1735 map of Haslemere. As he left, Wright exclaimed: 'Heaven be praised for this place. Everybody here seems happy.'

Wright then reached the little conical hills known as The Devil's Jumps, and ascended each in turn. On the Middle Jump he explored the remains of Richard Carrington's observatory and tunnels, and spoke to a woman who approached him carrying 'an oil painting of Galileo purchased at Carrington's sale'. But neither she, nor another local inhabitant, whom he met on another of the Jumps, seems to have told him about the tragic events which led to the deaths of Carrington and his wife.

Wright's next expedition was to Thursley, passing on the way the Hindhead houses of Sir Frederick Pollock, Aneurin Williams and Edward Nettleship. At Thursley, he visited the Vicarage, where Baring-Gould had stayed while writing his novel *The Broom Squire*. Wright mentions in his *Autobiography* that he had corresponded with him. He then went searching for Thor's Stone which features in that story. He managed to get a sight of it, but could not get near because of the swampy ground.

Although he lost his way on his return, Wright nevertheless got back to Grayshott in the late afternoon, and then went off to interview Richard Le Gallienne at his house at nearby Kingswood Firs. There, Wright and the novelist retired to the 'chalet on a gentle pine-clad hill where Mr Le Gallienne works' for 'an animated conversation'. Wright was pleased to find that his host was not as conceited as he was often alleged to be: 'everything was pleasant, easy and natural'. They ended the evening the warmest of friends, having 'electrified each other. I felt drawn to him as I have felt drawn to very few.' After Wright had got back to his lodgings he took up his copy of Le Gallienne's *The Quest of the Golden Girl*, and when he came to the final paragraph he 'could not restrain tears'.

Wright then journeyed to Liphook. On the way he passed High Pitfold, the residence of Professor Alexander Williamson, the retired chemist; then that of the sculptor Albert Bruce-Joy (Chase Lodge); and Bramshott Chase, of the late publisher Alexander Macmillan. This brought him to the Seven Thorns, which featured in Margaret Oliphant's novel *The Cuckoo in the Nest*. The inn got its name, according to Wright, from seven ancient trees, some holly and some hawthorn, on the opposite side of the road. The house itself, in better repair than it had been 'when Mrs Oliphant stayed there' (it is unlikely that she ever did stay there, for when she came to Hindhead she stayed with her friend Mrs Rogerson), is described as 'a long house, of moderate height, with good sized rooms and stables, which could take in half the horses in the county'. Wright identified the Grayshott Manor which features in *The Cuckoo in the Nest*, as Downlands, about a mile or less to the west. He then went on by way of Hammer to Liphook, 'famed for its carrots and tomatoes'.

The following day Wright was off to Blackdown. He gives an account of Aldworth and its late famous inhabitant. This is followed by a similar account of Frederic Harrison at Blackdown Cottage. This seems to have been one of several visits to Haslemere, whose architecture and history he describes in some detail. He was greatly impressed by the museum, and seems to have had some contact with Jonathan Hutchinson, who gave him a copy of his *The Centuries: A Chronological Synopsis of History on the Space-for-Time Method*. He was also impressed by the number of artists, scientists and writers living at Haslemere. There are accounts of the houses of Mrs Humphry Ward at Grayswood, and John Tyndall at Hindhead House.

Wright ends his book with a splendid peroration:

> never in all my experience have I seen so many cheery faces as during these two visits, and never have I witnessed scenery one half so lovely or a tithe so striking as that of the blowing woodlands and ample commons of aëry, amethystine, and oderiferous Hind Head.

As well as *Hindhead*, Wright also wrote a novel, *Ianthe of the Devil's Jumps* (1900), which is clearly based on his visits there.

The action mainly takes place in Haslemere and Hindhead, in about 1800. The plot is complex and melodramatic, involving a gang of smugglers, another of brutal robbers and an astronomical observatory on the Middle Jump, just where the astronomer Richard Carrington built his some seventy years later. Like Carrington's, the observatory was placed over a vertical shaft, which was linked to a long horizontal tunnel ... In the novel, this tunnel ends in a secret entrance to an old cottage, which is where the hero, Philip Diprose, first meets the heroine, Ianthe, who lives there. It is not long before they have their first embrace, but almost immediately afterwards the dastardly Hen Shott appears with his gang of ruffians, and they are in trouble from then on until near the end of the story. The picture of the wild and lawless heathlands, sinister rather than beautiful, is similar to that in Baring-Gould's novel *The Broom Squire*, depicted at the same period.

[Wright, 1898, 1900, 1936.]

Footnotes to Section Three

1 Richards, Grant, *Memories of a Misspent Youth*, p. 225.
2 Richards, ibid, pp. 31–35.
3 Dorson, Richard M., *The British Folklorists: A History*, pp. 251–71.
4 Wells, H.G., *Autobiography*, pp. 546–51.
5 Allen, Grant, *Twelve Tales*, pp. v–vi.
6 Wells, pp. 546–51.
7 Wright, *Hindhead*, p. 21.
8 Quoted in Syrett, p. 46.
9 Clodd, p. 207.
10 Quoted in Doyle, Arthur Conan, *Memories and Adventures*.
11 Allingham, *Diary*, pp. 290–304.
12 See Robertson, W. Graham, *Time Was*, p. 288.
13 Tennyson, Hallam, *Alfred Lord Tennyson: A Memoir*, vol. 2, p.369.
14 Duffy, Maureen, *A Thousand Capricious Chances: A History of the Methuen List, 1889–1989*, p. 27.
15 Cullen, Anthea, *Women in the Arts and Crafts Movement, 1870–1914*, p. 118.
16 The Wimshurst machine was invented by the London-born engineer James Wimshurst (1832–1903) in the 1880s. It had two glass disks, with metallic sectors attached, which were rotated by hand in opposite directions. This generated high-voltage electricity, capable of producing sparks between two brass balls. The construction of this apparatus demonstrates Buckton's grasp of yet another branch of science, and his practical ability as an engineer.
17 Allingham, *Diary*, p. 343.
18 Reported in *The Times*, 13th July 1925, p. 11.
19 James Simmons was described by Fenn as 'The Squire, a real English gentleman who possesses hounds and hunters, Alderney cows and tracts of meadowland. He is also Justice of the Peace and Captain of the Fire Brigade.' Fenn, Alice, *Century Magazine*, 'The Borderlands of Surrey', pp. 487–94.
20 Simpson's Forensic Medicine, 10th edition, revised by Bernard Knight, 1991, p. 140, says that 'smothering is virtually impossible to diagnose retrospectively at autopsy'.
21 Eggar, J. Alfred, *Life and Customs in Gilbert White's, Cobbett's and Charles Kingsley's Country*, p. 45.
22 Inquest reported in *The Times*, 7th December 1875, p. 11 and the *Surrey Advertiser*, 11th December 1875.
23 Benjamin Jowett (1817–93), classical scholar and Master of Balliol College Oxford, was a dominant figure in the Victorian intellectual scene, and so it is not surprising to find him turning up in the present work, in three separate contexts. He was one of Tennyson's closest friends, and a frequent visitor both at Farringford and Aldworth. Both Frank Costelloe and Logan Pearsall Smith were undergraduates at Balliol during his Mastership, and both at different times became Jowett's favourite pupils. Hence Costelloe was granted the privilege of a

Balliol wedding reception. Logan appreciated Jowett's great learning, and the rigour of his teaching, but deprecated his narrow academic attitude.

[24] Strachey, *Remarkable Relations*, pp. 77–126.

[25] MacKensie N., *The Letters of Sydney and Beatrice Webb*, p. 294.

[26] Quoted in Bell, Anne Oliver & McNeillie, Andrew (eds.), *The Diary of Virginia Woolf* vol. 5, 1936–41.

[27] Tennyson, Hallam (ed.), *Tennyson and his Friends*, p. 205.

[28] Reported in the *Surrey Advertiser*, 31st December 1898.

[29] Tennyson, H., *Tennyson and Friends*, pp. 188–205.

[30] Orel, p. 140.

[31] Thompson, *A Country Calendar, and other writings* pp. 170–71, and *Heatherley* pp. 29–31.

[32] Orel, pp. 184–93.

[33] Doyle, A.C., *Memories and Adventures*, pp. 100–01.

[34] Orel, pp. 46–47.

[35] Gilchrist, Herbert Harlakenden, *Anne Gilchrist: Her Life and Writings*, pp. 216–18.

[36] Cross, J.W., *George Eliot's Life*, vol. 2, p. 292.

[37] Cross, p. 253.

[38] Fenn, p. 487.

[39] Knies, p. 92.

[40] Quoted in Tennyson, H., *Tennyson: A Memoir*, vol. 2, p. 107.

[41] Quoted in Edel, Leon (ed.), *Henry James Letters*, vol. 1, 1974, pp.116–17; and in Bellringer, p. 12.

[42] These are reported in the *Surrey Advertiser* of 13th February, 22nd May and 12th June 1897.

[43] Dorson, pp. 310–13.

[44] Dorson, pp. 251–57.

[45] We know a good deal about the refurbishing of Brookbank, as it is frequently mentioned in the extensive diary kept by James Simmons senior, father of Anne Gilchrist's neighbour of the same name. It was one of a pair of labourers' cottages on the lane leading from Shottermill to Liphook. In 1860 it was bought by Simmons' son-in-law, John Small, a prosperous draper from Petersfield, and made fit for middle-class occupation. This involved extensive re-building, and the installation of a WC. The diarist recorded Mrs Gilchrist's arrival on 3rd April 1862, and Tennyson's visit in 1866. The attractive exterior of the little cottage is still substantially unchanged as seen from the road, although there have been extensive alterations to the rear and the interior. Its remarkable career as a centre of literary activity ended with Anne Gilchrist's departure in 1876.

[46] Gilchrist, p. 124.

[47] Gilchrist, pp. 161–71.

[48] Quoted in Alcaro, pp. 116–39.

[49] Quoted in Knies, p. 96.

[50] See Smith, L.P., *Unforgotten Years*.

[51] Harrison, Frederic, *Autobiographical Memoirs*, vol. 2, p. 103.

[52] Bockett, p. 195.

[53] Knies, p. 102.

[54] Harrison, A., p. 221.

[55] Martin, *Gerard Manley Hopkins*, p. 4.

[56] Martin, *Hopkins*, p. 6.

[57] *Cornhill Magazine*, Feb. 1914, pp. 230–239.

[58] Hutchinson, H., *Jonathan Hutchinson: Life and Letters*, pp. 77–78.

[59] Bockett, p. 206.

[60] Wright, pp. 36–40.

[61] Quoted in Thwaite, Ann, *Edmund Gosse: A Literary Landscape 1849–1928*, p. 338.

[62] Thompson, *A Country Calendar, and other writings* pp. 171–72, and *Heatherley* p.31.

[63] Cross, vol. 2, p. 283.

[64] Cross, vol. 2, p. 287.

[65] Knies, p. 102.

[66] MacKensie and MacKensie, *The Diaries of Beatrice Webb*, vol. 2, p. 252.

[67] Clark, p. 144.

[68] Quoted in Strachey, *Remarkable Relations*, p. 208.

[69] See Stewart, Jessie, *Jane Ellen Harrison: A Portrait From Letters*.

[70] Quoted in Russell, Bertrand, *The Autobiography of Bertrand Russell, 1872–1914*, vol. 1, p. 190.

[71] Branford, William, *Journal of Medical Biography*, vol. 2, pp. 162–67,1994.

[72] Nevill, Lady Dorothy, *Under Five Reigns*, p. 138.

[73] This is evidently a reference to Peter Aylwin (1827–1903) – Lady Dorothy was notoriously careless about names – who had a chemist's shop just across the High Street from Lady Dorothy's cottage. As well as being the postmaster of Haslemere, Aylwin also dealt in antiquities, and had Tennyson as a customer. The *Haslemere Herald* said in an obituary notice that his 'old-fashioned house in the High Street is full of curiosities and archaeological specimens of local interest, while his collection of oak carving, china and documents is very fine'. For Lady Dorothy, who was a maniacal collector of everything and anything, Aylwin' s shop would have been an irresistible attraction.

[74] Quoted in Gosse, Edmunds, 'Lady Dorothy Nevil: An Open Letter'; *Fortnightly Review*, vol. 101, pp. 278–87, 1914.

[75] Coghill, p. 10.

[76] Quoted in Jay, *Autobiography of Margaret Oliphant*, p. 16.

[77] Jay, ibid, p. 14.

[78] Reported in Jay, ibid, pp. 142–43.

[79] Hyde, H. Montgomery, *Henry James at Home*, p. 110.

[80] See Leavis's Introduction to Coghill, pp. 9–34.

[81] Jay, ibid, p. xx.

[82] Coghill, p. 356.

[83] The letters from 1890 and 1891 are held by the National Library of Scotland, while the 1895 source is in the British Library.

[84] Williams, pp. 202–05.

[85] Strachey, *Remarkable Relations*, p. 104.

[86] Jones, *Arthur Ponsonby*, pp. 111–12.

[87] Jay, *Margaret Oliphant*, p. 140.

[88] Richards, *Misspent Youth*, pp. 212–16.

[89] Quoted in a Memoir in vol. 1 of the memorial edition of the works of G.W. Steevens, pp. ix–xxvii.

[90] Gilchrist, pp. 138 & 145.

[91] Quoted in Jan Marsh's 1994 biography of Christina Rossetti, p. 312.

[92] Sharp, William, *Papers Critical and Reminiscent*, 1952, pp. 67–71.

[93] See Lang, Cecil Y. and Shannon, Edgar F. (eds.), *The Letters of Alfred Lord Tennyson*, vol. 3, p. 82.

[94] Russell, B., *Autobiography 1872–1914*, p. 179.

[95] Mentioned in Russell, B., *Autobiography 1914–1944*, pp.141 & 174.

[96] Clark, p. 326.

[97] Recorded in Shaw, Frank H., *Seas of Memory*.

[98] MacKensies, *Diaries of Beatrice Webb*, vol. 2, p. 96.

[99] Quoted in Usborne, Karen, *'Elizabeth': The Author of Elizabeth and her German Garden*, pp. 202 & 247.

[100] Russell, B., *Autobiography 1872–1914*, p. 141.

[101] Holroyd, *Bernard Shaw*, vol. 1, pp. 464–65.

[102] Shaw had stayed with the Webbs in 1893 and 1895 at The Argoed, the holiday home in the Wye Valley which Beatrice Webb had inherited from her parents. The reference may perhaps be to trees shattered in a storm while he was there, though I can find no mention of such an occurrence in her diary.

[103] Holroyd, *Shaw*, vol. 21, pp. 3–7.

[104] Quoted in Le Gallienne, *The Romantic '90s*, pp. 49–51.

[105] MacKensies, *Dairies of Beatrice Webb*, vol. 2, p. 208.

[106] Smith, Logan Pearsall, *Reperusals and Re-collections*, pp. 46–65.

[107] Woolf, Virginia, *Contemporary Writers*, pp. 74–76.

[108] Alas! Consultation of the *Alumni Cantabriensis* shows that Logan's delightful tale is wholly fictitious. While Logan was at Fernhurst (from 1889 to 1906), the incumbent of Linch was Henry Godwin Billingshurst. He had graduated at Cambridge in 1875, was ordained priest in 1876 and immediately became curate of Bringhurst in Leicestershire. He moved from there to Linch in 1883 as rector – not vicar, as in Logan's tale – and remained there until his death in 1912. So there would have been no time for studies of Greek deities at Oxford, and he was still in office after Logan had left Fernhurst.

[109] Moore, T. & Sturge, D.C. (eds.), *Works and Days, from the Journal of Michael*

Field, pp. 57–58.

[110] Smith, L.P., *Reperusals*, pp. 85–97.

[111] Smith, L.P., *Unforgotten Years*, p. 202.

[112] Quoted in Hobhouse, Janet, *Everybody who was Anybody: A Biography of Gertrude Stein*, pp. 29–30.

[113] MacKensies, *Diaries of Beatrice Webb*, vol. 2, p. 211.

[114] Wright, *Hindhead.*

[115] *The Lancet*, May 3rd and 24th, 1890.ii.972 & 1132 respectively.

[116] See Swinny, S.H., *Positivist Review*, 'In Memoriam Rayner Storr', No. 295, pp. 161–64, 1917.

[117] *Positivist Review*, No. 295, pp.145–46, 1917.

[118] See Unwin, S., *The Truth About A Publisher.*

[119] Unwin, P., *The Publishing Unwins.*

[120] Thompson, *A Country Calendar, and other writings* pp. 100–01.

[121] See Knies, *Tennyson at Aldworth: The Diary of James Henry Mangles.*

[122] Trotter, W. R., *Tennyson Research Bulletin*, 'The Search for a site for Aldworth', 1991, vol. 5, no.5.

[123] See White, *Journals*, pp. 166–67; Nairn and Pevsner, *Buildings of England*, 'Sussex', p. 106; Levi, Peter, *Tennyson*, p. 261; Mawson, T.H., *The Life and Work of an English Landscape Architect*, pp. 337–38; Bockett, *Some Literary Landmarks*, p. 211; Tennyson, C., *Aldworth*, p. 7; Metcalf, P., *James Knowles, Victorian Editor and Architect*, pp. 202–07.

[124] Quoted in Lang and Shannon, *The Letters of Alfred Lord Tennyson*, vol. 3, p. 150.

[125] Page, *Tennyson: An Illustrated Life*, p. 168.

[126] Quoted in Tennyson, H., *Tennyson and Friends*, p. 248.

[127] Knies, p. 62.

[128] Ricks, C., *The Poems of Tennyson*, Poem 361, xix.

[129] Quoted in Martin, *Tennyson*, p. 423.

[130] Harrison, *Memoirs*, vol. 2, p. 103.

[131] Martin, *Tennyson*, p. 132.

[132] Knies, pp. 49, 69, 121.

[133] Ricks, Poem 465.

[134] Ricks, Poem 349.

[135] Ricks, Poem 468.

[136] Ricks, Poem 390.

[137] Ricks, Poem 450.

[138] Martin, *Tennyson*, pp. 576-77; Pinion, E.B., *A Tennyson Chronology*, p. 175, Page, *Tennyson*, p. 172.

[139] Tennyson, H., *Tennyson: A Memoir*, vol. 2, pp. 384–86.

[140] Tennyson, C., *Aldworth*, p. 10.

[141] Quoted in Martin, *Tennyson*, p. 242.

[142] Quoted in Lang and Shannon, vol. III, p. 32.

[143] Published in *Blackwood's Magazine*, November 1892.

[144] Quoted in Martin, *Tennyson*, p. 427.

[145] Martin, *Tennyson*, p. 339.

[146] Quoted in Knies, p. 72. Quite apart from its propriety, this does seem a rather odd remark. A possible explanation is that what Tennyson actually said was: 'No luxury *like formication* – beats fornication all to pieces.' Mangles may not have been familiar with 'formication' – 'a sensation as of ants creeping over the skin' (OED) – and so missed the point of Tennyson's play on words.

[147] Tennyson, H., *A Memoir*, p. 99, note 1.

[148] See Wright, *Hindhead*.

[149] Tyndall, *Fragments*, p. 196.

[150] See Pollock, *For My Grandson: Reminiscences of an Ancient Victorian*.

[151] Eve and Creasy, *Life and Work of John Tyndall*, p. 259.

[152] Bockett, p. 220.

[153] The letter, dictated by Tyndall to his wife, is in the Haslemere Museum.

[154] At the inquest – reported in *The Times*, 8th December 1893 – Dr Winstanley, whom Louisa had summoned from Haslemere as soon as she realised what had happened, estimated that Tyndall must have taken 70–80 grains (4.5–5.2 grams) of chloral hydrate. The normal dose is 0.5 to 1.0 grams. The fatal dose is said to be about 10 grams, but death has been reported after only 4 grams (though there have been survivals after as much as 30 grams). Anyone with liver or kidney failure would be abnormally susceptible. There is nothing to suggest any damage to Tyndall's liver or kidneys, but there was no post-mortem, so this possibility cannot be excluded. Both Winstanley and Dr Buzzard, the London consultant who saw Tyndall in the terminal stages, thought that his chronic chest trouble would have made him unduly susceptible to chloral hydrate, though this seems unlikely.

[155] Sutherland, *Mrs Humphreys Ward*, pp. 185–87.

[156] MacKensies *The Diaries of Beatrice Webb*, vol. 1, p. 324.

[157] Seymour-Jones, p. 318.

[158] Webb, *My Apprenticeship*, pp. 408–10.

[159] Quoted in MacKensie, Norman (ed.), *The Letters of Sidney and Beatrice Webb*, vol. 1, pp. 294, 298.

[160] Seymour-Jones, pp. 236–37.

[161] Wells, *Autobiography*, pp. 546–53.

[162] Quoted in Whittington-Egan & Smerdon, *Richard Le Gallienne*, p.297.

[163] Wells,G.P. (ed.), *H.G. Wells in Love*, pp. 87–89, and Usborne K., *'Elizabeth': The Author of Elizabeth and her German Garden*, pp.156–58.

[164] Nevill, *Under Five Reigns*, p. 139.

[165] Nevill, *The Reminiscences of Lady Dorothy Nevill*, pp. 294–95.

[166] Edel, Leon, *Henry James: The Conquest of London,* 1870–1883, p.335.

[167] Wright, *Hindhead*, pp. vii–x.

[168] Thompson, *A Country Calendar, and other writings* pp. 175–76, and *Heatherley* pp. 35–35.

[169] Wright, *An Autobiography*, p. 69.

Bibliography

Alcaro, Marion Walker, *Walt Whitman's Mrs G: A Biography of Anne Gilchrist*, Associated University Presses, London and Toronto, 1991.

Allen, Grant, *The Woman Who Did*, John Lane, 1895; Oxford University Press, 1995.
The British Barbarians, A Hilltop Novel, John Lane, 1895.
The Evolution of the Idea of God, 1897.
Twelve Tales, Grant Richards, 1900.

Allingham, Helen, & Radford, D. (eds.), *William Allingham: A Diary*, Macmillan, 1907; Penguin Books, 1985.

Allingham, William, *Day and Night Songs*, Routledge, 1854.

Arthur, George (ed.), *The Letters of Lord and Lady Wolseley*, Heinemann, 1922.

Ashton, Rosemary, *G.H. Lewes: A Life*, Clarendon Press, 1991.

Barrus, Clara, *The Life and Letters of John Burroughs*, Houghton Mifflin, Boston, 2 vols., 1925.

Battiscombe, Georgina, *Christina Rossetti: A Divided Life*, Constable, 1981.

Bell, Anne Olivier, & McNeillie, Andrew, (eds.), *The Diary of Virginia Woolf*, Hogarth Press, 5 vols., 1977–84.

Bellringer, Alan W., *George Eliot*, Macmillan, 1993.

Beveridge, William, *India Called Them*, Allen & Unwin, 1947.

Boase, Frederic, *Modern English Biography*, Frank Cass, 6 vols., 1892–1921.

Bockett, F.W., *Some Literary Landmarks for Pilgrims on Wheels*, J.M. Dent, 1901.

Brock, W.H., McMillan, N.D. & Mollan, R.P., *Essays on a Natural Philosopher*, Royal Dublin Society, Dublin, 1991.

Burroughs, John, *Fresh Fields*, David Douglas, 1885.

Burton, Hester, *Barbara Bodichon, 1827–1891*, Constable, 1949.

Callen, Anthea, *Women in the Arts and Crafts Movement, 1870–1914*, Astragal, 1979.

Carr, John Dickson, *The Life of Sir Arthur Conan Doyle*, John Murray, 1949.

Chappell, Jennie, *Agnes Weston, The Sailor's Friend*, Pickering & Inglis, 1949.

Clark, Ronald W., *The Life of Bertrand Russell*, Jonathan Cape and Weidenfeld & Nicolson, 1975.

Clodd, Edward, *Grant Allen: A Memoir*, Grant Richards, 1900.

Cobbett, William, *Rural Rides*, Peter Davies, 1930.

Coghill, Mrs Harry, (ed.), *Autobiography and Letters of Mrs Margaret Oliphant*, Blackwood, 1899; Leicester University Press, with an Introduction by Q.D. Leavis, 1974.

Costelloe, B.F.C., *The Incidence of Taxation*, Ward & Foxlow, 1893.
Ethics or Anarchy, Catholic Truth Society, 1895.
The Gospel Story, Sands & Co., 1900.
with Muirhead, J.H., *Aristotle and the Earlier Peripatetics*, 2 vols., Longmans Green & Co., 1897.

Cross, J.W., *George Eliot's Life*, 3 vols., Blackwood, 1885.

Darley, Gillian, *Octavia Hill: A Life*, Constable, 1990.

Dickson, Lovat, H.G. *Wells: His Turbulent Life and Times*, Macmillan, 1969.

Dorson, Richard M., *The British Folklorists: A History*, Routledge & Kegan Paul, 1968.

Doyle, Arthur Conan, *Memories and Adventures*, Hodder & Stoughton,1924.

Drabble, Margaret, *The Oxford Companion to English Literature*, Oxford University Press, 1985.

Duffy, Maureen, *A Thousand Capricious Chances: A History of the Methuen List, 1889–1989*, Methuen, 1989.

Dunkel, W.D., *Sir Arthur Pinero: A Critical Biography with Letters*, University of Chicago Press, Chicago, 1941.

Edel, Leon, *Henry James: The Conquest of London, 1870–1883*, Hart- Davis, 1962.
   (ed.) *Henry James' Letters*, Macmillan, 1974.

Eggar, J. Alfred, *Life and Customs in Gilbert White's, Cobbett's and Charles Kingsley's Country*, Simpkin Marshall & Co., 1924.

Eve, A.S. and Creasy, C.H., *Life and Work of John Tyndall*, Macmillan, 1945.

Forrest, D.W., *Francis Galton: The Life and Work of a Victorian Genius*, Paul Elek, 1974.

Gilchrist, Herbert Harlakenden, *Anne Gilchrist: Her Life and Writings*, Fisher Unwin, 1887.

Haight, G.S., *George Eliot: A Biography*, Oxford University Press, 1968; Penguin, 1986.

Hamilton, Bernard, *The Light? A Romance*, Hurst & Blackett, 1898.
   A Kiss for a Kingdom, Hurst & Blackett, 1899.
   Wanted – A Man; Apply John Bull & Co, Late of Dame Europa's School, Simpkin Marshall & Co., 1900.

Hare, Augustus, J. C., *Biographical Sketches*, George Allen, 1895.

Harris, José, *William Henry Beveridge: A Biography*, Clarendon Press, 1977.

Harrison, Austin, *Frederic Harrison: Thoughts and Memories*, Heinemann,1926.

Harrison, Frederic, *Autobiographical Memories*, 2 vols., Macmillan, 1911.

Harrison, J.F.C., *Late Victorian Britain, 1875–1901*, Fontana Press, 1990.

Herrman, Luke, *Turner's Prints: The Engraved Works of J.M.W. Turner*, Phaidon, 1990.

Hobhouse, Janet, *Everybody who was Anybody: A Biography of Gertrude Stein*, Weidenfeld & Nicolson, 1975.

Hoge, James O. (ed.), *The Letters of Emily Lady Tennyson*, Pennsylvania State University Press, University Park, Pa., 1974.
   (ed.), *Lady Tennyson's Journal*, University Press of Virginia, Charlottes-ville,1981.

Holroyd, Michael, *Bernard Shaw*, 4 vols., Penguin, 1990–1993.

Hutchinson, Herbert, *Jonathan Hutchinson: Life and Letters*, Weidenfeld & Nicolson, 1947.

Hyde, H. Montgomery, *Henry James at Home*, Methuen, 1969.

Jay, Elizabeth, (ed.), *Faith and Doubt in Victorian Britain*, Macmillan, 1986.
   (ed.), *The Autobiography of Margaret Oliphant*, Oxford University Press, 1990.

Mrs Oliphant: 'A Fiction to Herself', Clarendon Press, 1995.

Jenkins, Roy, *Sir Charles Dilke: A Victorian Tragedy*, Collins, 1958.

Jennings, Louis J., *Field Paths and Green Lanes*, John Murray, 1877.

Jones, Kathleen, *Learning not to be First: The Life of Christina Rossetti*, Oxford University Press, 1992.

Jones, Raymond A., *Arthur Ponsonby: The Politics of Life*, Christopher Helm, 1989.

Kevles, Daniel J., *In the Name of Eugenics*, Penguin, 1986.

Knies, Earl A. (ed.), *Tennyson at Aldworth: The Diary of James Henry Mangles*, Ohio University Press, Athens, Ohio, 1984.

La Chard, Therese, *A Sailor Hat in the House of the Lord: The Autobiography of a Rebellious Victorian*, George Allen & Unwin, 1967.

Lang, Cecil Y., & Shannon, Edgar F. (eds.), *The Letters of Alfred Lord Tennyson*, 3 vols., Clarendon Press, 1981–90.

Lankester, Ray, *Degeneration: A Chapter in Darwinism*, Macmillan, 1880.

Laurence, Dan H. (ed.), *Collected Letters of George Bernard Shaw*, Max Reinhardt,1972.

Le Gallienne, Richard, *The Religion of a Literary Man*, Elkin Matthews & John Lane, 1893.

   The Quest of the Golden Girl, John Lane, 1896.

   The Romantic '90s, Putman, 1926.

Levi, Peter, *Tennyson*, Macmillan, 1993.

Lindsay, Gillian, *Flora Thompson: The Story of the Lark Rise Writer*, Hale, 1990.

MacCarthy, Desmond & Russell, Lady Agatha, *Lady John Russell: A Memoir*, Methuen, 1910.

Macdonald, Greville, *Maude Egerton King 1867–1927; A Portrait in Miniature*, Privately printed, 1927.

MacKensie, Norman (ed.), *The Letters of Sidney and Beatrice Webb*, 2 vols., Cambridge University Press, 1978.

with MacKensie, Jeanne (eds.), *The Diaries of Beatrice Webb*, 4 vols., Virago and London School of Economics, 1982–83.

Marsh, Jan, *Christina Rossetti: A Literary Biography*, Jonathan Cape, 1994.

Martin, Robert Bernard, *Gerard Manley Hopkins: A Very Private Life*, Putnam, New York, 1991.

   Tennyson: The Unquiet Heart, Faber & Faber, 1980.

Matthews, E.C., *The Highlands of South-West Surrey*, Adams & Charles Black, 1911.

Mawson, Thomas H., *The Life and Work of an English Landscape Architect*, Richards Press, 1927.

May, J. Lewis, *George Eliot: A Study*, Cassell, 1930.

Metcalf, Priscilla, *James Knowles: Victorian Editor and Architect*, Clarendon Press, 1980.

Millgate, Michael, *Testamentary Acts: Browning, Tennyson, James, Hardy*, Clarendon Press, 1992.

Mix, Katherine Lyon, *A Study in Yellow: The Yellow Book and its Contributors*, Constable, 1960.

Moore, T. & Sturge, D.C. (eds.), *Works and Days: From the Journal of Michael Field*, John Murray, 1933.

Nairn, Ian & Pevsner, Nicolaus, *Sussex*, in *The Buildings of England*, Penguin,1965.

Nevill, Lady Dorothy, *The Reminiscences of Lady Dorothy Nevill*, Edward Arnold, 1907.

  Leaves from the Note-Books of Lady Dorothy Nevill, Macmillan, 1907.

  Under Five Reigns, Methuen, 1910.

Nevill, Guy, *Exotic Groves: A Portrait of Lady Dorothy Nevill*, Michael Russell, 1984.

Nevill, Ralph, *The Life and Letters of Lady Dorothy Nevill*, Methuen, 1919.

Nicholls, David, *The Lost Prime Minister: A Life of Sir Charles Dilke*, Hambledon Press, 1995.

Oliphant, Margaret, *Miss Marjoribanks*, Blackwood, 1866; Virago, 1988.

  Kirsteen: The Story of a Scotch Family Seventy Years Ago, Macmillan, 1890.

  The Cuckoo in the Nest, 3 vols., Hutchinson, 1892.

Orel, Harold (ed.), *Sir Arthur Conan Doyle: Interviews and Recollections*, Macmillan, 1991.

Page, Norman, *Tennyson: An Illustrated Life*, Allison & Busby, 1992.

Paterson, Arthur, *The Homes of Tennyson*, Adam & Charles Black, 1905.

Pearson, Hesketh, *Conan Doyle*, Methuen, 1943.

Pearson, Karl, *Life, Letters and Labours of Francis Galton*, 4 vols., Cambridge University Press, 1914–1930.

Pinion, E. B., *A Tennyson Chronology*, Macmillan, 1990.

Pollock, Frederick, *For my Grandson: Reminiscences of an Ancient Vic- torian*, John Murray, 1933.

Randell, J.O., *Yaldwyn of the Golden Spurs*, Mast Gulley Press, Melbourne, 1980.

Reynolds, A.M., *The Life and Work of Frank Holl*, Methuen, 1912.

Richards, Grant, *Memories of a Misspent Youth 1872–1896*, Heinemann, 1932.

  Author Hunting, by an Old Literary Sportsman, Hamish Hamilton, 1934.

Ricks, Christopher (ed.), *The Poems of Tennyson*, 3 vols., Longman, 1969.

Robertson, W. Graham, *Time Was*, Hamish Hamilton, 1931.

Rossetti, William Michael (ed.), *The Poetical Works of Christina Georgina Rossetti, with Memoir and Notes*, Macmillan, 1904.

Rubinstein, David, *Before the Suffragettes: Women's Emancipation in the 1890s*, Harvester, 1986.

Russell, Bertrand, *The Autobiography of Bertrand Russell*, 3 vols., George Allen & Unwin, 1967–69.

Russell, John, *A Portrait of Logan Pearsall Smith*, Dropmore, 1960.

Russell, Rollo, *Epidemics, Plagues and Fevers: Their Causes and Prevention*, Stanford, 1892.

  First Conditions of Human Prosperity, Longmans, 1904.

  The Distribution of Land, P.S. King & Son, 1907.

  Psalms of the West, Longmans, 1922.

Seymour-Jones, Carole, *Beatrice Webb: Woman of Conflict*, Allison & Busby,1992.

Sharp, William, *Papers Critical and Reminiscent*, William Heinemann, 1952.

Shaw, Frank H., *Seas of Memory*, Oldbourne, 1958.

Smith, John Owen, *On the Trail of Flora Thompson*, John Owen Smith 1997.

Smith, Logan Pearsall, *Reperusals and Recollections*, Constable, 1936.

Unforgotten Years, Constable, 1938.

Smythe, F.S., *Edward Whymper*, Hodder & Stoughton, 1940.

Spittles, Brian, *George Eliot, Godless Woman*, Macmillan, 1993.

Steevens, Mrs Christina, *A Motley Crew: Reminiscences, Observations and Attempts at Play-writing*, Grant Richards, 1901.

Stewart, Jessie, *Jane Ellen Harrison: A Portrait from Letters*, Merlin Press, 1959.

Strachey, Barbara, *Remarkable Relations: The Story of the Pearsall Family*, Gollancz, 1980.

Strachey, Ray, *A Quaker Grandmother*, Fleming H. Revell, New York, 1914.
> *The Cause*, G. Bell & Sons, 1928.
> *Millicent Garrett Fawcett*, John Murray, 1931.
> *Group Movements of the Past*, Faber & Faber, 1934.

Sutherland, John, *The Longman Companion to Victorian Fiction*, Longman, 1988.
> *Mrs Humphry Ward: Eminent Victorian, Pre-eminent Edwardian*, Oxford University Press, 1991.

Swanton, E.W., *The Rise and Development of the Haslemere Natural History Society*, Haslemere Museum, 1939.

with Woods, P., *Bygone Haslemere*, West, Newman & Co., 1914.

Syrett, Netta, *The Sheltering Tree: An Autobiography*, Geoffrey Bles, 1939.

Tennyson, Charles, *Aldworth, Summer Home of Alfred Lord Tennyson*, The Tennyson Society, 1977.

Tennyson, Hallam, *Alfred Lord Tennyson: A Memoir*, Macmillan, 1897.
> *Tennyson and his Friends*, Macmillan, 1911.

Thompson, Flora, *A Country Calendar, and other writings*, Oxford University Press, 1979.
> *Heatherley*, John Owen Smith, 1998.

Thwaite, Ann, *Edmund Gosse: A Literary Landscape* 1849–1928, Secker & Warburg, 1984.

Trevelyan, Janet, *The Life of Mrs Humphry Ward*, Constable, 1923.

Tyndall, John, *Fragments of Science*, 2 vols., Longmans, 1892.

Unwin, Philip, *The Publishing Unwins*, Heinemann, 1972.

Unwin, Stanley, *The Truth about a Publisher*, Allen & Unwin, 1960.

Usborne, Karen, *'Elizabeth', The author of Elizabeth and Her German Garden*, Bodley Head, 1986.

Veitch, James, *George Douglas Brown*, Herbert Jenkins, 1952.

Vogeler, Martha, *Frederic Harrison; The Vocations of a Positivist*, Clarendon, 1984.

Wales, Hubert, *The Yoke*, John Long, 1907.
> *The Purpose: Reflections and Digressions*, John Long, 1913.

Wearing, J.P. (ed.), *The Collected Letters of Sir Arthur Pinero*, University of Minnesota Press, Minneapolis, 1974.

Webb, Beatrice, *My Apprenticeship*, Cambridge University Press, 1979.

Wells, G.P. (ed.), *H.G. Wells in Love*, Faber & Faber, 1984.

Wells, H.G., *Experiment in Autobiography*, Victor Gollancz & The Cresset Press, 1966.

Weston, Agnes, *My Life among the Bluejackets*, James Nisbet, 1909.

White, Walter, *The Journals of Walter White*, Chapman & Hall, 1898.

Whittington-Egan, Richard & Smerdon, Geoffrey, *The Quest of the Golden Boy: The Life and Letters of Richard Le Gallienne*, Unicorn Press, 1960.

Williams, Merryn, *Margaret Oliphant: A Critical Biography*, Macmillan, 1986.

Wilson, Duncan, *Gilbert Murray OM, 1866–1957*, Oxford University Press, 1987.

Woolf, Virginia, *Contenporary Writers*, Hogarth Press, 1965.

Wright, Thomas, *Hindhead, or the English Switzerland*, Simkin, Marshall & Co., 1898.

   Ianthe of the Devil's Jumps, The Rambler's Library, 1900.

   An Autobiography, Herbert Jenkins, 1936.

Wright, T.R., *The Religion of Humanity*, Cambridge University Press, 1986.

Index

acknowledgements, 5, 17
Aitken, Reverend George Herbert, 71, 106, 135
Aldworth, 43, 173, 192, 197, 207, 226
  Alys Buckton at, 95
  Anne Gilchrist at, 121
  architectural merits of, 192
  built by Tennyson, 23
  convalescent lunatics at, 193
  death of Tennyson at, 198
  Frederic Harrison at, 34, 124
  Garnet Wolseley at, 223
  George Buckton at, 95
  Hallam Tennyson at, 200
  James Henry Mangles at, 30, 144, 145
  John Addington Symonds and Henry Dakyns at, 105
  Leweses at, 113
  purchase, 192
  Russell family at, 170
  séance at, 196
  views from, 194, 197
  visitors to, 194
  William Allingham at, 89
Allen, Ellen (Nellie) *née Jerrard*, 82
Allen, Grant, 20, 23, 44, 52, 81–87, 110, 163, 187, 188, 204, 225
  and Conan Doyle, 87, 106, 107, 110
  and Edward Clodd, 87, 116
  and H.G. Wells, 215–16
  arrives in Hindhead, 35
  at Haslemere Microscope and Natural History Society, 37
  consoles Richard Le Gallienne, 139
  death of, 39, 87
  described by
    Grant Richards, 86
    Netta Syrett, 86
  memorial address, 159
  on feminism, 60–62
  on religion, 62–63

works
  Force and Energy, 82
  Hilda Wade, 87
  Origin of the Idea of God, 83
  Philistia, 83
  Physiological Aesthetics, 82, 83
  Strange Stories, 83
  The British Barbarians (Hilltop Novel), 21, 53, 62, 84, 85
  The Evolution of the Idea of God, 63, 82
  The Evolutionist at Large, 82
  The Woman Who Did (Hilltop Novel), 52, 61, 62, 84, 85, 215, 225
  Twelve Tales, 83
Allingham family, 146
Allingham, Helen *née Paterson*, 87, 200, 222
Allingham, William, 20, 32, 44, 87–90, 192, 211
  and Garnet Wolseley, 222–23
  discussion with William Morris, 69
  last words, 90
  on religion, 69–70
  works
    A Diary, 88
    Laurence Bloomfield, 88
altitude sickness, 221
Alton
  John Burroughs at, 98
Amberley, Lady, on feminism, 51
Amberley, Lord and Lady, 171
Andes, the, 221
Anstead Brook
  Therese La Chard at, 92
Argoed, Gwent, The, 177, 214, 231
Arnim, Elizabeth von, 39, 216
  affair with H.G. Wells, 216
  Elizabeth and her German Garden, 216
Arnold, Matthew, 195, 210

Arnold, Thomas, 210
Arts and Crafts, 92–93, 137–39
Ashridge, Herts, 211
Astor, Lady Nancy Witcher, 104
Aylwin, Peter (Mr Elwin), 153, 230
Ball (architect of Undershaw), 107
Balliol College, Oxford, 103, 183,
   228
Barbellion, W.N.P., 161
Barford
   Gilbert Murray at, 36, 147
   Jane Harrison at, 148
Baring-Gould, Reverend Sabine, 90
   works
      Onward Christian Soldiers, 90
      The Broom Squire, 35, 90, 146,
         225
Baroda, Gaekwar of, 95, 193, 200
Beacon Hotel, Hindhead
   Bernard Shaw at, 178
Bedford College, London
   Annette Beveridge at, 91
Beesley, Edward F., 224
Bel Alp, 206
Berenson, Bernard, 103, 148, 160,
   184, 214
   marries Mary Costelloe, 103
Berenson, Mary née Pearsall Smith,
   later Costelloe, 148, 184
   meets Walt Whitman, 183
   shocked by Gilbert Murray, 149
Berensons, The
   The Golden Urn, 149
Beveridge, Annette Susannah née
   Akroyd, 91–92, 176, 220
   described by Bernard Shaw, 91
   on feminism, 53
   on religion, 65
   works
      The Bábar-Náma, 92
      The History of Humayun, 92
      The Key to the Hearts of
         Beginners, 92
Beveridge, Henry, 91, 176
Beveridge, Lord William Henry, 44,
   92
   on degeneracy, 49
   works

      Full Employment in a Free
         Society, 92
      Social Insurance and Allied
         Services, 92
      Unemployment – A Problem of
         Industry, 92
Blackdown, 23, 24, 30, 31, 145, 197,
   201, 226
   F.W. Bockett on, 124
   H.G. Wells at, 215
   National Trust and, 33
   proposed road over, 131, 132
   scenery on summit of, 197
   site for Aldworth, 119
Blackdown Cottage
   and Mrs Warren's Profession, 123,
      178
   Beatrice Webb at, 35, 214
   Bernard Shaw at, 178
   Frederic Harrison at, 34, 123, 195,
      226
   Yaldwyn family at, 126
Blackdown House, 123, 127, 176
Blackdown, height of, 19
Blake, William, 117, 160, 223
Blen-Cathra, Hindhead
   Bernard Shaw at, 36, 177
   Sidney Webb visits, 214
Blount, Ethel née Hine, 92–93
   works
      The Story of the Homespun Web,
         93
Blount, Godfrey, 92–93
   works
      Arbor Vitae, 93
      The Blood of the Poor, 93
      The Song of the Sower, 93
Bockett, Frederick William, 25, 27,
   123, 124, 190, 207
   a Positivist, 67
   at Fox & Pelican, Grayshott, 38
   at Haslemere Museum, 136
   at Sir Jonathan Hutchinson's
      lecture, 134–35
   on Aldworth, 193
   Some Literary Landmarks for
      Pilgrims on Wheels, 27
Bodichon, Barbara

friend of George Eliot, 141
Bodichon, Dr
  on degeneracy, 48
Bodleian Library, 210
Boer War, 45–47, 218–19
Borough Farm, Milford
  Henry James at, 211
  Humphry Wards at, 211
  Webbs at, 214
  William Allingham at, 211
Bowley, Sir Arthur, 40
Bramshott Chase, 226
Briar Cottage, Hindhead
  G.D. Brown at, 94
Bridges, Dr John Henry, 188
Bridges, Robert, 95, 129, 184, 186
British Mycological Society, 191
Brookbank, Shottermill, 224
  Anne Gilchrist at, 30, 117–22
  Christina Rossetti at, 30, 165, 166–68
  G.H. Lewes and George Eliot at, 32, 111–12, 141–42
  George Smith at, 112
  refurbishing at, 229
  Tennyson at, 30, 192
Brooke, Emma, 122
Brooke, Gerald, 190
Brooke, Winifred *née Storr*, 190
broom squires, 22, 25, 35, 90, 146
Brown, Ford Madox, 118, 120
Brown, George Douglas, 39, 94
  The House with the Green Shutters, 94
Brown, T.E., 106
Brownscombe, Shottermill
  R.S. Whiteway at, 219
Bruce-Joy, Albert, 226
Buckton, Alys Mary, 32, 95–96
  on Tennyson's knee, 95, 146
  works
    Eager Heart, 95
    Through Human Eyes, 95
Buckton, George Bowdler
  makes a Wimshurst machine, 95
Buckton, George Bowdler, 32, 94–96
  works

The Natural History of Eristalis tenax, or the Drone Fly, 95
Buckton, Mary Ann *née Odling*, 94
Burroughs, John, 24, 33, 44, 96–98
  and Anne Gilchrist, 96, 98, 121
  and Walt Whitman, 96
  hears the nightingale, 98
  works
    Birds and Poets, 96
    Fresh Fields, 96
Butler, Samuel, 66
Byron, Lord, 196
Campbell, Thomas, 196
Carlisle, Lady
  Gilbert Murray's mother-in-law, 147
  model for Bernard Shaw's Lady Britomart, 147
Carlyle, Jane *née Baillie*, 30, 117, 118
Carlyle, Thomas, 30, 117, 118, 155, 198, 200
Carrington, Richard Christopher, 21, 32, 98–102, 225
  at his wife's inquest, 100
  dies, 101
  marries Rosa (Rose) Jeffries, 99
  on religion, 63
  works
    A Catalogue of 3735 Circumpolar Stars, 98
    Observations on the Spots on the Sun, 98
Carrington, Rosa (Rose) *née Jeffries*
  attacked by William Rodway, 100
  dies, 100
  marries Richard Carrington, 100
Carroll, Lewis (Charles Dodgson), 166
Castle, Agnes, 39
Castle, Egerton, 40, 159
  Schools and Masters of Fence, 159
Cauteretz, Tennyson and Dakyns at, 105
Cayley, Charles, 167
Chamberlain, Joseph, 45, 57, 212
Chapel Street, London, 67, 124
Chapman, Ernest, 46
Chapman, Walter, 203

becomes psychotic, 203
kills wife Emily, 203
Chenies Street, London, 135
Cherrimans, Shottermill
  James Simmons Jnr at, 97, 118
  Leweses at, 111–12
Chesham Cottage
  David Ker at, 137
Cheyne Row, London
  Anne Gilchrist at, 117
Churchill, Lord Randolph, 45
Churt, 30, 172, 192, 225
  Gilbert Murray at, 147
  Lloyd George at, 40
Clark, Dr R. Oke
  at inquest on
    Richard Carrington, 101
    Rose Carrington, 100
Clodd, Edward, 83, 87, 116
Cobbett, William, 22
Cobden, Richard, 45
Cochet Farm
  H.G. Wells at, 39, 216–17
Collinson, James, 167
Comte, Auguste, 67, 68, 124, 188, 189
  Cours de philosophie positive, 67
Congreve, Richard, 67, 124, 188
contents, 9
Costelloe, Benjamin Francis Conn
  (Frank), 44, 102–5, 183
  dies, 103
  marries Mary Pearsall Smith, 103
  on religion, 74
  works
    *Aristotle and the Earlier
      Peripatetics*, 103
    Ethics or Anarchy, 104
    Frédérick Ozanam, 104
    The Gospel Story, 104
    The Incidence of Taxation, 103
Costelloe, Karin. *see* Stephen, Karin
Costelloe, Mary Pearsall. *see*
  Berenson Mary
Costelloe, Ray. *see* Strachey, Ray
  The World at Eighteen, 104
Courts Hill Lodge, Haslemere,
  Hopkins family at, 129

Cowper, William, 223
Crane, Walter, 37
Crawford, Donald, 162
Crawford, Mrs, 162
Croft, Hindhead, The
  Conan Doyle at, 110
  Grant Allen at, 35, 81, 225
Cross, J.W., 113
Cust, H.J.C., 164
Daffarn, Daphne *née Mangles*, on
  Tennyson's knee, 146
Dakyns, Henry Graham, 35, 45, 105–
  6, 201
  at Doyle's Christmas Ball, 105, 107
  works
    The Education of Cyrus, 106
    The March of the Ten Thousand,
      106
    Xenophon, 106
Dangstein, Rogate, Lady Dorothy
  Nevill at, 151
Darwin, Charles, 82, 87, 114, 205
Defoe, Daniel, 223
degeneracy, 47–49, 114, 174
Devil's Jumps, The
  observatory at, 98
  Richard Carrington at, 21, 32, 98–
    102
  Tennysons at, 118, 192
  Thomas Wright at, 99, 225
Devil's Punch Bowl, The, 22, 35, 81,
  90, 122, 141, 187, 197, 224
Dickens, Charles, 171
Dilke, Sir Charles, 162
Dimbleby, Richard, 40
Disraeli, Benjamin, 1st Earl of
  Beaconsfield, 154
Diver, Maud, 39
Dolmetsch, Arnold, 138
Dorking, Grant Allen in, 81
Dorson, Richard, 116
Downlands, Bramshott, 226
Doyle, Jean *née Leckie*, 110
Doyle, Sir Arthur Conan, 20, 45, 47,
  106–11, 122, 211, 215
  as motorist, 108
  at Grant Allen's deathbed, 87

at Haslemere Microscope and
Natural History Society, 37
builds Undershaw at Hindhead, 35
described by Flora Thompson, 108,
204
dual personality, 109
gives Christmas Ball, 105, 107
Grant Allen's advice to, 106
in Egypt, 107
leaves for Crowborough, 39, 110
marries Jean Leckie, 110
on Boer War, 46, 108
on Lady Dorothy Nevill, 153
on religion, 74–75
on spiritualism, 74–75
organises Rifle Club, 108
Sherlock Holmes, new series of
stories, 109
works
A Study in Scarlet, 106
Hilda Wade, 87
Micah Clarke, 209
Rodney Stone, 109
Sir Nigel, 108, 109
The Great Boer War, 108
The Hound of the Baskervilles,
109
The Study in Scarlet, 110
The Tragedy of the Korosko, 107
*The War in South Africa – Its
Cause and Conduct*, 46
The White Company, 108
Dunrozel, Hindhead
Bertrand Russell at, 171
Lady Russell at, 170
Rollo Russell at, 171, 173
Earls Colne, Essex, 119, 120
Eashing
John Burroughs at, 97
Edge, S.F., 40
Eggar, J. Alfred, on death of Rose
Carrington, 101
Egmont, Lord, 192
Eliot, George (Marian Evans, later
Mrs Cross), 20, 21, 51–52, 111–13,
143
as Mrs Lewes, 111, 141–42
at Brookbank, 31, 111–12, 141

at Cherrimans, Shottermill, 112
death of, 39
described by
Henry James, 113
Tennyson, 113
marries J.W. Cross, 113
on feminism, 51
on Positivism, 125
on religion, 63–64
talks to farmer's wife, 43, 112
works
Impressions of Theophrastus Such,
113
Middlemarch, 32, 111, 112, 141
O May I Join the Choir Invisible,
125
The Mill on the Floss, 51
Eliot, Thomas Stearns, 75
Ellis, Henry Havelock, 50
Emma, Queen of Hawaii, at
Hampstead, 129
Ensleigh, Grayshott, Miss Weston
and Miss Winz at, 217
Etheridge, Reverend Sanders, 85
eugenics, 49, 113–15
Evans, Marian. *see* Eliot, George
Eyre, General John Edward, 205
Fabian Society, 213, 215
Faraday, Michael, 205
Farringford, Isle of Wight, 23, 192,
193, 198, 207
William Allingham at, 89
Fawcett, Mrs Millicent Garrett, 57,
61, 105
feminism, 50–62
Fenn, Alice Maud, 112, 228
Fernhurst, Sussex
Bertrand and Alys Russell at, 35,
172
Elizabeth von Arnim at, 39, 216
Osbert Salvin at, 33, 176
Pearsall Smiths at, 103, 172, 181
Webbs at, 172, 214
Field, Michael, 185
Fielding, Reverend James, 191
Foster, Dr, 182
Foundry Cottage, Haslemere,
Godfrey and Ethel Blount at, 92

Fox and Pelican
  described by
    Flora Thompson, 203
Fox and Pelican, Grayshott, The, 37–38, 148, 150, 160, 178, 188
  described by
    F.W. Bockett, 38
    Flora Thompson, 38
Fox, Dr Wilson, 169
Foxholes, Blackdown, 145, 197
Friday's Hill
  barbecue at, 214
  Beatrice Webb at, 35, 186
  Bernard Berenson at, 103
  Bertrand and Alys Russell at, 172
  Frank and Mary Costelloe at, 103
  Gertrude and Leo Stein at, 186
  Michael Field at, 185
  Pearsall Smiths at, 35, 39, 103, 172, 181
  Ray Strachey at, 35, 104
  Sidney Webb at, 35, 103, 214
Fringford, Oxon, 201
Friswell, James Hain, 195
Fry, Roger, 160
Gaika War, 218
Galton, Sir Francis, 20, 113–15, 130, 205
  cousin Charles Darwin, 65, 114
  death of, 39, 113
  on degeneracy, 48
  on religion, 65
  works
    Essays in Eugenics, 115
    Hereditary Genius, 114
    Kantsaywhere, 114–15
    Memories of my Life, 115
    The Art of Travel, 115
Garland, Mrs, 119, 141
Garnett, Lucy Mary Jane, 115–16
  on feminism, 53
  works
    Greek Folk Songs, 116
    The Women of Turkey and their Folklore, 116
Garth, Haslemere, The, Hopkins family at, 129, 130
Georgian Hotel, Haslemere, 151, 187

Gilchrist, Alexander, 117
Gilchrist, Anne and Alexander, *Life of William Blake*, 21, 30, 117
Gilchrist, Anne *née Burrows*, 21, 30–31, 117–22
  and G.H. Lewes, 119, 141
  and George Eliot, 111, 119
  and John Burroughs, 96, 98, 121
  and Tennyson, 30–31, 118–19, 192
  and the Rossettis, 118–20, 165–66, 168
  and Thomas and Jane Carlyle, 117, 118
  and Walt Whitman, 119–21
  death of, 39, 98
  in Hampstead, 121
  in Philadelphia, 121
  works
    An Englishwoman's Estimate of Walt Whitman, 120
    Life of Mary Lamb, 118
Gilchrist, Grace
  and Bernard Shaw, 122
  and Christina Rossetti, 121, 165
  on Tennyson's knee, 122, 146
Gladstone, William Ewart, 45, 150, 200, 210
Godalming, John Burroughs at, 97
Godfrey, Miss Alice, marries Rollo Russell, 173
Gooch, Reverend F.H., 90
Goodwyns, Haslemere, Montagu White at, 218
Gosse, Edmund, 140, 153
Gosse, Philip, 142
Grayshott and District Refreshment House Association, The, 32, 37–38, 159, 178, 188
Grayshott and Hindhead Temperance Guild, 218
Grayshott Farm
  Tennyson at, 119, 192, 197
Grayshott, Hants, 23
  Agnes Weston at, 217
  Flora Thompson at, 36, 46, 201–4
  Galton at, 113
  post office, 203–4
  Thomas Wright at, 35, 37–38, 224

Grayswood
  Arthur Pinero at, 35, 158
  Henry Dakyns at, 35, 105
  Joseph and Maude King at, 35, 137,
    138
  Mrs Humphry Ward at, 35
Grayswood Beeches
  Conan Doyle at, 107
  Humphry Wards at, 211
Grayswood Commons, 131
Grayswood Vicarage, R.S. Whiteway
  at, 220
Grey, Sir Edward, 211
Gutch, Reverend, 170
Haines, William, 117, 165
Hamilton, Bernard, 39, 47, 122–23
  his allegorical booklet, 122
  on Boer War, 46
  on religion, 71
  works
    A Kiss for a Kingdom, 122
    The Light?, 122
Hamley, General, 197
Hammer, 23, 226
Hampstead
  Anne Gilchrist at, 96, 121
  H.G. Wells at, 216
  John Burroughs at, 96
  Manley Hopkins at, 129
  Rayner Storr at, 188
Hardy, Thomas, 52
  works
    Jude the Obscure, 52
    Tess of the d'Urbervilles, 52
Harrison, Austin, 125
Harrison, Frederic, 20, 32, 34, 87,
  123–26, 214, 226
  and Positivism, 67–69, 124–25, 188
  death of, 69, 125
  on Boer War, 45, 219
  on feminism, 57
  on Irish Home Rule, 45
  on politics, 44, 47
  on Tennyson, 195, 196
  works
    Cromwell, 124
    *Studies in Early Victorian
      Literature*, 124

*Theophano – the Crusade of the
  Tenth Century*, 124
Harrison, Jane, 148–49
Harrison, Mrs Frederic, on feminism,
  53, 56
Harvard, Pearsall Smiths at, 103, 183
Haslemere
  anti-Boer riot at, 219
  described by
    F.W. Bockett, 25
    Hubert Wales, 209
    Lady Dorothy Nevill, 151–53
  drains of, the *Lancet* on, 174, 188
  in 1859, 29
  Montagu White at, 218
  Morley's 1735 map of, 225
  Peasant Arts in, 93, 137
  remoteness, 187
  too bourgeois for Mrs Ward, 211
  unemployment, 92
  William Allingham at, 32, 89
Haslemere Educational Museum, 17,
  32, 37, 135–37, 190, 219, 226
Haslemere Microscope and Natural
  History Society
  Bernard Shaw at, 178
  early history, 32, 36, 191
  Edward Nettleship at, 150
  Flora Thompson at, 191, 202
  Frederick Pollock at, 159, 205
  Gilbert Murray at, 147, 178
  Grant Allen at, 85, 86
  John Tyndall at, 207
  R.S. Whiteway at, 220
  Rayner Storr at, 186, 188, 190
  Rollo Russell at, 174
Hawaii, Kingdom of, 20, 129
Hawksfold, Salvin at, 176
Hazel Grove, Frederick Pollock at, 34
Heights, Witley, The, Leweses at,
  113, 142
Henley, W.E., 164
Herald, The, newspaper, 177, 179
Hesse, Revd James Legrew, 218
Higginson, T.W., 198
High Building, Fernhurst, Logan
  Pearsall Smith at, 183
Highcombe Edge, Hindhead

Rayner Storr at, 33, 123, 187
S.H. Swinny at, 188
Thomas Wright at, 225
Highercombe, Grayswood
  Arthur Pinero at, 158
  Henry Dakyns at, 105
Hill Farm, Camelsdale
  Bernard Shaw at, 137
  Joseph King at, 137
Hill, Octavia, 51, 131
Hilltop Novels, 21, 35, 52, 84, 139,
  209
Hilltop Writers, location of, 14
Hindhead, 21–22, 203, 225
  air of, 34, 113, 207
  and The National Trust, 131
  Christina Rogerson at, 35
  described by
    Agnes Weston, 217
    F.W. Bockett, 25
    Grant Allen, 21, 81
    H.G. Wells, 215–16
    Helen Mathers, 23
    Louis Jennings, 22
    Netta Syrett, 39
    Richard Le Gallienne, 139
    Thomas Wright, 24, 224, 226
    William Cobbett, 22
  English Switzerland, 34, 36, 207,
    224
  Frederick Pollock at, 34
  Grant Allen at, 35
  height of, 19
  Hindhead's turn will come!, 25
  Hubert Wales at, 208
  John Tyndall at, 34, 206–8
  Margaret Oliphant at, 35, 155
  Russell family at, 170–73
  sketched by
    J.M.W. Turner, 22
  suburbanisation, 24, 25, 39, 158,
    179, 204
Hindhead Brae, Bernard Hamilton at,
  122
Hindhead Copse, Frederick Pollock
  at, 34, 158
Hindhead House, 226
  screens, 206, 209

Tyndalls at, 206–8
Hine, Henry, 138
Hine, Maude Egerton. see King,
  Maude Egerton
Hird-Jones, Miss Catherine, 138
Hirst, T.A., 208
Hodgson, Agatha Stewart, 223
Holl, Henry, 126–28
  works
    The King's Mail, 127–28
    The Old House in Crosby Square,
      126
Holl, William, 126
Homeward Heath, Hindhead, Hubert
  Wales at, 208
Honeyhanger, Shottermill, Algernon
  Methuen at, 35, 146, 209
Hooker, Sir Joseph Dalton, 145, 206
Hooker, Sir William Jackson, 145
Hopkins, Arthur, 130
Hopkins, Charles, 129
Hopkins, Cyril, 130
Hopkins, Everard, 130
Hopkins, Gerard Manley, 72, 128,
  129
Hopkins, Grace, 130
Hopkins, Kate, 130
Hopkins, Lionel, 130
Hopkins, Manley, 20, 34, 128–30
  and the Kingdom of Hawaii, 129
  on religion, 72
  opinion of Tennyson's poems, 129
  works
    A Handbook of Average, 129
    A Manual of Marine Insurance,
      129
    Hawaii – The Past, Present and
      Future of its Island-Kingdom,
      129
    Spicilegium Poeticum, A
      Gathering of Verses, 130
    The Cardinal Numbers, 130
Hopkins, Millicent, 130
Houghton, Lady, 142
Houghton, Lord, on Aldworth, 194
Hunter, Sir Robert, 33, 130–31, 132

The Preservation of Open Spaces, Footpaths and Other Rights of Way, 131
Hutchinson, A.S.M., 40
Hutchinson, Jane *née West*, 131
Hutchinson, Sir Jonathan, 20, 32, 131–37, 190, 226
and Edward Nettleship, 149
as teacher, 134
invests in property, 132
lectures, 134–35, 188
marries Jane West, 131
medical practice, 132
on leprosy, 133–34
on purpose of museums, 136
on religion, 71, 135
on syphilis, 136
starts Haslemere museum, 37, 135–37, 190
visits Norway, 133
visits South Africa, 133
works
On Leprosy and Fish-Eating, 134
Illustrations of Clinical Surgery, 136
The Centuries – A chronological Synopsis of History as the 'Space-for-Time' Method, 137
Huxley, Thomas Henry, 205
I Tatti, Italy
Berensons at, 103, 148–49
Gilbert Murray and Jane Harrison at at, 148–49
illustrations, list of, 10
imperialism, 47, 76, 122
Inval, Haslemere, Sir Jonathan Hutchinson at, 32, 132, 135, 190
Irish Home Rule, 45, 205
Jackson, Hughlings, 131
James, Henry, 143, 154, 162, 184
Jay, Elizabeth, 64
Jeffries, Rosa (Rose). *see* Carrington, Rosa
Jekyll, Gertrude, 147, 183
Jenner, Sir William, 169
Jennings, Louis, 22
Joachim, Gertrude. *see* Russell, Gertrude

Joachim, Henry, 173
Joachim, Joseph, 173
Jowett, Benjamin, 103, 183, 228
Jumps House, 98
Kamehameha IV, King of Hawaii, 129
Kelvin, William Thomas, 1st Baron, 205
Kemble, Mrs, 143
Kempis, Thomas à, 68, 123, 189
Imitation of Christ, 68
Ker, David, 39, 137
works
Among the Dark Mountains, Or Cast Away in Sumatra, 137
The Wild Horsemen of the Pampas, 137
Kernahan, Coulson, on Doyle, 110
Kilmainham, 123
King, Joseph, 35, 44, 92, 137–38
marries Maude Hine, 137
on religion, 72
political career, 138
works
Filius Nullius, 138
Peasant Arts, 138
The School Manager, 138
King, Maude Egerton *née Hine*, 35, 92, 138–39
marries Joseph King, 138
works
The Country Heart and Other Stories, 139
The Vineyard, 138
Kingswood Chase, Grayshott, Richard Le Gallienne at, 140, 225
Kipling, Rudyard, 148
Knowles, James, 145, 192, 207
Krakatoa, eruption of, 174
Kruger, Paul, 47, 123
La Chard, Therese, 92
Ladysmith, siege of, 164
Lane, John, 85
Lawson, Cecil, 89
Le Gallienne, Richard, 20, 39, 139–40, 216, 225
contribution to the *Yellow Book*, 140

described by Flora Thompson, 140, 204

marries Irma Hinton Perry, 140

marries Julie Norregard, 139

on religion, 70

works

  Sleeping Beauties and other prose fancies, 140

  The Quest of the Golden Girl, 35, 139, 225

Lea Park, 132, 215

League Against Women's Suffrage, 53, 91, 220

Leake, Helena Isabel *née Whiteway*, 220

Leake, Revd, first vicar of Grayswood, 220

Lear, Edward, 199

Leavis, Q.D., on Margaret Oliphant, 155

Leckie, Jean, marries Conan Doyle, 110

Leigh, Augusta, 196

Lewes, George Henry, 20, 141–43

as scientist, 142

at Brookbank, 31, 141–42

death of, 39, 113

described by

  Charles Eliot Norton, 143

  Henry James, 143

encounters Tennyson, 141

misses his train, 141

on religion, 63

with George Eliot, 111–13

works

  A Biographical History of Philosophy, 142

  Problems of Life and Mind, 141

  Sea-side Studies at Ilfracombe, Tenby, the Scilly Isles and Jersey, 142

  The Life and Works of Goethe, 142

Lewin, Edith May, marries Edward Whymper, 221

Linch, Sussex, deranged vicar of, 184–85, 231

Linnean Society, 191

Lion Green, 121

Liphook, Hants

Flora Thompson at, 39, 191, 202

John Burroughs at, 97

Leweses at, 141

Thomas Wright at, 226

Webbs at, 215

Lloyd George, David, 40

Loder, Gerald, 146

Lodge, Haslemere, The, Montagu White at, 218

Log House, Hindhead, The

Christina Rogerson at, 163

Margaret Oliphant at, 156, 164

London School of Economics, founding of, 215

Long House, Hindhead, The, 156, 208

Longdown Hollow, Hindhead, Edward Nettleship at, 150

Longfellow, Henry Wadsworth, 171

Lower Birtley, Joseph King at, 137

Lower Grayswood, Humphry Wards at, 211

Ludshott Common, 131

Lurgashall, 146

MacCarthy, Desmond, 184

  Lady John Russell, A Memoir, 171

MacDonald, Greville, 138

Maclean, Alastair, 40

Macmillan, Alexander, 226

Mangles, Agnes (daughter of J.H. Mangles), 144

Mangles, Alice (daughter of J.H. Mangles), 146

marries William Daffarn, 146

on Tennyson's knee, 146

Mangles, Charles Edward (father of J.H. Mangles), 144

Mangles, Isabella (wife of J.H. Mangles), 90, 144, 146

invited to Aldworth, 146

Mangles, James Henry, 21, 30, 32, 113, 143–46, 201, 216

advises Tennyson about plants, 196

against railway nationalization, 144

as rhododendron hybridiser, 145

death of, 146

discovery of diary, 144

in Bengal, 144
relations with Tennyson, 144, 192,
  195, 196
works
  Rhododendron Notes, 146
  *Tennyson at Aldworth
    The Diary of James Henry
    Mangles*, 144
Manor House, Haslemere, The,
  Wolseleys at, 222
Map of Haslemere, circa 1867, 15
Marley, 131, 141
Marvin, F.S., 125
Mason, Colonel William H., 36
Mason, Mr, neighbour of Tyndall,
  207
Mathers, Helen, 23
Matterhorn, Edward Whymper climbs
  the, 221
Matthews, E.C., 19
Mawson, Thomas, 193
Maxwell, James Clerk, 205
Meadfields, Haslemere, Robert
  Hunter at, 130
Menken, Adah, 196
Meredith, George, 81
Merton Abbey, 164
Methuen, Sir Algernon *formerly
  Stedman*, 35, 90, 146–47, 161, 209
and politics, 44
and unemployment in Haslemere,
  92
changes name to Methuen, 90, 147
on Boer War, 45
works
  *A Simple Plan for a New House of
    Lords*, 147
  An Alpine ABC, 147
  An Anthology of English Verse,
    147
  The Tragedy of South Africa, 147
Milford
  Humphry Wards at, 211
  Webbs at, 214
Mill, John Stuart, *The Subjection of
  Women*, 53
Millais, John Guille, 146
Millhanger, Fernhurst

Bertrand and Alys Russell at, 172
described by Beatrice Webb, 172
Webbs at, 214
Milton, Winifred Maria, marries
  Rayner Storr, 190
Moorcroft, Hindhead, Richard Le
  Gallienne at, 139
Moorlands, Hindhead, 107
Morley, John 1st Viscount, 189
Morley's 1735 map of Haslemere,
  225
Morris, William, discussion with
  William Allingham, 69
Mowatt, Fanny Louise *née Akroyd*,
  91
Mozley, H.W., 151, 187
Mud House, Fernhurst, The, 104, 183
Mudie's lending library, 204, 210
Muirhead, James Fullerton, 103
Munstead Wood, Logan Pearsall
  Smith at, 183
Murray, George Gilbert, 20, 36, 44,
  65–66, 102, 147–49, 189
arrives at Barford, 147
at Haslemere Microscope and
  Natural History Society, 37, 147
Bernard Shaw's quip, 147, 178
model for Bernard Shaw's Adolphus
  Cusins, 147
on Boer War, 45
on feminism, 59
on politics, 44
on religion, 65
visits Berensons with Jane Harrison,
  148–49
works
  Andromache, 147
  Euripedes, 147
  Five Stages of Greek Religion, 66
Murray, Lady Mary, 148, 178
Museum Hill, Haslemere, 136, 190
Mycological Society, British, 191
Myers, Frederic William Henry, on
  religion, 63
National Trust, The, 24, 33, 131, 206
Nettleship, Edward, 20, 37, 149–50,
  160, 178, 220, 225

Anomalies and Diseases of the Eye, 150
described by Queen Victoria, 150
operates on William Gladstone, 150
Nettleship, Elizabeth *née Whiteway*, 220
Nevill, Lady Dorothy *née Walpole*, 43, 151–54
and Montagu White, 218, 219
at Tudor Cottage, Haslemere, 187
at Tudor Cottage, Haslemere, 151–52
described by
  Conan Doyle, 153
  Edmund Gosse, 153
garden at Rogate, 151
marries Reginald Nevill, 151
on Boer War, 46
on feminism, 56
on politics, 45
works
  Leaves from the Notebooks of Lady Dorothy Nevill, 153
  Mannington and the Walpoles, 153
  The Ailanthus Silkworm, 153
  The Reminiscences of Lady Dorothy Nevill, 153
  Under Five Reigns, 153
Nevill, Ralph, 153
New Place, Hindhead, Methuen at, 147
Newton Hall, London, 67
Nicolson, Harold, 201
Norman, Mrs Iris, discovers J.H. Mangles diary, 144
Norregard, Julie, marries Richard Le Gallienne, 139
Norton, Charles Eliot, 143
Nutcombe Hill, Hindhead, Edward Nettleship at, 150
Oliphant, Margaret *née Wilson*, 20, 154–57
and Christina Rogerson, 156, 162, 163, 164
death of, 39
death of daughter, 72, 155
encounter with Tennyson, 155
Henry James on, 155

on feminism, 52–53, 55
on religion, 72
Q.D. Leavis on, 155
vast output, 154
works
  Kirsteen, 154
  Memoirs of the Life of Laurence Oliphant, 157
  Miss Marjoribanks, 154
  The Cuckoo in the Nest, 35, 156, 226
Olney, Bucks, Thomas Wright at, 223
Onions, Oliver, 40
Pall Mall Gazette, 163
Palmer, Samuel, 117, 118
Pannell, Charles Jnr
  120 Years of Non-conformity in Haslemere, 37
  A Short account of the Land and Freshwater Molluscs of Haslemere, 37
  Secretary of Haslemere Microscope and Natural History Society, 36
Parry, Sir Hubert, 160
  Jerusalem, 160
Passfield Corner, Webbs at, 215
Pater, Walter, 223
Paterson, Arthur, at Aldworth, 200
Paterson, Helen, marries William Allingham, 87
Payne-Townshend, Charlotte, marries Bernard Shaw, 176
Peasant Arts in Haslemere, 93, 137–39
Pembroke Lodge, Richmond Park, 170, 171
Penfold, John Wornham, 129, 190, 206
Penfold, Kate, 130
Perry, Irma Hinton, marries R. Le Gallienne, 140
Petworth House, 176
Philadelphia
  Anne Gilchrist at, 96, 121
  Pearsall Smiths in, 181
Philipson-Stowe, Sir Frederick and Lady, 123

Pinero, Sir Arthur Wing, 20, 35, 39, 158
works
Lady Bountiful, 158
The Profligate, 158
Pite, Beresford, 152, 187
Pite, William A., 151, 152, 187
Pitfold House, Shottermill
Bernard Shaw at, 36, 91, 176–77
Beveridges at, 35, 91–92
Pius X, Pope, praised *Concordance*, 20, 189
Polecat Hill
Galton at, 113
John Burroughs at, 97
Pollock, Sir Frederick, 20, 158–60, 225
and Fox & Pelican, 37, 159, 178
as fencer, 159
as mountaineer, 159, 206
at Doyle's Christmas Ball, 107
at Haslemere Microscope and Natural History Society, 37, 65, 205, 207
at Hazel Grove, Hindhead, 34, 158
dances the 'kitchen lancers', 163
leaves Hindhead, 39
works
First Book of Jurisprudence for Students of the Common Law, 159
Mountaineering, 159
Ponsonby, Arthur Augustus William Harry, 1st Baron of Shulbrede, 20, 160–61
marries Dolly Parry, 160
on feminism, 58
on politics, 44
peerage, 137, 160
works
English Diaries, 161
More English Diaries, 161
Scottish and Irish Diaries, 161
The Camel and the Needle's Eye, 161
The Priory and Manor of Lynchmere and Shulbrede, 161
Positivism, 27, 67–69, 87, 123–26

Potter, Beatrice. *see* Webb, Beatrice
Potter, Richard, on feminism, 57
Poyle, Mangles family at, 144
Pradeau, Gustave, 188, 189
Priory, London, The, 111, 119, 141, 143
Punch Bowl Inn, Hindhead, 170, 173
Quedley, Galton at, 113
Quell, The, 127
railway, 19, 30, 43, 131, 144, 194, 220
Rawnsley, Canon Hardwicke Drummond, 131, 198
Redhill, Richard Carrington at, 98
religion, 62–75
Rhodes, Cecil, 47, 123
Richards, Grant, 85, 86, 163
Robertson, Graham, 90
Rodway, William, 100
Rogerson, Christina *née Stewart*, later Steevens, 35, 161–64, 226
A Motley Crew Reminiscences, observations and attempts at playwriting, 164
described by Grant Richards, 163
described by Margaret Oliphant, 163
encounter with Christina Rossetti, 166
her home for slum children, 156, 163
in Dilke divorce case, 162–63
marries George Steevens, 163
on feminism, 53
Rolleston, Sir Humphrey, 40
Ropes, Fernhurst, Charlotte Waterlow and Elizabeth von Arnim at, 216
Rossetti, Christina, 20, 21, 30, 164–70
described by Grace Gilchrist, 165
develops exophthalmic goitre, 168–69
dies of breast cancer, 169, 170
on feminism, 55, 168
on religion, 72–73, 168
prefers town to country, 166
works
A Farm Walk, 166–67

Bird or Beast?, 168
Goblin Market, 165
In the bleak mid-winter, 73, 169
Maiden Song, 118, 166
Seek and Find, 55
Songs in a Cornfields, 167
Twilight Night, 118, 168
Rossetti, Dante Gabriel, 30, 117, 118, 165, 196
Rossetti, William Michael, 30, 72, 117, 118–20, 165, 169
Rothenstein, Sir William, 185
Rothschilds, 211
Royal Institution, 206
Rozeldene, Hindhead
  Bernard Russell at, 170
  Lady Agatha Russell at, 170
Ruck, Berta, 40
Russell Square, Humphry Wards at, 211
Russell, Alys *née Pearsall Smith*, 35, 172
  on feminism, 56
Russell, Bertrand Arthur William, 3rd Earl Russell, 20, 170, 171–72
  and Gilbert Murray, 148
  and Jane Harrison, 148
  and politics, 45
  and the Webbs, 172, 214
  described by Elizabeth von Arnim, 172
  impressing John Tyndall, 207
  marries Alys Pearsall Smith, 35, 172
  on Boer War, 45
  on Hannah Pearsall Smith, 182
  on religion, 64
  works
    An Essay on the Foundations of Geometry, 172
    German Social Democracy, 172
    Principia Mathematica, 172
    The Principles of Mathematics, 172
Russell, Gertrude *née Joachim*, 170, 173
Russell, Hon Rollo, 33, 158, 171, 173–75
  advocates nationalism on land, 175

and politics, 45
  at Haslemere Microscope and Natural History Society, 37, 173, 174, 207
  builds Dunrozel, 170, 173
  marries Alice Godfrey, 173
  marries Gertrude Joachim, 173
  on degeneracy, 49, 174
  on religion and science, 175
  works
    Break of Day, and Other Poems, 175
    Preventable Cancer – A Statistical Research, 174
    Psalms of the West, 175
    The Atmosphere in relation to Human Life and Health, 174
    The Distribution of Land, 175
    Epidemics, Plagues and Fevers, 174
Russell, Lady Agatha, 90, 170–71
  builds Rozeldene, 170
  on feminism, 56
  parodies Longfellow, 171
  rumours about her chauffeur, 170
  teaches Bertrand Russell to read, 170
  works
    Gleanings Grave and Gay, 171
    Lady John Russell, A Memoir, 171
    Thoughts of Many Minds, 171
Russell, Lady John, 171, 173
Russell, Lord John, 171
Salvin, Anthony, 176
Salvin, Osbert, 33, 176
  Biologia Centrali-Americana, 176
Santayana, George, 184
Saville Gardens, 146
Selby, Sir Jonathan Hutchinson at, 135, 136
Selwyn, Canon Edward Carus, 111, 212
Seven Thorns Inn, 139, 156, 226
Severn, Alice, marries Rayner Storr, 190
Severn, Joseph, 190
Shackleford, John Burroughs at, 97
Sharp, William, 166

Shaw, Capt Frank, describes Lady
  Agatha Russell, 170
Shaw, Charlotte *née Payne-
  Townshend*, 176–78, 214
Shaw, George Bernard, 20, 44, 87,
  160, 176–79
  and Fabian Society, 213
  and Fox & Pelican, 37, 178
  and politics, 45
  at Blen-Cathra, 36, 177–78, 214
  at Haslemere Microscope and
    Natural History Society, 37, 178
  at Pitfold House, 36, 91, 176–77
  described by Flora Thompson, 204
  flirts with Grace Gilchrist, 122
  gives books to Fox & Pelican, 37
  marries Charlotte Payne-
    Townshend, 176
  on feminism, 58
  on Gilbert Murray's translation of
    Euripedes, 147
  on honeymoon, 91
  on Irish Home Rule, 45
  on religion, 66–67
  works
    Back to Methuselah, 66
    Caesar and Cleopatra, 177
    Captain Brassbound's Conversion,
      177
    Major Barbara, 147
    Misalliance, 25, 178
    Mrs Warren's Profession, 123,
      178
    The Perfect Wagnerite, 91, 177
    Three Plays for Puritans, 178
Shottermill
  Anne Gilchrist at, 30, 31, 117–22
  Christina Rossetti at, 166–68
  G.H. Lewes and George Eliot at,
    111–13, 141–42
  James Simmons Snr diarist at, 29,
    220
  John Burroughs at, 33, 96, 97, 121
  Tennyson at, 118, 141, 192
Shulbrede Priory, Ponsonbys at, 160
Sillick, William Austen, 17, 25, 179–
  81, 208
  and Flora Thompson, 180

describes Bank Holiday at
  Hindhead, 180
on Conan Doyle, 180
Simmons, Ann (wife of James
  Simmons Jnr), 112
Simmons, James Jnr, 97, 112, 207
  helps Tennyson find site for
    Aldworth, 31, 118, 192
Simmons, James Snr, 29, 144, 220,
  229
Small, John, 117, 229
Smith, Alys Pearsall. *see* Russell,
  Alys
Smith, George, 112
Smith, Hannah Pearsall *née Whittall*,
  21, 35, 104, 181–82, 184
  described by Bertrand Russell, 182
  described by Carey Thomas, 182
  disapproves of daughter's marriage,
    103
  leaves Fernhurst, 39
  men should be castrated, 56, 182
  on men and on feminism, 55, 103,
    182
  religion and religious sects, 105,
    181–82
  *The Christian's Secret of a Happy
    Life*, 181
Smith, Logan Pearsall, 20, 104, 183–
  86
  and Gertrude Jekyll, 183
  and Walt Whitman, 121, 183
  at Balliol College, 183
  at Friday's Hill, 35, 183
  at High Buildings, Fernhurst, 183
  described by Beatrice Webb, 186
  leaves Fernhurst, 39
  on Ray Costelloe's novel, 104
  works
    The Golden Urn, 149, 184
    The Youth of Parnassus, 184
    Trivia, 184–85
Smith, Mary Pearsall. *see* Berenson
  Mary
  marries Frank Costelloe, 103
Smith, Robert Pearsall, 181, 182
Smiths, Pearsall, 44, 160, 172, 214
Spencer, Herbert, 82, 87, 119

Splatt, Mrs, 144
St Cross, Haslemere
  described by Therese La Chard, 92
  Geoffrey and Ethel Blount at, 92
Stawell, Miss, 105
Stedman, Algernon. *see* Methuen
Stedman, Dr John Buck, 146
Steevens, Christina. *see* Rogerson
Steevens, George Warrington
  death of, 164
  marries Christina Rogerson, 163
Stein, Gertrude, 185
Stein, Leo, 186
Stephen, Adrian, brother of Virginia
  Woolf
  marries Karin Costelloe, 104, 105
Stephen, Karin *née Costelloe*, 104,
  105
Stevenson, Robert Louis, 81
Stewart, Mrs Duncan, 161
Stillands, Arthur Pinero at, 158
Stoatley Farm, Haslemere
  Hutchinsons at, 131
  Tennysons at, 131, 192
Stocks, Bucks, Humphry Wards at,
  70, 211
Stopes, Dr Marie, 40
Storr, Alice Mary (daughter of Alice),
  190
  marries Stanley Unwin, 190
Storr, Alice *née Severn*, 190
Storr, Milton (son of Winifred
  Maria), 190
Storr, Rayner, 20, 151, 160, 178,
  186–90, 225
  and Fox & Pelican, 38, 188
  and Positivism, 67, 188–89
  at Haslemere Microscope and
    Natural History Society, 37, 186,
    188
  leaves Hindhead, 25
  marries Alice Severn, 190
  marries Winifred Maria Milton, 190
  on Boer War, 45, 188
  on religion, 189
  works

*Concordance to the Latin original
  of De Imitatione Christi*, 20, 33,
  186, 189
*Record of Lectures and Addresses
  of the Haslemere Microscope
  and Natural History Society*, 186
Storr, Wilfred (son of Winifred
  Maria), 190
Storr, William Bromfitt (father of
  Rayner), 187
Storr, Winifred (daughter of Alice),
  190
  marries Gerald Brooke, 190
Storr, Winifred Maria *née Milton*, 190
Strachey, Lytton, 201
Strachey, Oliver, marries Ray
  Costelloe, 104
Strachey, Rachel (Ray) Conn *née
  Costelloe*, 35, 104–5
  at Mud House, Fernhurst, 183
  on feminism, 56
  works
  Group Movements of the Past,
    105, 181
  Millicent Garrett Fawcett, 105
  The Cause, 105
Stuart-Glennie, John Stuart, 116
Stubbs, Bishop of Oxford, 37
Sutton Place, 124
Swanton, Ernest William, 133, 136,
  190–91
  works
  A Country Museum, 191
  Bygone Haslemere, 190
  Country Notes, 191
  Fungi, and How to Know Them,
    191
  *The Rise and Development of the
    Haslemere Natural History
    Society*, 191
Swinburne, Algernon Charles, 81,
  195, 196
Swinny, S.H., 67, 188
Syrett, Netta, 39, 86
Tagore, Rabindranath, 171
Tennyson, Alfred 1st Baron
  Tennyson, 20, 21, 47, 125, 129, 131,
  145, 155, 171, 192–99, 207, 216

and Frederic Harrison, 34, 75, 124, 195
and politics, 45
and William Allingham's last words, 90
and William Gladstone, 45
at Brookbank, 118, 141
at Cauteretz, 105
at The Devil's Jumps, 98, 118, 192
death of, 39, 198
described by
  Anne Gilchrist, 118
  T.W. Higginson, 198
  Thomas Carlyle, 198
  William Allingham, 88–90
distrust of biographers, 201
enjoys literary gossip, 196
enjoys scratching, 201, 233
friendship with James Mangles, 144–45, 192, 196
marries Emily Sellwood, 199
on feminism, 58–59
on Irish Home Rule, 45
on life after death, 196
on plants, 196
on religion, 75
on the scenery of Blackdown, 194, 197
on Walt Whitman, 121
quizzes Buckton about the ant, 95
remembered by Alys Buckton, 95
sensitivity to criticism, 195–96
sings *John Brown's Body*, 89
Wolseley's opinion of, 223
works
  All along the valley, 105
  Balin and Balan, 197
  Crossing the Bar, 75
  Flower in the crannied wall, 197
  Gareth and Lynette, 196
  Guinevere, 142
  Idylls of the King, 197
  In Memoriam, 75, 129, 195
  June Bracken and Heather, 197
  Maud, 51, 149
  The Death of Oenone and other poems, 197

  The Holy Grail and other Poems, 197
  The Princess, 58–59, 129
Tennyson, Hallam, 23, 200–201
  in Australia, 200
  preserves image of his father, 201
  works
    Alfred Lord Tennyson, A Memoir, 59, 199, 200
    Tennyson and his Friends, 200
Tennyson, Lady Emily *née Sellwood*, 105, 197, 198, 199–200, 207
  and Thomas Carlyle, 200
  and William Gladstone, 200
  at Brookbank, 142
  described by Edward Lear, 199
  marriage, 199
  mysterious illnesses of, 200
  on Walt Whitman, 121
  works
    Journal, 199
    Letters, 199
Tennyson, Lionel, 105
Tennyson, Sir Charles, 193, 197, 198
Tennyson's Lane, funeral procession along, 198
Thomas, Carey, 182
Thompson, Flora Jane *née Timms*, 20, 43, 201–4
  alarmed by Walter Chapman, 203
  at Haslemere Microscope and Natural History Society, 191
  describes some Hilltop Writers, 108, 140, 204
  describes William Sillick, 180
  on Boer War, 46
  on feminism, 50
  on Fox & Pelican, 38
  on religion, 74
  post office, Grayshott, 23, 36, 202, 203–4
  works
    A Country Calendar, 202
    Heatherley, 36, 180, 202, 224
    Lark Rise to Candleford, 201
    Peverel Papers, 191, 202
Thompson, John William, 202
Thor's Stone, Thursley, 225

Thursley, 35, 90, 225
Tilford, 148, 172
Town House, Haslemere, 29, 220
Toynbee Hall, 92
Transvaal, Republic of, 218
Treves, Sir Frederick, 134
Tristram, Ernest, 40
Trotter, Wilfred Robert, 7
Tudor Cottage, Haslemere
  Lady Dorothy Nevill at, 151–52,
    219
  Rayner Storr at, 187
Turner, Joseph Mallord William, 22
Tyndall, John, 20, 33, 34, 44, 158,
  171, 204–8, 215, 226
  as mountaineer, 30, 159, 205
  as scientist, 204
  at Haslemere Microscope and
    Natural History Society, 37
  at his Hindhead hut, 206
  death of, 39, 208, 233
  Frederick Pollock's memorial
    address, 65, 159, 205
  in Switzerland, 205
  indigestion and insomnia, 208
  inquest on, 233
  on Irish Home Rule, 205
  on politics, 205
  on religion, 64–65, 205
  protective screens, 206–7, 209
  sinks well at Hindhead, 206
  works
    Fragments of Science for
      Unscientific People, 208
    New Fragments, 208
Tyndall, Louisa, 206, 208
Tyndall's Wood, 206
Undershaw Commando, The, 108
Undershaw, Hindhead
  Conan Doyle at, 35, 107–11, 225
  E.C. Selwyn at, 111, 212
  French Naval Officers at, 110
Unwin, Alice Mary *née Storr*, 190
Unwin, Philip, 189
Unwin, Sir Stanley, 189
Valewood House
  Allinghams at, 90, 146
  Mangles family at, 30, 144, 146

Tennyson at, 145
Victoria, Queen
  on Edward Nettleship, 150
  on Lady Amberley, 51
Voysey, C.F.A., 147
Waggoners Wells, 131, 140, 180,
  197, 224
Wales, Hubert (William Piggott), 39,
  208–10
  on qualification for the franchise,
    210
  works
    The Purpose
      Reflections and Digressions, 210
    The Yoke, 208–9
Walkley, A.B., 158
Walpole, Horace, 151
Walpole, Horatio, 3rd Earl of Orford,
  151
Walpole, Sir Robert, 151
Ward, Humphry, 210–12
  The Reign of Queen Victoria, 212,
    222
Ward, Mary Augusta *née Arnold. see*
  Ward, Mrs Humphry
Ward, Mrs Humphry, 20, 47, 210–12,
  217
  and politics, 45
  at Borough Farm, 211–12
  at Grayswood, 35, 211–12, 226
  at Stocks, 211
  on Boer War, 47
  on feminism, 53–57
  on religion, 70
  works
    Robert Elsmere, 210, 211
    The History of David Grieve, 211
Warner, Oliver, 40
Warr, Mrs Fanny, 204, 224
Warren, Herbert, 198
Waterlow, Charlotte, 216
Waverley Abbey, 109
Weaving House, Haslemere, 93
Webb, Beatrice *née Potter*, 20, 123,
  148, 177, 212–15
  affair with Joseph Chamberlain, 212
  and politics, 45
  at Friday's Hill, 35, 181, 186

at Millhanger, 172
at The Argoed, 214, 231
on degeneracy, 48, 49
on feminism, 56–57
on Positivism, 69
The Co-operative Movement in Great Britain, 213
Webb, Sidney and Beatrice
ashes in Westminster Abbey, 215
at Borough Farm, 211, 214
English Local Government, 214
Webb, Sidney, Baron Passfield, 20, 212–15
and politics, 45
at Friday's Hill, 35, 214
described by Beatrice, 213
marries Beatrice Potter, 214
on degeneracy, 48, 49
reluctantly enobled, 215
Webster, Augusta, on feminism, 55
Wells, H.G., 20, 164, 215–17
and Elizabeth von Arnim, 39, 216–17
and Grant Allen, 81, 83, 85
and Richard Le Gallienne, 139
at Cochet Farm, Blackdown, 39, 216–17
on feminism, 61
works
Ann Veronica, 85
Experiment in Autobiography, 215
Marriage, 216
The New Machiavelli, 85, 216
Tono Bungay, 215
West, Jane, marries Jonathan Hutchinson, 131
West, Rebecca, 217
Westminster Abbey, 72, 75, 198, 215
Weston, Dame Agnes, 217–18
at Grayshott, 217–18
founds Sailors' Rests, 72, 217
My Life Among the Bluejackets, 218
on religion, 72
Weycombe House, Haslemere
George Buckton at, 32, 94
Whistler, James McNeill, 162
White House, Haslemere, The, 187
White, Montagu, 44, 218–19

appointed Consul-General for Boer Republics, 45, 218
attacked by mob, 219
death in South Africa, 219
described by Lady Dorothy Nevill, 219
The Story of the Boers, 219
White, Walter, 30, 118, 192
Whitehead, Alfred North, *Principia Mathematica*, 172
Whiteway, Mrs, 220
Whiteway, R.S., 150, 219–20
works
The Portuguese Expedition to Abyssinia 1541–43, 220
The Rise of the Portuguese Power in India 1497–1550, 220
Whitman, Walt
and Anne Gilchrist, 21, 119–21
and Emily Tennyson, 121
and John Burroughs, 96, 121
and Pearsall Smith family, 121, 183
and Tennyson, 121
Leaves of Grass, 70, 120, 121
Whymper, Annette, 30, 220, 221
works
Celia's Fortunes, 221
Kesiah Crabbe, Spinster, 221
Whymper, Edward, 20, 29, 220–21
as mountaineer, 205, 221
as wood engraver, 220
works
Scrambles among the Alps, 221
Travels among the Great Andes of the Equator, 221
Whymper, Emily, *Beauty in Common Things*, 221
Whymper, Josiah Wood, 29, 220
Whyte, Frederick, 107
Wilberforce, Samuel, 129
Wilde, Oscar, 55, 140
Williams, Aneurin, 44, 225
Williamson, Professor Alexander, 226
Winz, Sophia, 217
Wisley, 146
Witley Hospital for Convalescent Lunatics, 193

Witley Park, 132
Witley, William Allingham at, 89
Wollstonecraft, Mary, *Vindication of
the Rights of Woman*, 50
Wolseley, Garnet Joseph, Field-
Marshall Viscount, 34, 44, 212,
222–23
described by
Henry James, 223
Lady Dorothy Nevill, 223
William Allingham, 222
in Egypt, 223
Life of Marlborough, 222
on degeneracy, 49, 222
opinion of Tennyson, 223
Woman Question, The. *see* feminism
Woods, Percy, *Bygone Haslemere*,
190
Woolf, Virginia, 104, 182, 184

Wright, Lord, 159
Wright, Thomas, 24, 99, 102, 187,
188, 196, 203, 204, 211, 223–28
and Richard Le Gallienne, 140, 225
works
Autobiography, 224
*Hindhead, or the English
Switzerland*, 36
Ianthe of the Devil's Jumps, 102,
226
Hindhead, 224
Wright, Whittaker, 132
Yaffles, Galton at, 113
Yaldwyn, General John Whitehead,
126
Yaldwyn, Richard, 126
Yaldwyn, William Henry, 126
Zola, Emile, 153

Made in the USA
Charleston, SC
11 April 2016